DEFENDING
CAMBRIDGESHIRE

DEFENDING CAMBRIDGESHIRE

The Military Landscape from Prehistory to the Present

MIKE OSBORNE

First published 2013

The History Press
The Mill, Brimscombe Port
Stroud, Gloucestershire, GL5 2QG
www.thehistorypress.co.uk

British Library Cataloguing in Publication Data.
A catalogue record for this book is available from the British Library.

ISBN 978 0 7524 9330 5

Typesetting and origination by The History Press
Printed in Great Britain

Contents

Acknowledgements

Thanks are due to the following:

Colin Alexander; Adrian Armishaw; Tony Baggs; Mike Bardell of East Anglia RFCA; Bob Beales; Paul Bellamy; Guy Bettley-Cooke; Michael Bowyer; Mrs Boyall of Chapel Cottage, Maxey; Barry Britain; Graham Cadman; Wayne Cocroft of English Heritage; Darby Dennis of Walcot Hall for allowing access; Paul Francis of the Airfield Research Group/AiX for Figure 17; John Goldsmith of the Huntingdon Museum for permission to include Figures 3, 4 and 5; Richard Hillier of Peterborough, Chris Jakes of Cambridge and David Hufford and Lesley Akeroyd of Huntingdon local studies libraries; Sir William Proby of Elton Hall for providing photographs; Martyn Smith for information regarding the Huntingdonshire Cyclists; Ray Smith; Keith Ward; Dr William Ward.

All illustrations are the author's unless otherwise credited.

Abbreviations

NB In several places, especially where RAF buildings are concerned, they are often described by their Drawing Numbers. These consist of a sequential number and a year: thus 343/43 refers to the Watch Office for All Commands, built to the 343rd design to come out of the Air Ministry in 1943. The term 'tb' refers to buildings with walls which are a single brick in width and officially known as 'temporary brick'.

AA	anti-aircraft
ACF	Army Cadet Force
ADGB	Air Defence of Great Britain (1924 scheme)
AFS	Auxiliary Fire Service
ARP	Air Raid Precautions
ASP	Aircraft Servicing Platform
AT	anti-tank
ATC	Air Training Corps
ATS	Auxiliary Territorial Service (forerunner of WRAC)
BEF	British Expeditionary Force
BHQ	Battle Headquarters
CBA	Council for British Archaeology
CD	Civil Defence
CO	commanding officer
CRO	Civilian Repair Organisation (aircraft repair workshops)
CUOTC	Cambridge University Officer Training Corps
DFW3	Directorate of Fortifications & Works, Department 3
DL	defended locality
(E & R) (S)FTS	(Elementary & Reserve) (Service) Flying Training School
EH	English Heritage
ELINT	electronic intelligence
FIDO	Fog Information and Dispersal Organisation (on airfields)
FRIBA	Fellow of the Royal Institute of British Architects
GDA	gun-defended area (AA)
GHQ	General Headquarters (GHQ Line, GHQ Reserve etc.)
GL	gun-laying (radar for AA artillery)
HAA	heavy anti-aircraft

HAS	hardened aircraft shelter
ICBM	inter-continental ballistic missile (e.g. POLARIS)
IRBM	intermediate-range ballistic missile (e.g. THOR)
LAA	light anti-aircraft
LDV	Local Defence Volunteers, later Home Guard (HG)
lmg	light machine gun
MAP	Ministry of Aircraft Production
MI4,5,6 etc.	Military Intelligence departments
MOD	Ministry of Defence
MU	maintenance unit (RAF)
NCO	non-commissioned officer
OCU	Operational Conversion Unit
ORs	other ranks
ORP	operational readiness platform
OTU	Operational Training Unit (usually RAF Bomber Command)
PBX	private branch exchange
pdr	pounder (as in weight of projectile) 1 pound = 454 grams
PR	photographic reconnaissance
PSP	pierced steel planking (for runways and hard standings)
QF	quick-firing (gun)
RAAF	Royal Auxiliary Air Force (until 1957)
RAC	Royal Armoured Corps
RAF	Royal Air Force (from 1 April 1918)
RAFVR	Royal Air Force Volunteer Reserve
RAMC	Royal Army Medical Corps
(R)AOC	(Royal from 1918) Army Ordnance Corps
(R)ASC	(Royal from 1918) Army Service Corps
RBL	Royal British Legion
RCHM(E)	Royal Commission on the Historical Monuments of (England)
RE	Royal Engineers
REME	Royal Electrical and Mechanical Engineers (from 1942)
RFC	Royal Flying Corps (up to 31 March 1918)
RFCA	Reserve Forces and Cadets' Association
RIMNET	Radioactive Incident Monitoring Network (from 1988)
RNAS	Royal Naval Air Service
(R)OC	(Royal from 1941) Observer Corps
SAA	small arms ammunition
SAM	surface-to-air missile (AA weapons)
SAS	Special Air Service
SEBRO	variously permutations of: 'Short Brothers', 'Engineering', 'Rochester and Bedford', and 'Repair Organisation'
SIGINT	signals intelligence
S/L	searchlight

SOE	Special Operations Executive
STS	Special Training School (SOE)
TA	Territorial Army (from 1920–39 and 1947–present)
TAC	Territorial Army Centre (drill hall post-1947)
tb	temporary brick (single brick with buttresses in RAF buildings)
TDS	Training Depot Station
TF	Territorial Force (from 1908–1918)
UKWMO	United Kingdom Warning & Monitoring Organisation
UP	unrotated projectile (as in Z battery, AA rockets)
USAAF	United States Army Air Force (Second World War)
USAF(E)	(E)United States Air Force (Europe) (post-Second World War)
VAD	Voluntary Aid Detachment (First World War)
VP	vulnerable point
VTC	Volunteer Training Corps (First World War Home Guard)
WAAF	Women's Auxiliary Air Force
WRAC	Womens' Royal Army Corps
WT	Wireless Telegraph
WVS	Women's Voluntary Service

Introduction

This volume, the sixth in a series covering the military landscapes of individual counties, includes all those local authorities which combined as Cambridgeshire in 1974: old Cambridgeshire, the Isle of Ely, Huntingdonshire, Peterborough and the Soke. Over the years continuous boundary changes have led to an eclectic mix of military affiliations. Infantry units representing Cambridgeshire, Suffolk, Northamptonshire, Bedfordshire and Huntingdonshire have been recruited from and based in the county, as have Yeomanry cavalry units from Suffolk, Norfolk, Bedfordshire and Northamptonshire. The Northamptonshire battery of a parent artillery unit based in Hertfordshire, and a specialist engineer unit, nominally from Northamptonshire, have both been closely associated with parts of the county. Successor units, such as the Royal Anglian Regiment, have continued to maintain these territorial connections.

For the almost twenty-five years that I worked in the county, avoidance of the A14 enabled me to drive most of the county's by-roads and so discover the wealth of heritage often overshadowed by the dominance of Cambridge, Ely and Peterborough. There are sites ranging from the lowest-lying hill-fort in Britain, through to bases devoted to the collection of electronic intelligence. Many of these sites have been re-used over the centuries – Stonea Camp, the Cambridgeshire Dykes and Earith Bulwark all figured in conflicts from ancient times, through the Civil Wars or into the Second World War. It is no coincidence that in those latter two conflicts, the same line was chosen for Cambridge's inner defensive perimeter.

Whilst giving a talk at Duxford's Imperial War Museum, I made the mistake of noting the absence of coast defences in land-locked Cambridgeshire forgetting, as was pointed out to me that, not 100 yards away was one of the 9.2-inch turreted guns from Gibraltar, along with all sorts of other exhibits from campaigns near and far, all shown within an almost unique historic setting. Having always been fascinated by castles and forts, it was in Peterborough that my interest in more recent anti-invasion defences was kindled when I came across Barry Allen, of the Soke Military Society. The pillbox in his back garden had prompted him to record such structures across a wide swathe of the north of the county. That was thirty years ago and many which had survived until then have now gone. Demolition on brown-field sites is gathering pace and Oakington, Waterbeach and Alconbury airfields will soon have largely disappeared. This makes the process of recording doubly vital. The confusion between disc barrows and searchlight sites is now a cliché but such mistakes still occur. Humps and bumps on Peterborough's Stanley recreation-ground, for instance, identified as evidence of mediaeval ridge and furrow, actually represent former air-raid shelters, and unless we note what was once there it will be lost forever. This book seeks to show how rich Cambridgeshire is in its military heritage, but also how quickly the evidence is disappearing. However, new discoveries are still out there waiting for us, and any reader lucky enough to uncover items of interest is asked to observe three principles: to respect private property and privacy; to take appropriate care in potentially hazardous locations; and to report discoveries to local authority Historic Environment Officers or museum staff.

Mike Osborne, 2013

one

Prehistoric, Roman and Saxon Cambridgeshire

Prehistoric Fortifications

One of the earliest forms of defence work is the causewayed enclosure. That at Haddenham is the largest in England, covering a little over 20 acres (8.5ha) surrounded by a single ditch and palisade. Other examples have been found at Great Wilbraham and Maxey/Etton. At Rectory Farm, Godmanchester, is an enclosure of 16 acres (6.3ha) with an entrance to the north-east and twenty-four massive timber posts spaced around the inside of the perimeter. The Early Iron Age was largely characterised by loose unenclosed villages which had developed from farms set in field systems. Throughout the Iron Age, right up until the Roman invasion and beyond, isolated settlements consisted of round huts within an enclosure. A typical example was found at Werrington, where a single hut lies in a roughly square enclosure of bank and ditch, with sides of around 50 yards.

In the period between the third and the first centuries BC, the so-called Iron Age 'hillforts' made their appearance. There is still disagreement amongst historians as to the purpose of these monuments which would have required an enormous investment of materials and labour. It is quite possible that individual examples fulfilled different functions, but it is clear that many were never permanent residential sites. Assuming at least an element of military intention, it is possible to draw distinctions between those in our area. Some, such as Belsars Hill, were of only local importance, whilst others suggest themselves as being of more strategic significance, guarding frontiers. A line of forts, which includes Wandlebury, Arbury and War Ditches, stretched from the Thames to the Fens using the valleys of the Lea, Stort and Cam to separate the Trinovantes to the east from the Catuvellauni, controlling Huntingdonshire and West Cambridgeshire, in the west. Further to the north, the Corieltauvi marked their boundary with the Iceni with the fort at Borough Fen and a series of smaller defended enclosures which extended into Lincolnshire. Borough Fen (**1**), 4.5 miles (7km) north-north-east of Peterborough, on Peakirk Moor, had been built with a rampart 24 feet (7.5m) wide and reinforced with a revetment and a surrounding ditch, 32 feet (10m) wide and nearly eight feet (2.5m) deep, but these clear defensive features apparently enclosed empty space which was soon put to pasture. Recent *Lidar* mapping has

shown an outer bank and ditch on the west, and emphasised that the fort stands 'a diz-
zying 4m' (13 feet) above sea level. Arbury, too, appears to lack interior structures and
it has been suggested that it was an enclosure for migrating stock, but its substantial
timber gateway, ramparts and ditches nevertheless suggest a defensive function. There
is continuing uncertainty regarding the purpose of many Iron Age forts, and explana-
tions of their use as emergency refuges are perfectly plausible. Arbury's low-lying
position is contrasted by that of Wandlebury, a bi-vallate fort on the Gog Magog
hills south of Cambridge. Here there is evidence of settlement, but not necessarily
contemporaneous with the defences. A smaller fort at Cherry Hinton, War Ditches
is, again, roughly circular, whilst Borough Hill at Sawston, much more extensive than
all those mentioned above, appears to anchor its double ditches on natural marshy
obstacles. Along with these forts, tribal boundaries were often marked by linear dykes,
many of which are traceable through their re-use in Anglo-Saxon times.

It has been suggested that the major Fenland fortress of Stonea Camp, covering
nearly 24 acres (9.5ha) and the most extensive such structure in East Anglia, was an
important focus for Iceni gatherings. It enjoys the status of *oppidum*, or tribal centre,
putting it on a level with Colchester, St Albans and Leicester. Stonea lies a little to
the south-east of March on a ridge that dominates the southern Fens, close to the
old courses of the Ouse and the Nene, and at a point where fresh-water met sea-
water. The Iron Age fort occupies a site which in Neolithic times accommodated
a settlement, a *cursus*, and burial mounds. The camp dates from the third or second
centuries BC, from which time an inner defensive rampart and ditch have been found,

1 BOROUGH FEN CAMP on Peakirk Moor: this circular Iron Age camp may have defended
a tribal frontier. In this low-lying landscape the bank and ditch nowadays appear insignificant as
fortifications.

2 STONEA CAMP near Wimblington: this Iron Age site may have served as a tribal centre, a refuge and a settlement. Its inner banks and ditches still appear to fulfil a defensive function.

entered through staggered entrances, an arrangement commonly found in such forts across the country. There are three distinct lines of banks and ditches, the two inner of them forming D-shapes with outer ones to the north and east (**2**). The ditches are cut through different ground conditions and this may account for variations in their dimensions and profiles. The excavators have postulated a four-phase construction for the camp, which began with the outer enclosure, and finished with the outer of the two D-shaped enclosures, suggesting a re-modelling towards the end of the Iron Age occupation. Ditches were generally around 16 feet (5m) across and up to 7 feet (2m) deep which, added to the height of the rampart, would have produced an impressive fortification in this low-lying landscape. To the surprise, and apparent disappointment of the excavators, no evidence was discovered for timber gate-defences. This may be explained by the lack of settlement evidence, as it seems likely that Stonea Camp was a site for gatherings and rituals, its defences being more of an insurance policy for emergencies rather than of permanent and continuous usage. The weakness of the defences on the south facing the watery approaches has been cited as a case for dismissing the structure's defensive integrity but, as at Borough Hill, the marshy nature of the land on that side may have been deemed sufficient defence in itself.

Despite archaeologists' and historians' ambivalence over the purpose of these Iron Age forts, it would appear that at least one Cambridgeshire example, War Ditches at Cherry Hinton, may have met a sudden and violent end. Although much of the fort has been destroyed by quarrying, excavators found that the ditch had not filled by natural processes but had been back-filled with the rubble and stone blocks which had formed the rampart, apparently intentionally, rapidly and by human agency. Not only was there charcoal in the ditch indicating the burning of, at the very least, the timber palisade, but there were large numbers of skeletons, both articulated and disjointed, some bearing cut-marks, and constituting possible evidence of injuries received in conflict. All this was dated to the middle of the first century AD, and may relate to the northward progress of the Roman army, or may simply represent the product of an intertribal spat.

Roman Fortifications

Having reconnoitred Britain in the previous century, but penetrated no farther than Hertfordshire, the Romans invaded Britain in AD 43, this time showing every intention of staying. Although the native British tribes had made some collective effort to resist the earlier incursions of the Belgic tribes from France, they were generally not given to co-operation, which gave the Roman troops a clearer run than they might have expected. Having secured London, and especially the major tribal centre of Colchester, their major thrust was towards the Trent and Humber, with the line of the Fosse Way marking a temporary western frontier. The valley of the Great Ouse appears to have provided one approach for the Roman forces who established forts at Godmanchester to secure a ford on the road north from Sandy (Bedfordshire), and at Longthorpe, on the Nene a little to the west of Peterborough, to act as a base for further operations. By AD 48 the Romans felt sufficiently well-established to demand that the British disarm, but powerful tribes such as the Iceni unsurprisingly resisted this demand, and military action, possibly taking place near Stonea Camp, was necessary for the policy to be enforced. Amongst human remains uncovered at Stonea was the skeleton of a child which appeared to carry sword-cuts. Following their subjugation, the Iceni were allowed to retain their own leader, a source of later misunderstandings, but became a subject people under Rome.

At Godmanchester (*Durovigutum*) the earliest fort, of the usual playing-card shape and oriented east-west, was large enough to hold half a legion. It had a double ditch and a timber rampart revetted in turf. It appears to have had timber interval turrets, the four corner-posts of one having been found on the south side of the fort. At Cambridge, the early settlement on the promontory overlooking the river was surrounded by a ditch outside a bank topped by a palisade. The original fortress at Longthorpe was squarer in plan with double ditches and an earthen rampart, 20 feet (6m) wide, surmounted by a timber palisade with a wall-walk or fighting-platform. The fortress, again designed to accommodate half a legion, covered 27 acres (11ha). It was south-facing on a site on the north bank of the Nene and close to important roads. Its four gates were each defended by flanking timber turrets mounted on six posts, allowing them to project beyond the two gate-passages, which were each 12 feet (3.6m) wide. The interior of the fort held barracks, a headquarters building, stores and granaries. It was in occupation from some time in the mid-AD 40s, but whether or not it pre-dated the initial problem with the Iceni cannot be determined with any certainty. Given that only auxiliaries rather than legionaries were involved in that particular campaign, might suggest that it came after the rebellion had been put down. It had a number of functions which included providing a reserve force behind the Fosse Way and a blocking force to prevent military collusion between the Iceni and their neighbours, the Coritani and Catuvellauni. It was also the nearest garrison to the newly established *colonia* at Colchester. As well as providing the base for a mobile strike-force, it offered winter quarters for troops on campaign, and a permanent storage facility for grain and equipment. The mobility required by a quick-reaction force would have been provided by the stationing of auxiliary cavalry in the fortress, and one of the buildings, excavated in the 1960s and '70s, has been interpreted as stabling. The nature, proportions and dimensions of the buildings and the spaces in which they are set, enabled the excavators to infer a garrison of around 1,700 legionaries and 1,000 auxiliaries, including cavalry. About 500 yards to the east, a military depot produced pottery and other wares for the army.

In AD 60 Boudicca led a full-scale revolt of the Iceni against Roman rule. Hearing of the sack of Colchester, Petillius Cerialis, legate of the IXth Legion, led his troops from Longthorpe but was surprised by a vastly greater force of Iceni and defeated. A draft of reinforcements to the legion the next year contained 2,000 legionaries and is likely to represent the scale of losses sustained in the battle. Cerialus escaped back to Longthorpe with his cavalry, and appears to have shrunk the area of the fortress to reflect his reduced defence capability. The new fort, nearer to the typical playing-card shape, covered 11 acres (4.4ha) within the perimeter of the old fortress. The new defences were on a smaller scale to the earlier ones although it is likely that the old timbers, particularly those of the gate-towers (**Fig. 1**), were re-used. Those buildings which fell within the new enclosure were used as they were, with no visible evidence either of adaptation or rebuilding. The old outer defences were allowed to erode and the now unused buildings were dismantled. After the inevitable defeat of the Iceni, the Roman army shifted its focus northwards once more, and around AD 60

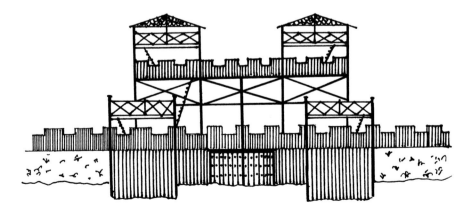

Fig. 1 LONGTHORPE: a reconstruction of the gateway of this Roman legionary fortress of the first century AD, based on other examples and archaeological evidence.

the IXth Legion's base was established in a new legionary fortress in Lincoln, rendering Longthorpe redundant. Military occupation there appears to peter out after AD 61, although it is not impossible that the fort continued in use for some years after.

Following the shock of the Boudiccan revolt in which three major Roman towns had been razed and their inhabitants slaughtered, the urgent re-establishment of Roman control was essential. Cambridgeshire contained important hubs in the network of roads in the region. From Colchester, a road ran to Braintree and Great Dunmow (Essex) entering the county at Great Chesterford, and continuing on to Cambridge and Godmanchester, finishing up in Leicester. Another road led from Royston to Durobrivae via the river crossing at Godmanchester (Ermine Street) and linked to the Longthorpe fort. The Fen Causeway ran from Whittlesea to Denver (Norfolk), and King Street ran from Durobrivae north along the fen edge to Lincoln. To protect these routes, and the settlements which grew up associated with them, forts were newly built or up-dated. New forts were built along the Fen Causeway, at Grandford near March and at Eldernell. The Grandford fort replaced an earlier one which may have been built around AD 47 at the time of the brush with the Iceni. Its successor, of a size appropriate to the accommodation of 500 auxiliaries, most likely represents the installation of a garrison along the Fen Causeway charged with ensuring that the remnants of the Iceni army caused no further problems. The fort at Eldernell, also located on the Fen Causeway, appears to have been of a similar size. At Cambridge (*Durolipons*) the defensive site above the river-crossing and track-way junction was enlarged with renewed defences as a military supply base, located near New Hall on the road out of the North Gate to Godmanchester, and in use around the turn of the first century. It was later adapted for domestic use, and by AD 150 the fort had been redeveloped as a town laid out in *insulae*. The fort at Godmanchester, which had in the meantime become a civilian settlement apparently destroyed during the Boudiccan revolt, was re-built in its aftermath slightly further to the north of its original site. With the winding-down of the legionary base at Longthorpe, it was nevertheless necessary to maintain a military presence in the Nene Valley, and a double-ditched auxiliary fort covering 5 acres (2ha) was established at Water Newton, where Ermine Street crossed the Nene. An industrial settlement, probably supplying the needs of the army, developed outside the fort, and this was most likely the stimulus for the later town of Durobrivae. A further fort at Lynch Farm near Peterborough probably dates from this first century of Roman rule. At Tort Hill, Sawtry, it was once thought that a possible Roman signal station had been built, presumably one in a chain which must have followed the line of Ermine Street. However, subsequent excavation revealed the square earthwork as a Civil War fort. The former presence of a Roman watchtower at Pilsgate, overlooking Ermine Street, has been recorded in a local history of neighbouring Barnack, along with a marching camp in Burghley Park to its west. To the south of the Coneygeare in St Neots are traces of what has been interpreted as a Roman marching camp, perhaps sited to protect a crossing of the Great Ouse, since signs of a Roman road, entering Eynesbury from the south and aligning with the old Stanestrete to Crosshall and Hail Weston, have been inferred.

The important centre of the Iceni at Stonea was chosen as the site of a Roman town around AD 125. Functioning as an administrative centre, possibly of an Imperial estate under the patronage of Hadrian, exploiting the fertility of the Fenland soil as well as a focus for trade, this town boasted several sophisticated and imposing structures. One of these was a substantial square building, constructed in stone and possibly rising to four storeys, interpreted as either a town hall or a temple. Most of the rest of the town, spread over at least a dozen *insulae*, were of timber and daub. The settlement flourished until well into the third century when it appears to have shed its official status, and become the nucleus of a farming community. Thus at the time that other similar-sized towns were renewing or acquiring fortifications, Stonea lacked the status, the motivation and the resources.

Durobrivae has been described as a ribbon development straggling along Ermine Street, in essence a definable centre and two suburbs, with plots fronting onto the main road, and lanes going off in all directions behind this frontage. In the late second or early third century, the central part of the town was walled. These walls, in the shape of an irregular hexagon enclosing 44 acres (15ha), consisted of clay banks supporting a stone wall. In common with other such towns, the unrest of the late fourth century led to bastions being added to the walls. Despite a thriving mosaic industry and evidence of wealth as exemplified by the early Christian Water Newton treasure, the town contracted, the suburbs dwindled and the town died with the exodus of the Romans. The nearby settlement of Castor was centred on a high-status villa often described in palatial terms. The owner has never been identified but it has been suggested, possibly somewhat fancifully, that he could have been someone as important as the Count of the Saxon Shore, the Roman commander of the *Classis Britannica*, responsible for the defence of Britain's coastline against Saxon raids during the second half of the fourth century.

Godmanchester's replacement fort was itself subsumed by the town defences following the line of the fort's walls, and utilising its north gate. These town walls date from just before AD 300, enclose an area of 27 acres (11ha), and consisted of a 10 foot (3m) wide masonry wall built onto a contemporary rampart with a 32 foot (10m) wide ditch, incorporating rectangular external interval towers. The South Gate in Pipers Lane, almost 30 feet (9m) wide, had a pair of projecting towers. The construction of these walls was interrupted by a fire which destroyed the *mansio*, leaving gaps. A later wall partitioned off the town's official buildings, and may point to a general contraction of the defended area. A hundred years later the defences were refurbished with stone robbed from the buildings in the town centre, an artillery bastion was added to the south-east corner, and a new 40 foot (12.5m) wide ditch was dug around the perimeter.

In Cambridge, the major part of the town, 25 acres (10ha), was walled in stone (**3**) late in the fourth century, with gates located on each side. That on the west on Mount Pleasant, at the junction with Albion Row, had been excavated. Only the northern half of the gate could be examined, and this consisted of a rectangular footing measuring 25 feet (7.5m) by 15 feet (4.5m). The roadway between this and its corresponding

3 CAMBRIDGE, Mount Pleasant: here Storeys Almshouses stand on the bank which marks the north-west angle of the Roman town defences.

footing on the south side measured nearly 30 feet (9m). The excavator suggested that this gate-arch would have been flanked by rectangular or D-shaped gate-towers projecting forward from the wall. Since so much of the Roman circuit disappeared under the castle and the later Civil War earthworks, it has not been possible to locate bastions on the course of the wall, if indeed they ever existed.

A number of other possible town sites have been identified in the northern Fens. Most appear to have been composed of groups of ditched enclosures containing either circular or rectangular timber huts, temples, barns and evidence of agricultural and associated industrial processes. At Fen Drove, Earith, there are suggestions of defences in the form of a ditch enclosing a roughly rectangular area, measuring about 300 yards by 100 yards, alongside a drove-way, and containing many of the elements of the settlement. Camp Ground at Colne Fen, Earith was a similar settlement estimated to have had a population of up to 120 inhabitants. Covering an area of 17 acres (7ha), its perimeter was marked by double-ditched embankments and ditched trackways. The excavators reckoned that, had these banks been topped with thick thorn hedges, then they would have constituted a viable defence against both casual aggressors and wild beasts.

After a dip which lasted through much of the fourth century, the Fens appear to have experienced a degree of economic recovery marked by new stone buildings, at Stonea and Chatteris for instance. There is evidence that occupation of such sites continued beyond the end of Roman rule in the early 400s.

Saxon and Danish Fortifications

After the Romans left, the inhabitants attempted the continuation of their Romano-British life-style often, but not exclusively, in a rural context. Saxon incomers appeared early in East Anglia and are recorded in the chronicles as having assumed a predominance by the mid-fifth century. There would have been examples of peaceful co-existence in some places, and violent seizure of land and ejection of the native population in others. Evidence for reoccupation at Stonea Grange, where timber halls of Anglo-Saxon date occupied the former administrative quarter, has been found. In Peterborough, Godmanchester and in Cambridge (Grantaceastr north of the river Cam), timber halls, sunken huts and cemeteries have all been uncovered. Clusters of sunken huts have been found all over the county at, among other locations, Maxey, Waterbeach and Willingham. The location of Anglo-Saxon cemeteries in locations such as Haddenham and Witchford airfield may indicate the occupation of strategic sites controlling access to the islands in the Fens, and evidence for the fifth-century reoccupation of the long-abandoned fort at Longthorpe may point to a parallel attempt to control the Nene crossing. At Orton Hall Farm, a Saxon timber hall had been built on the ruins of a Roman house, alongside a group of sunken huts and a granary.

Throughout much of the Anglo-Saxon period, the Cam represented a political boundary between East Anglia and Mercia, and Cambridge was the furthest north it was possible to access the Midlands from East Anglia before the traveller disappeared into the impenetrable Fens. To the east of the river there is a series of defensive dykes of fifth and sixth-century date, apparently positioned to protect East Anglia from hostile approaches from the south-west. The four dykes, south-west to north-east, were Bran Ditch east of Royston; Brent Ditch, between the rivers Granta and Cam; Fleam Dyke/High Ditch between the Cam and the Icknield Way south of Wilbraham; and the Devil's Dyke between Burwell and the Swaffhams. The latter two, probably earlier than the others, were also more substantial. It has been suggested that having been constructed soon after the Roman withdrawal, they would have figured both in local power struggles, and also against the growing incursions of Anglo-Saxon invaders. It is possible that the origins of these dykes may lie in earlier Iron Age boundary ditches. Devil's Dyke is the most impressive of these monuments running for a continuous 7.5 miles (11km), its bank 23 feet (7m) wide at its base and its ditch to the west, 16 feet (5m) deep. Excavations have revealed some of the construction techniques and also that the Bran Ditch was preceded by much less impressive double ditches with a timber palisade between them. A succession of re-builds show that construction continued through into the seventh century. Across the border in Suffolk further pairs of similar ditches occur, straddling Roman roads and suggesting that together, all these dykes may represent a co-ordinated attempt to both define and defend territory. It has been suggested on the basis of female dress excavated in sixth-century graves at Edix Hill, that Cambridgeshire failed to develop a regional identity of its own as did, say, Essex, and maybe it was this unsettled life in a buffer state which precluded that.

Mercia only cemented its hold over its easterly area of influence by re-establishing the town of Cambridge late in the eighth century. King Offa picked up on the Danish use of fortified camps by building a network of defensive centres known as burhs. Many of these were well-established towns, previously fortified by the Romans, whilst others were on green-field sites of strategic value. Cambridge, preserving its Roman walls and gates, and representing a gateway to Mercia, became one of Offa's burhs, Grantabrycge. As well as the fortified core, he also built a bridge across the Cam and encouraged the growth of trade by establishing wharves by the river-side and a market. There may also have been a minster-church on the site later chosen by the Normans for their castle. The king's reeve or alderman may have had a house within its own ditched and banked enclosure in the north-east corner of the Roman enclosure, referred to as Alderman's Hill.

Susan Osthuizen has shown how the settlements in the more stable East Anglia have 'ham' place-names, whereas the more latterly occupied estates to the west have more 'tons'. Peterborough had been founded in 655 by Peada, the first Christian king of Mercia, as Medehamstead, with an important monastery and at the centre of exten- sive land-holdings bestowed by King Wulfhere. Other important monasteries were founded across the county at this time, among them, Thorney, Ely and Ramsey.

The Danes, first appearing off the coast of Britain in 789 on exploratory expeditions, and having previously carried out mainly small-scale raids, stepped up their efforts throughout the ninth century, often over-wintering with up to 300 ships in prepared water-side laagers. In 870, after King Edmund had died attempting to evict the Danish host from East Anglia, attacks increased in ferocity; Peterborough abbey was burnt to the ground, and the abbot and his monks slaughtered. This was but one defeat which heralded a sustained period of Danish dominance, and England was partitioned, with the Danes establishing the Danelaw in the counties to the east of Watling Street under Guthrum. From around 873, outside their heartland of East Anglia, four separate outer territories centred on Bedford, Cambridge, Huntingdon and Northampton were set up, each ruled by an earl with his own standing army. In 875, the Danes built a new burh in Cambridge extending south of the river with St John's Ditch marking its southern boundary. In 876, Guthrum assembled an army at Cambridge to embark on the subjugation of Wessex, a struggle which finally ended with his defeat by Alfred. The Danes converted to Christianity and retreated into East Anglia, and by 886 Alfred had managed to ally Wessex and Mercia to produce a durable state that might defend against dormant Danish ambitions.

Under peaceful Danish rule, the county saw the growth of up to 250 village com- munities replacing the scattered farmsteads of earlier times. Members of the Danish aristocracy lived in small defended enclosures known as 'holds', examples of which have been identified at Spaldwick and Wistow, with that of the earl himself at Shelford, where his coin was minted. The Danes continued to carry out coastal raiding but they were not the only aggressors. According to the version of the *Anglo-Saxon Chronicle* written by the monks of Peterborough, in 903 the Danes were lured into breaking the truce giving Edward the excuse to ravage all the land between the Devil's Dyke, the Fleam Dyke and the Ouse.

By 917, the success of the Danish economy was attracting the covetous attention of Edward the Elder and of Aethelflaed the Lady of Mercia. Having lost Bedford and Northampton, the Danes left their fortified base at Huntingdon and moved to a new camp on the Ouse at Tempsford, seeing it as more convenient for attacks into Mercia. Retiring there, having been repulsed by Edward's garrison in Bedford, the Danes were overwhelmed by the Mercians and forced back into Essex where they faced further defeats. Edward's men took Huntingdon, repairing the damage and making it defensible once more. The Danes of Cambridge were particularly keen to accept Edward as their overlord, welcoming his commitment to increase the importance of the town by extending the area south of the river, establishing a mint and awarding them the status of county-town. On the basis of archaeological evidence, RCHM(E) regards the Kings Ditch as being pre-Conquest, being re-cut around 1200, and the church of St Bene't is dated to between 950 and 1050. There is a theory that stone Saxon church-towers (4) fulfilled defensive and civic functions alongside ecclesiastical ones, and both these monuments point to a developing settlement complementary to the town on the hill. Edward is known to have established burhs across his lands, and it is likely that he was responsible for the Kings Ditch which served as both a drain and a defence. Excavations at St Neots, ideally situated on the Ouse to be a trading hub, have revealed that a flourishing settlement existed by, perhaps, the tenth century, defended

by a substantial ditch enclosing nearly 30 acres (12ha). This ditch ran along Cambridge Street and Church Street and may have linked to the Brook to form a secure settlement site on good arable land some way from the river. Within this enclosure were sunken huts and boat-shaped timber halls, one measuring 40 feet by 25 feet (12 x 7.5m), whilst a monastery, founded in 974 by Earl Leofric of Mercia, probably lay outside.

Under Edward, and then Athelstan, the county enjoyed three generations of peace and prosperity. However, this was to change. After 980 the resumption of Danish raids culminated in a shattering defeat for the combined forces of Wessex and Mercia at Maldon (Essex) in 991. For some twenty years the Danes landed an army virtually every year in order to collect Danegeld, a particularly unsophisticated form of protection racket. In 1010 it was a larger army than normal that landed at Ipswich and marched towards Cambridge.

4 CAMBRIDGE, ST BENE'T'S CHURCH: this Saxon tower dating from 950–1050 may have contributed to the defences of the town south of the River Cam.

Deserted by most of the East Anglians, the men of Cambridge stood firm but were defeated, losing many of their leaders. The Danes fired Cambridge and Thetford (Norfolk), after which their cavalry ravaged the counties of Buckingham, Oxford and Bedford before meeting up with their ships again at Tempsford. They sailed for home laden with plunder and avoided belated attempts to intercept them. Within a few years the Danish Swein was occupying the throne to be followed by Cnut and, following the blinding of Alfred the Atheling, Aethelred's son, at Ely in 1036, by Harthacnut. Not until Edward the Confessor, in 1043, was the throne again occupied by an English king.

The monastery of Medehamstede sought to protect itself from the worst of the Danish depredations by building a precinct wall between 992 and 1006. Excavations reported by Don Mackreth appear to have confirmed the local tradition and the assertion in Aelfric's *Life of St Aethelwold*, that Abbot Kenulph (992–1005) built a precinct wall around the monastery, thus prompting a name-change to Petreburgh, the fortified place of St Peter, later Peterborough. The base of a stone wall with foundations over 7 feet (25m) thick, was found lying between the cathedral and the later motte on the north side. It may have run across the west front of the present cathedral midway between that and the Outer Gate. On the south side it probably followed the same line as the present wall which follows the course of a stream. On the east it is more difficult to be certain of its course, as it is still unknown how much of the settlement would have lain within this wall. The important Bolhithe Gate, however, gave access on that side to the market and houses of Burgh. In 1997, further excavation, within the present precincts and near the inferred location of the Bolhithe Gate, uncovered the wall, a defensive ditch and two sharpened wooden stakes, thought to be evidence of the Saxon defences.

two

The Early Mediaeval Period in Cambridgeshire 1066-1300

After William I's victory over the Saxon army at Hastings, his rapid march on London, and his coronation, there was still much for him to do in the way of consolidation. Not only was there a potentially rebellious Saxon population to subdue, but also the real and constant threat of an invasion by the descendants of Cnut, those whom Harold had recently defeated at Stamford Bridge (Yorkshire) just prior to William's arrival. One way of securing the country against both these threats was to build castles in the county towns. These, largely novel, structures would fulfil a number of functions. They would provide bases for Norman garrisons; they would act as administrative centres for dispensing justice and collecting taxes; and above all, provide psychological dominance by literally towering over a subject populace. This emphasis on the new Norman rulers as a dominant force was underlined by the ruthless way in which existing dwellings were swept away to provide suitable sites for the imposition of these castles, an act paralleled by the, sometimes violent, substitution of Norman officials for Saxon aldermen and churchmen alike.

The castle as a private fortress was almost unknown in Britain. A few Saxon nobles and some of the Normans at the court of Edward the Confessor had built their own castles in the years prior to the Conquest and a few key defensive sites, such as Dover, appear to have had earthwork and timber forts. However, the concept of the castle as a fortified residence, military garrison and administrative centre, was essentially new to the Saxons. The castles built by the Normans in the first decade after Hastings were of earth and timber and followed two basic patterns: the motte and the ring-work. The motte was a high artificial mound of earth built with the spoil from its surrounding ditch, or else a natural mound, scarped to provide steep sides. Either way, it had a flat top on which was built a timber tower, sometimes on posts which stood on firm ground with the mound piled around them, or sometimes on a stone cellar embedded in the mound. Most mottes were large enough to have a palisade around the rim, often with a timber gate-tower approached by a flying bridge over the moat. The ring-work was an enclosure within a bank and ditch, again surrounded by a palisade which might have interval turrets and a fortified gate-tower. Either model could have one or more outer courtyards known as baileys, which could accommodate a hall, chapel, stables and workshops, as well as living quarters for the garrison, its families and servants.

Depending on the castle's situation, the moats might be wet or dry. Again, depending on the local soil, the motte might need layering with clay, terracing or revetting, particularly if it were intended ultimately to bear the weight of a stone tower. A number of factors influenced the choice of pattern, and each enjoyed both disadvantages and benefits. Mottes provided less accommodation in the most secure part of the fortress, but could be defended by fewer soldiers and had the added benefit of greater two-way visibility – the garrison could see what was going on below them, and the townsfolk were constantly aware of the Norman presence. The ring-work offered more space in the kernel of the fortress but was less obtrusive in the landscape although, as with Iron Age forts, in the low-lying Fens even a modest rampart might appear disproportionately dominant. The choice of pattern might be determined by military considerations or could simply come down to personal taste or even fashion. Across the country the ratio of mottes to ring-works is roughly 4:1. In present-day Cambridgeshire there were ten mottes, four apparent ring-works, seven further early earthwork castles of individual design (mainly rectangular moated platforms) and four vanished ones of form unknown.

The earliest network of Norman castles included two in Cambridgeshire, and these were both mottes. The castle at Cambridge was begun in 1068, when twenty-seven houses were demolished to make way for its construction on the end of the promontory overlooking the river from the north. This had been the location of the Roman town and the earliest Anglo-Saxon settlement and it dominated both the bridge, and the town which had grown up south of the river. At a number of other places, including Cardiff and Chichester, the Normans had placed their mottes within Roman perimeters. The Cambridge motte was 40 feet (12m) high with a diameter of 200 feet (60m) at its base, and was separated from the bailey to the north by a ditch, measured in the early nineteenth century as 16 feet (5m) deep. Allowing for erosion, and even without the tower which stood on the summit, the motte today retains a striking prominence (5). The castle was founded by William himself, on his return from accepting the subjugation of York. On that same journey south, William also established a castle in Huntingdon. The main feature of this, too, was a motte, later radically altered, on the river-bank overlooking the bridge. This motte, along with two baileys, displaced twenty houses, part of a town owned by Earl Waltheof, which formed part of his daughter's inheritance, and passed into Norman hands on her marriage to Simon de Senlis. It is worth emphasising that the core element of both these early castles was the motte, that very element best-suited to an urban situation where it might daily reinforce the reality of Norman rule.

As well as these strategically placed royal castles, there were a number of private fortresses such as that of Picot, sheriff of Cambridgeshire at Bourn. Recorded in Domesday, this appears to have been built by 1086 as a ring-work, now occupied by Bourn Hall, and a bailey. Aubrey de Vere received the manor of Castle Camps from William in the land share-out which followed the conquest. It consists of a large ring-work with a small bailey, enlarged at a later date prior to the building of the church. It occupies a site on a low spur which is easily defended but not necessarily attractive

5 CAMBRIDGE CASTLE: the eleventh-century motte was built by William the Conqueror as part of his campaign to dominate England's traditional centres of power and influence.

as a settlement site, suggesting that the castle was sited to satisfy military considerations and that the dependent settlement followed.

Whilst the Normans employed a number of strategies to maintain their conquest, ranging from indiscriminate violence to integration through marriage, there were instances of armed resistance, possibly the best-known being associated with the Cambridgeshire Fens. Immediately after William's victory at Hastings, when it was still uncertain how successful his attempt at conquest might prove, there was a possibility that Saxon resistance might be rallied behind Edgar the Atheling, whose great-uncle had been Ethelred. In fact, it was to Edgar that Brand of Peterborough turned when, following the death of Abbot Leofric, probably from wounds received at Hastings, he sought official approval for his election to the abbacy. However, the Saxon earls' promises of backing for Edgar failed to materialise and he capitulated. As the great and good of the land submitted to William, changes were made only gradually. It may only be coincidental, but when Abbot Brand died in 1069 he was replaced by the Norman Turold. This was after William, as the *Chronicle* reports, had begun to plunder the richer monasteries, further alienating senior churchmen. Aethelric of Durham was seized from sanctuary at Peterborough, and his outlawed brother, Bishop Aethelwine, hastened to the inaccessible monastery of Ely in order to foment rebellion from that secure retreat. Abbot Brand had been required to pay a huge fine for his insolence in appealing to Edgar, and now all the cathedrals and abbeys were burdened with having to provide knight service in return for retaining their estates. In Peterborough's case, it was sixty knights, a blatantly punitive assessment, and in the reckoning following Hereward's revolt, Ely was assessed at a similar level, which it successfully appealed only some time later.

Hereward's Rebellion

William's planted castles were clearly intended to fulfil a strategic function, but a group of castles constructed only a few years later were very much a solution to a particular tactical problem. Hereward, a nephew of Abbot Brand of Peterborough, had failed to carry out some contractual responsibilities and had been exiled to Flanders in the early 1060s. He probably served as a mercenary until 1069 when he returned to England. Finding that he and his companions had lost their lands to the Normans, he became an outlaw and joined the monks of Ely who, providing a haven for rebels, were blockaded by William's troops. After the death of Brand, it was heard that the Norman Turold, a notorious fighting abbot, had been appointed to Peterborough and charged with implementing William's policy of appropriating the abbey's portable wealth. When Turold had reached Stamford, with a significant force of 160 knights, Hereward hi-jacked a Danish force which was raiding around the Humber. Several motives lay behind this treasonous act, which some might have described as playing with fire. In the short term he wanted to pre-empt Turold by saving the treasures of the abbey with which he had an affinity through his uncle. In the long term he hoped to persuade the Danes to stay on and support the Saxon resistance to William. The Danes agreed to help, but then it all began to go wrong. Hereward and his Danish allies, whose eyes were solely on the promise of plunder, attacked the monastery but met unexpected resistance from the monks who mistrusted Hereward's motives. Setting fire to the Bolhithe Gate, the Danes forced their way in and sacked the church, taking every item of value they could carry and retreating into the Fens. At this point the Danes heard from William that they could keep their loot so long as they sailed away at once, which is what they did, only to lose all their treasure in a storm at sea. This left Hereward and his band of rebels, along with other rebel leaders including Earl Morcar and Bishop Aethelwine, high and dry on a blockaded Isle of Ely. Fresh from his ruthless and successful campaign in the north of England, William was determined to crush this last rebel stronghold in the Fens and moved his forces there by land and water in the autumn of 1071, using the recently completed Cambridge Castle as his base.

The Isle of Ely, surrounded by un-drained marshes and wide expanses of water, relied heavily on these natural defences, which had been further enhanced by fieldworks constructed of peat. William's blockade made use of existing works such as the Devils Ditch and Belsar's Hill at Willingham, both re-fortified with palisades. Access to Ely relied on hidden and tortuous causeways which often led to open water where the final approach had to be made by boat. The Normans attempted to strengthen these causeways by dumping sand and earth, by building timber trestles and pontoons and by using inflated sheep-skins as buoyancy aids. In order to attack the defenders, William built fighting decks for his archers, belfries or siege towers to overlook the defenders' positions, and four circular platforms which could mount catapults, designed to protect the labourers constructing the causeways. Many of these structures were set on fire and destroyed by the defenders' sallies. One timber belfry was fired whilst occupied by a witch, engaged by William to harangue the defenders with curses, an early use of psychological warfare. Hereward's men made regular sorties to fire the reeds surrounding the Normans' camps and their dumps of building materials, causing peat fires which could burn for days, trapping Norman patrols yet to come to terms with this alien environment. At the end, however, it was treachery which undid the Saxon defenders. Whilst Hereward was away on a raid, the other leaders, particularly the monks of Ely who were severely financially embarrassed by their lodgers' activities, decided to accept William's terms and meekly surrendered, leaving the rank and file to face the final assault. Whilst use was made of the causeways his troops had worked so hard to widen and strengthen, William drew on his previous experience of amphibious warfare; his final approaches to the Isle were made by punts which were even used to ferry his heavy cavalry. The defenders were quickly subdued and the rebellion soon fizzled out. As well as Belsar's Hill, the Normans used the earthwork at Braham's Farm, on the Roman road from Cambridge, as a base. This has sometimes been labelled as a Roman camp, but may actually date from these later times. The unidentified site of 'Alrehethe', 'Alderethe' or 'Alderede' mentioned in the chronicles may have been one of a number of locations, but probably not Aldreth which fails to meet the topographical criteria. Weapons, characteristic of those used at that time, have been found in a number of places including Brahams Farm, Burwell Fen and Wicken, confirming that the theatre of operations covered a wide area all around the Isle, or more exactly, isles.

At the end of the campaign, William planted an earthwork castle at Wisbech, probably oval in shape, and on the line still marked by The Crescent. In Peterborough, Abbot Turold sought to secure his new abbey by building a motte on the north side of the monastery precinct, outside Abbot Kenulph's wall. This mound, known as Tout Hill and still standing 20 feet (6m) high in the Prior's garden, was in use for a century or so, but was never defended by anything other than timber palisades. Wisbech, on the other hand, occupying a strategic position at the Nene outfall and constituting one of the gateways to the Fens, was rebuilt in stone in 1087, when it appears to have consisted of a circular shell-keep, perhaps occupying an original motte, within an oval enclosure, walled in stone with a gatehouse facing Museum Square. In Ely itself William constructed a *praesidio* within the monastery precincts, something to which the monks took grave exception. This structure may have been Cherry Hill, the motte and bailey castle still to be seen immediately south of the cathedral, but could simply have been a royal residence with a palisade around it. It is thought by some authorities that Cherry Hill may date only from the time of Henry I. The existing motte is 40 feet (12m) high with a diameter on its summit of 50 feet (15m). Its bailey is roughly square and surrounded by a bank, but no traces of a ditch survive. With remarkable foresight, for he could not have known that within the next two centuries the Isle would figure in three further rebellions, William initiated work to consolidate the causeways and bridges leading onto the Isle, including one which went through the middle of Belsar's Hill, over the river, and on through Aldreth to Haddenham (**Fig. 2**).

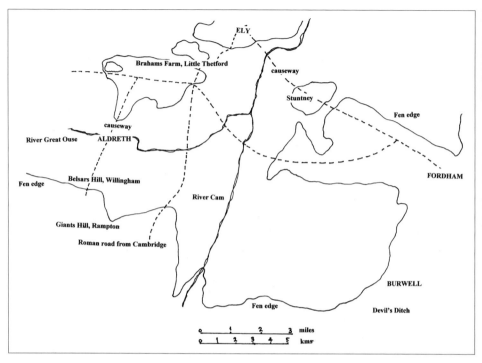

Fig. 2 Sketch map to show sites mentioned in the campaigns around the Isle of Ely.

The Anarchy

When Stephen took the throne in 1135, contrary to his father's will, he inherited the previous regime's officers of state. Given that it was these very men, Bishop Roger of Salisbury and two of his nephews, who had supported Henry in naming the Empress Matilda as his heir, it was imperative that Stephen curb their influence as soon as possible. Inciting a brawl between their retainers at court, he accused them of treason and deprived them of their ministerial status. One nephew, Nigel, Bishop of Ely and Treasurer of England, gave up his castle of Downton (Wiltshire) and fled to Ely, which he fortified against Stephen. It is recorded that he brought two fortifications into a state of readiness there in 1138, one a castle, perhaps Cherry Hill, and a strong fort by the river. Although a bridge is mentioned at Aldreth in 1082, presumably built by the monks of Ely on the orders of William after the campaign against Hereward, it had fallen into disrepair, and anyone approaching Ely by this main route through Belsar's Hill, was, once again, forced to cross by pontoon. This may have been one of the considerations which persuaded Stephen against an assault on Bishop Nigel. Instead, he got his brother, Henry de Blois, Bishop of Winchester, to fabricate an ecclesiastical case against Nigel which would force him to travel to Rome to plead before the Pope. With the main rebel side-lined for at least two years this appeared to have defused the Ely situation.

However, Stephen's problems in this quarter were only just beginning. Geoffrey de Mandeville, Earl of Essex and constable of the Tower of London, had been a powerful ally of Stephen, but previous offences against his vindictive king meant that he remained vulnerable to royal revenge. In 1143 he was stripped of his offices and fortresses but allowed to go free. De Mandeville immediately made for Ely, filling the vacuum created by Nigel's forced departure. Using Ely as a base he quickly established a chain of castles from which his men could dominate the hinterland pursuing a policy of extortion, kidnap and ransom, robbery, rape and murder. All those things the *Peterborough Chronicle* ascribed to the nation's criminal lords were practised by de Mandeville. His castles at Chatteris, Fordham, Benwick and Wood Walton screened Ely from attack and kept Stephen's troops at arm's length. His success took him further from Ely. When Abbot Walter of Ramsey declared for the Empress, Stephen deposed him, replacing him with a monk named Daniel who may have helped the king in his initial reconnaissance of the area back in 1138. Within a few weeks, de Mandeville was in Ramsey not, as the monks imagined, to re-instate Walter, but to take advantage of a confused situation by turning out the monks and converting the monastery into a fortress, and building the motte and bailey fortress of Booth's Hill in the abbey grounds. Despite attempts at resistance by Daniel, who set fire to the wooden gatehouse and the tents of de Mandeville's troops, Ramsey became another springboard for attacks on the local settlements. As de Mandeville's power increased he felt more able to threaten Stephen himself, attacking the royal castle of Cambridge. This was possibly one of the factors which led Stephen to bring an army to the Fens to put a stop to his banditry.

To counter de Mandeville's screen of fortresses, Stephen began his own containing cordon of castles. It was imperative that a linkup be prevented between the Earl of Chester in Lincoln and Hugh Bigod, controlling much of East Anglia and both supporters of the Empress, so Stephen built his first two barrier forts at Weeting (Norfolk) and Lidgate (Suffolk). To protect the royal base of Cambridge by countering the threat from de Mandeville's fortresses in the Huntingdon area, he built forts at Eaton Socon and at Caxton. To seal off the Aldreth causeway, he built two more castles at Swavesey and Rampton. One idea put forward to explain the enigmatic Round Hill, Conington, is that it was built as a siege castle for Wood Walton. The final gap to be plugged was Burwell, which would also provide a base from which the final advance on Ely could be made along the Stuntney ridge. Squeezed tighter and tighter, de Mandeville realised that the Burwell works had to be destroyed before they could provide the stranglehold Stephen sought. Half-expecting such a move, the troops were alert to the danger of an attack and de Mandeville was hit by an aimed spear whilst attacking the building works. He died a few days later, probably from blood poisoning. With his death the campaign came to an end as Stephen had driven the necessary wedge between the sources of Matilda's support in the east. It still took the monks of Ramsey some time, however, to eject de Mandeville's son from Booth's Hill.

Whilst nothing is known of the shape of most of de Mandeville's castles, it may be inferred that they were simple moated earthworks with timber gates and towers astride palisades. Wood Walton has recently been re-surveyed to show that the motte has been removed, but that it once appears to have occupied the centre of a bailey. This may have formed the pattern for de Mandeville's other castles. Stephen's castles appear to share a similar design in that each comprises a rectangular platform inside wet moats. Neither Rampton nor Burwell was completed and both exhibit only the general outline of their defences, whilst retaining spoil-heaps and ramps for the use of the builders. Caxton, with strong defences and a barbican, had a life subsequent to the campaign, as did Swavesey. Burwell appears to have been intended as a more substantial and permanent fortress, displacing two houses from the village. A range of stone buildings along the east side, their outer walls of clunch faced with flint, has been excavated. In the middle of this range was a stone gatehouse accessed by a timber bridge, evidenced by post-holes, over the moat. The north-east corner was marked by a diagonal buttress, and there were latrine-chutes in the wall. Despite the effort and expense, the site was abandoned on de Mandeville's death and later handed over to the monks of Ramsey as a manorial site.

As well as the abandoned and unfinished sites at Burwell and Rampton, it is likely that there were other castles built at this time which were either similarly abandoned by their builders, or demolished on the orders of Henry II. These might include the mottes at Kimbolton and Orwell, the low motte with a small bailey at Sapley, and two of the three ring-works at Southoe, one of which, at Boughton, is known to have been abandoned by 1153, whilst the other (TL178638), its yard paved with Collyweston slates, produced only Saxo-Norman pottery. The motte at Knapwell, only 5 feet (1.5m) high, was built by the monks of Ramsey, to protect their estates there from the depradations of de Mandeville, and would have quickly decayed after the danger had passed, probably not surviving beyond the end of the Anarchy in 1154. A possible motte and bailey at Four Mile Stable, Swaffham Bulbeck (TL589597) may also come into this category of short-lived strongholds. Excavated pottery at the castle at Eaton Socon, held by Hugh de Beauchamp, has shown it to have been occupied around 1140. It consisted of a motte, probably surmounted by a timber tower, and two baileys which enclosed any living quarters. Though pre-existing houses on an Anglo-Saxon settlement site were destroyed in its construction, it appears to be unfinished and was destroyed soon after work on it ceased. A mention in 1210 may refer to a later manor house.

Other Earthwork Castles

Twenty years later another very temporary fortress was built at Huntingdon. The Conqueror's castle passed through marriage to King David of Scotland, and by 1174 was in the possession of his grandson, Scottish King William the Lion, who gave his support to the young Prince Henry. Young Henry was in rebellion against his father, Henry II. William's castle of Huntingdon was besieged by Richard de Lucy, Justiciar of England, who erected a siege castle described by Benedict of Peterborough in the abbey chronicles. It lies on the river-bank, west of the castle, and consists of a mound,

150 feet (45m) in diameter at its base, rising 5 feet (1.5m) to a level platform, 60 feet (18m) in diameter. This would have provided both a secure base for the besiegers, and cut off the castle from supplies or reinforcements from the west. Excavations in 1967 uncovered traces of timber revetments. When de Lucy's troops finally stormed the castle they used hooks on the ends of long poles to pull down the defences, which must have been made of timber.

At least two of the early earthwork castles enjoyed longer lives, even though they were probably never rebuilt in stone. Great Staughton consists of a trapezoidal enclosure with double moats on the south side and single ones on the other three sides. Within this bailey is a low motte, rising to around 15 feet (4.5m) above its surrounding wet ditch. Although its build is credited to Sir Adam de Creting, a commander in Edward I's army in Gascony, it is more likely that the earthwork fortress in this manor, mentioned in Domesday, was in existence much earlier. De Creting, who died in 1295 on service in France, is likely to have transformed it into a fortified house in 1275. One of Southoe's three ring-works (TL184644) was occupied from late in the eleventh century right through to the fourteenth.

Civil Strife

Two episodes during the thirteenth century saw Cambridgeshire castles involved in martial activity. Although castles are generally seen as fulfilling a primarily military function, the majority never saw action. According to generally agreed figures, Cambridgeshire's twenty-two castles together saw a total of eleven actions, quite a high proportion compared to a national average, and the reign of John saw a peak in castles being besieged. During the struggle for power between king and barons which culminated in the signing of Magna Carta, one group of dissidents took refuge in the Isle of Ely, only to be flushed out by a force of royal mercenaries, probably some of the Flemings which King John employed to subdue his own people. The castle was subsequently dismantled and, by 1229, was the site of a windmill. Dating from around this time, and recorded as in use by 1219, is the castle of Kirtling, a rectangular moated enclosure with a higher platform inside, later the site of a Tudor strong house. Kirtling was defended by banks and ditches with palings, sharpened stakes, some of which have been found in modern times.

The defeat of Simon de Montfort's army at Evesham (Worcestershire) in 1265 brought another band of asylum-seekers to the Isle. These were the 'Disinherited', knights who had forfeited their lands by being in rebellion against their lawful king, Henry III. They fortified Ely, using it as a base for raiding expeditions, arguing that in their enforced state as landless knights they now had no alternative means of survival. One of their targets was Swavesey, the manor held by the staunchly Royalist de la Zouch family. It is likely that the earlier defences were expanded and refurbished after they had been over-run in 1266, and all the valuables looted from the church strong-box. These defences, of banks, wet ditches and palisades, encompassed more than the extent of the existing settlement and it has been suggested that de la Zouch was planning a new town, exploiting the existing market and inland port facilities, and that the attacks merely sped up the process by securing the putative burgesses against further attacks. Present-day street names such as 'Turnbridge' memorialise the defended town with its ditches and drawbridges. The 'Disinherited' under John d'Eyvill pointed out the impossibility of them ever raising the five-times annual revenue required to redeem their lands, but even though a compromise was reached with the Church levying a tax to provide them with financial help, the impasse carried on for over a year. Finally Prince Edward took advantage of inside information from the disenchanted and a period of dry weather in August 1267, to seize the Isle and evict the remaining rebels, amongst whom, by chance, was one Baldwin Wake.

Town Defences

Both the conflicts just described resulted in attempts to strengthen the defences of Cambridge. The Kings Ditch runs from the Cam at Mill Lane eastwards and northwards in a loop around the city centre to rejoin the river on the west side of Jesus Green. It may have originated as part of Edward the Elder's burh, but was insignificant as a defence. Both King John in 1216, and Henry III in 1265, are said to have had the

dyke cleared, deepened and widened in order for it to become a viable defence work. There were two gates guarding bridges over the ditch: Trumpington Gate north of Pembroke College, and Barnwell Gate by Christ's. Henry III expressed an intention that the line of the ditch should be walled in stone, linking the gates with defences of substance. There are no records of murage grants for Cambridge and it must be assumed that no action was taken; in fact by 1278 it hardly figured in the topography of the town.

6 PETERBOROUGH ABBEY: the Great Gate onto the marketplace, originally built by Abbot Martin of Bec soon after 1200 when he changed the focus of the town from the east to the west, and then rebuilt in 1308.

The ditch became more and more of an embarrassment and was perceived as a veritable health hazard until it was sluiced out in 1610. Slight traces of the ditch may be seen in the fellows' Garden of Sidney Sussex College.

Despite Peterborough's former burh status and its 'Gate' street names (from the Norse word for street), it was never walled. The early settlement had been on the east of the abbey, but when Abbot Martin of Bec established a new marketplace in front of the abbey's west gate (**6**) soon after 1200, this new focus of the town was not given defences.

Stone Castles of the Thirteenth Century

Whilst Wisbech was rebuilt in stone within twenty years of its original foundation, others like Cambridge and Castle Camps lasted two centuries before improvements were undertaken. At Cambridge an ambitious reconstruction in stone commenced in 1284 under Edward I, when the bailey was walled in masonry. A rectangular gate-tower with a chamber over the gate-passage from which the portcullis and drawbridge might be operated, was further protected by a barbican. Between the gate and the motte, a tower with a massive base was built at the vulnerable south-west corner, with a further three towers on the north curtain and another on the east. The motte was crowned with a circular tower, replacing the previous one of timber. Within the bailey, a Great Hall and a chapel were built along with other domestic structures. The hall was origi-nally of two storeys over a basement stable. Surprisingly, given the danger of fire caused by accident or malign intent, the curtain walls and even the barbican outside the gate were thatched with reed which needed replacing every four years. The roof of the gate-house, however, was covered more securely in lead. Much of this work had essentially been completed by 1288, and Edward visited in 1293. He apparently objected to the smells which permeated the hall from the stables below, and a separate stable was put up soon after, one of the final projects before the castle was deemed finished in 1299. One of the reasons that the castle had been strengthened was its weakness in the war of the 'Disinherited' twenty years previously, so with its own water supply, the improved defences and stores of weapons and food-stuffs, it was now considered capable of with-standing a siege. However, its garrison was small, increased to only thirty men in 1317, and it was never called on to be anything other than an administrative centre and store-house. Castle Camps also remained an earthwork and timber edifice until 1265, when extensive building works were started, which involved enlarging the original enclosure which would now encompass a new village church. It must be assumed that the previ-ous timber buildings occupying the inner ring-work were replaced in stone at this time. Further reconstruction was carried out here in 1331.

Some castles were started around this time, built in stone from the beginning. The so-called John of Gaunt's House at Bassingbourn was licensed to Warin of Bassingbourn in 1266, when he was given leave to surround his house with a bat-tlemented stone wall. An inner enclosure is set inside a larger moated area accessed by a causeway, which appears to run between two semi-circular gate-towers. Outside this

inner double enclosure was a much larger outer one, surrounded by a bank and ditch.

Near to the site of Torpel, a manor owing knight service to Peterborough Abbey, lies the lower stage of a masonry structure that was described, when uncovered in 1969, as 'keep-like'. At around 70 feet (20m) square with walls 11 feet (3.5m) thick, other details indicated a turret with a spiral stair, and the possible presence of a fore-building. Despite all these features, the most likely explanation is that it was probably a hunting-lodge as it sits in the middle of a deer-park, first embanked in 1198. Masonry has also been found in the earthworks of the manorial site, and a re-erected archway, traditionally originating from Torpel, stands beside a house in nearby Helpston (**7**), with neighbouring 'College House' containing more mediaeval details.

The second half of the thirteenth century saw radical changes in castle design, exemplified by the buildings of Edward I in Wales. In these the keep was replaced as the focal point by a strong gatehouse set astride a curtain wall with projecting towers. Clearly Edward's castles, often with several concentric enclosures, were designed for use in a war zone, so in the generally peaceful English shires elements of this advanced military architecture were adapted for incorporation in fortified residences. At Kimbolton the motte, probably raised in the eleventh century and still in existence in 1221, appears to have been replaced by a quadrangular, moated stone castle on a different site, probably the one mentioned in 1275. This castle was completely remodelled starting in 1525 and nothing of the original fabric is now discernible. It is likely to have had a square tower at each corner, a gatehouse in the centre of one side, and buildings around a central courtyard. Another castle of similar design stands at Woodcroft, but here the surviving corner-tower is circular (**8**), and the gatehouse is flush with the curtain wall. No evidence for gate

7 HELPSTON: a doorway traditionally thought to have been brought from the mediaeval hunting-lodge at nearby Torpel.

8 WOODCROFT CASTLE: one of the circular corner towers of the castle built in around 1280.

defences exists but an interruption in the string-course suggests that there was some sort of timber platform projecting above the gate. The building dates from 1280 and exhibits what are said to be 'Caernarvon-style' arched windows. The castle has undergone much alteration but still presents very much as a mediaeval fortified dwelling.

Licences to Crenellate

The mechanism by which the nobility, both secular and ecclesiastical, applied to the crown and were granted licence to crenellate, a sort of mediaeval planning permission, has never really been understood. Although we have consistently been informed about the 'adulterine' castles of the Anarchy, and their subsequent destruction by Henry II, there appears to be little evidence differentiating between those and legitimate castles. Not altogether successful attempts have been made to link the granting of licences to particular reigns or to particular periods of unrest. It has been suggested that the granting of a licence was a reward for loyal service, or a mark of royal approbation, but it is impossible to extrapolate from these notions, often linked to specific personages. The fact remains that of all the hundreds of buildings put up in the mediaeval period which might have been eligible for a licence, only a very few actually received one. The licence to crenellate was taken to indicate royal approval for the fortification of one's home whether it be castle, monastery, rural manor or urban mansion and, by extension, for the applicant himself. The licence, issued to a named person, noble, cleric, lawyer or merchant, allowed him (or occasionally her) to build a wall of stone and lime topped with battlements around a property, to build turrets, and to defend the entrance. Licensed properties ranged from large moated enclosures with veritable fortresses inside, to small tower-houses. Whilst Cambridgeshire boasts a large number of fortified or defensible properties, only a handful of licences were apparently issued during the four centuries of their use, and only two in the period covered by this chapter. One is Bassingbourn, already noted; the other was Biggin 'Abbey', recorded as 'Ditton', licensed to the Bishop of Ely in 1276. This was a summer residence of the bishops of which there remains a range of buttressed stone buildings with later features which include fifteenth-century windows. Other monastic sites were to be fortified, with or without a licence in the next century.

Homestead Moats

The dividing line between castles, such as Swavesey or Bassingbourn, and moated sites is a very narrow one. At sites invested with the title 'castle', one might expect to find, within the moat, evidence of some defensive structure which is reckoned to have fulfilled one or more of the military, judicial, administrative or domestic functions generally associated with what we know as castles. The definition of a moated site is much looser, merely identifying a platform with a moat, usually wet, round it.

Moats are known to have been dug around farms, homesteads, abbey granges, live-stock enclosures and orchards. More moats are found in low-lying areas than in others, as the terrain makes it easier to dig a wet moat around a house, and it is also beneficial in that a moat will drain the land around a house. Status is also thought to have played a part, in that socially aspirational families may have dug moats around their houses as a way of keeping up with the de Mandevilles. Many moats will have had the purely practical purpose of providing water, or the fish which was prescribed as food on nearly half the days of the year. They will have kept farm-animals in, and wild ones out, providing, whatever their prime purpose, a degree of security for those dwelling inside. Outlaws, discharged soldiers, peasants in revolt, or merely those seek-ing to steal one's cash crop, might be delayed, or even deterred by a moat. Whatever the purpose, there were around 400 moats in Cambridgeshire, a figure exceeded by only Essex (550) and Suffolk (500). Six of those in Cambridgeshire are scheduled Ancient Monuments, and a similar number have been excavated. So many un-investi-gated sites may indicate that some may be masquerading as moats but really represent something else. Conversely, that total may have missed genuine moats which have not hitherto been recognised as such. Just as functions were varied, there is no solution to be found in morphology. Moats could be circular, square, rectangular, single-ditched, double-ditched, single, multiple and any combination of those. A rectangular moat at Boxworth, for example has adjacent fish-ponds, one at Gamlingay has only ever

been moated on three sides of a square, and another, at Harlton, comprises three or more separate moats sur-rounding platforms serving different functions. Access to the platform, which in most Cambridgeshire exam-ples is rarely more than a metre higher than the sur-rounding land, can also vary. Commonest are causeways such as at Tadlow, but at Eltisley, the remains of what may have been a stone bridge-abutment have been found.

Given all these variations in form and function it is hardly

9 HEMINGFORD GREY: the rare survival of a stone Norman manor house with a first-floor hall entered by an external timber stair.

surprising that firm dating of any particular site is difficult without excavation, and even then being specific can be problematic. Fowlmere, for instance, following its excavation in 1906, was only pronounced to be 'mediaeval'. Yen Hall at West Wickham can trace its origins to a farmstead chartered in 974 by Edgar, and a number of sites in the county can with certainty be assigned to the period pre-1300. Twelfth-century pottery has been found at Yelling, and at Wintringham traces of four successive timber houses were found, built at intervals of fifty years from 1150, the last being abandoned by 1350. At Elton, on the banks of the Nene west of Peterborough, the abbey of Ramsey had a manorial complex consisting of a group of substantial, buttressed, stone buildings most probably dating from the thirteenth century, standing on a platform within a moat which appeared to incorporate fish-ponds. The site was walled and accessed by a stone gateway approached via metalled track-ways. At Ellington Thorpe, a timber house with a tiled roof, dated to the twelfth century, was found inside a moated enclosure. The house consisted of a hall with a central hearth and a dais at one end, with a covered-way along one side and across one end, separating it from a kitchen. Finds from the twelfth and thirteenth centuries were uncovered.

Many of the moats which can be identified as containing manorial buildings would have provided the only defensive feature on site. Mainly timber buildings were vulnerable to fire and enjoyed only a limited life-span as seen at Wintringham. However, at Hemingford Grey (9) there is an example of a very rare structure, a Norman manor house built in stone, dated to the middle of the twelfth century. Moated on three sides with the Great Ouse on the fourth, the house contained a first-floor hall accessed by a timber stair leading to a doorway in the end wall. There may have been a timber-framed cross-wing at the opposite end, possibly containing a chapel. The raised hall is clearly a feature associated with security and defensibility, and the stairs to the upper door may have been retractable. Another stone Norman manor house was the so-called Bishop's Palace at Barnack. Here, on a site north of the church, was a moat containing a stone house whose last vestiges were demolished in 1977. Despite serious fires in 1830 and 1903, some details survived, and from the slender evidence of the existence of two arches from an arcade, the tenuous inference was made that there had been an aisled hall here, comparable to that remaining at Oakham Castle (Rutland).

three

The Later Mediaeval and Tudor Periods 1300-1600

The first two centuries examined in this chapter were times of great turmoil, spanning the Black Death, the Peasants' Revolt, the Hundred Years War and the Wars of the Roses. Although many individuals, whilst enduring the drudgery and general insecurities of their everyday lives, may have been relatively untouched by these events, none, in town or country, could have been completely insulated against the knock-on economic and social consequences. Typical of the physical threats to be withstood were the raids carried out in the northern part of the county by outlaws based in the Forest of Rockingham, which was then very much more extensive than it is now, a risk recognised by the king himself in 1348. It was therefore vital that those who were able, took every precaution against threats to their already precarious livelihoods and their very lives.

Fortified Manor Houses

With or without licence to crenellate, the nation's great and good continued to ensure that their homes were defensible against all but a determined army with a siege-train. Work continued at some established castles as at Castle Camps which was in process of being reconstructed in 1331. Other sites were wholly new, some of them reflecting the rise of new men in trade or in royal service. Sir Robert Thorpe and Sir William Thorpe were neighbours, contemporaries (dying within three years of each other), fellow officers of state and, presumably, relatives. Sir Robert (d.1372) was Edward III's Chancellor, and Sir William (d.1375) was Lord Chief Justice until 1350, when he was impeached. Sir Robert's house may have been Longthorpe Tower, now on the western outskirts of Peterborough. Here a stone manor house, probably built along with the village church in the 1260s by Sir William de Thorpe, consisted of a hall and solar. His son, Sir Robert, Steward of Peterborough Abbey from 1310–29, added a solid, square tower (**10**) in the early years of the fourteenth century, and it is likely that either he, or *his* son, also Sir Robert (and possibly the Sir Robert who was Chancellor of England) added the decorations which represent such a rare survival today – wall-paintings depicting, amongst other motifs, the wheel of the five senses, and the seven ages of man. A tower of this

10 LONGTHORPE TOWER, Peterborough: the fortified tower of this fourteenth-century manor house of the Thorpes, now administered by the City Council on behalf of English Heritage.

type would have been a commonplace in the warfare-ridden borderlands of Scotland or Wales, but here it is an anomaly. Very similar to a pele-tower, it was designed to be defensible. It could only be entered from the hall at the level of the vaulted ground-floor and again at first-floor level, also vaulted, with no internal link between those two floors. There is a stairway within the thickness of the 7 foot (2.3m) thick wall giving access to the second-floor, and then a spiral stair up to the Collyweston-tiled roof, which has a wall-walk protected by a parapet with open turrets at the corners.

Sir William de Thorpe's house was at Maxey. He must have recovered some of the estates he forfeited on his impeachment, and regained the approval of the king for he was granted licence to crenellate in 1374. Maxey Castle appears from later documents to have been quadrangular with a tower at each corner, a gatehouse and a further, central tower. Only the moat now remains though some architectural details survive in Chapel Cottage opposite (**11**), representing the castle's chapel of St Mary. The present house, within the moat, is much later and exhibits no mediaeval features externally. The design which was common at this time reflects the shift from military duty based on feudal dues and knight service, to the employment of mercenaries. Buildings were grouped around the interior walls of the castle, and these included lodgings for the family and retainers. A strong tower or gatehouse which could be cut off from the rest of the castle could often give peace of mind to the lord and his family, whose household might now contain troops whose loyalty was susceptible to purchase. Throughout the Hundred Years War, European knights who had been captured, and were being held either as hostages or for ransom, would be lodged in suitably appointed castles. In fact it was the ransom itself which sometimes financed an enterprising knight's house-building. John of Angouleme was given up as a hostage in 1412, and joined in 1415 by his elder brother, Charles of Orleans, who had been found uninjured, but trapped by his armour under a pile of bodies on the field of Agincourt. Nowadays, Charles is best remembered for his poetry, but as leader of the Armagnac faction of the French royal house, he was considered too important to be ransomed. He was only released in 1440, as was John, four years later. At least part

11 MAXEY CASTLE: the two-light window in the gable wall of Chapel Cottage, represents the only visible remnant of St Mary's, the chapel belonging to Margaret Beaufort's castle, whose only other remains are the earthworks of former moats and fishponds.

of John's captivity was spent at Maxey castle, from whence he wrote a letter in 1420, and where he would have been treated as an honoured guest rather than a prisoner, having given his word (*parole*) not to escape.

Not all castle-builders were from knightly families. The successful merchant and financier Sir John Pulteney served four terms as Lord Mayor of London, and in 1341, he was granted licence to crenellate three properties. These were the Manor of the Rose, a fortified tower on the Thames waterfront; Penshurst Place in Kent; and Cheveley Castle in Cambridgeshire. Cheveley occupies a rectangular island, 30 yards by 20, surrounded by a deep ditch some 20 feet (6m) deep and crossed by a causeway on its north side. The castle appears to have had curtain walls of rubble masonry with at least one round tower at the north-west angle, and a twin-towered gatehouse. Odd lengths of wall, some bolstered by, possibly later, brick buttresses also survive. The island slopes up to a slightly higher mound on the south side.

At Burrough Green, there are three moated sites. That near the church enclosed the manor house of the de Burghs. In 1330, Thomas, now an MP, was granted licence to create a deer-park. Park Wood (TL642549), a moated site consisting of two adjoining rectangular enclosures surrounded by banks and ditches, is associated with this development. Four years later he was licensed to crenellate his Yorkshire home of Walton, so Park Wood may have been a trial run as the presence of masonry was recorded in the early nineteenth century. The third moat in the parish belonged to the Bretton family.

Other sites exhibit features which may indicate the former existence of strong houses. At Lolham Hall, near Maxey, a later house retains the three stone doorways from a screens passage, giving access from the hall into the kitchen, the buttery and the pantry. At Stonea, Stitches farm-house had external stone stair-towers, possibly representing a later-mediaeval house on this historic site.

Fortified Monastic Precincts and Houses

It may have been the lurid tales in the *Peterborough Chronicle* which caused the monks to fortify their precinct, or it might have been the general unpopularity of the Norman abbots. The Outer Gate had originally been built in the twelfth century, but in 1308 Peterborough Abbey received a licence to crenellate 'the gate of the abbey and two chambers', essentially the structure which faces onto the Marketplace today. The Gatehouse into the Great Court, now occupied by the gardens of the later Bishop's Palace, dates from a decade or so earlier and consists of a square tower with turrets, inside which is a cross-wall containing separate carriage and pedestrian archways (**12**). Also surviving are the Prior's Gate, again with separate arches, and built by Abbot Kirton whose rebus of a church and a barrel still top the carriage arch, and fragments of the Almoner's Gate in the south-east corner. Long stretches of the precinct wall can be seen, which are successive re-buildings of Abbot Kenulph's original wall.

At Ely, the precinct was also enclosed by a wall with several gates, the most impressive of which is the three-storey Ely Porta (**13**) started in 1397. It is a massive rectangular block with four square angle turrets, and is pierced by the usual two gate-openings, merging into a single gate-passage. Many of the monastic buildings survive within the walled precinct, in use by the Cathedral and by King's School. On the north side, the precinct is

12 PETERBOROUGH BISHOP'S PALACE: the fourteenth-century gatehouse of the Abbott's lodging showing the outer arch and the inner one split into two, one for carriages and the other for pedestrians.

13 ELY PORTA: the main gate into Ely's monastic precinct, licensed in 1397.

14 ELY: the Sacristy Gate of 1325 gives access to the precinct from the High Street.

bounded by the High Street (formerly Steeple Row), onto which open the Sextry (or Sacristy) Gate of 1325–26 (**14**), the Steeple Gate with a timbered upper storey of around 1500, and the Goldsmith's Tower, begun by Alan of Walsingham around 1335, and subsequently adapted as another entrance into the precinct. The main gateway on the north has disappeared.

Documents show that the priory at St Neots, founded in 974 and re-founded in 1080, at some time in its life acquired a defensive wall, probably refurbished at regular intervals into the fifteenth century. Facing onto the river was the gatehouse, still standing in 1814, whilst the walled area extended as far as New Street. A conjectural plan of the priory shows a rectangular block pierced by a gate arch with a lodge to one side. There are burials outside the southern line of this wall, which would thus appear to be a later addition.

Prelates too felt the need to fortify their houses, and there are two fine examples from the fourteenth century in the county. Northborough consists of a domestic block comprising a full-height hall attached to a two-storey solar-block, the whole forming a T-shape. The hall measures 36 feet (10.8m) by 24 feet (7.2m), and is connected by a screens passage to the ground-floor kitchen, pantry and buttery. Above these three rooms, and reached by an internal spiral stair is a private solar, measuring 37 feet (11m) by 15 foot six inches (4.5m), into which the family might retire. In front of the hall-block and facing north up the Lincoln road, is the slightly earlier gatehouse, built in around 1330, with its gate-passage arrangement modelled on that at the Abbot's Gate in Peterborough (**15**). The likely builder of the manor house is Roger de Norburgh, bishop of Lichfield and Coventry, whose master-mason,

15 NORTHBOROUGH MANOR: the gatehouse with a cross-wall forming separate carriage and pedestrian archways.

16 CHESTERTON TOWER: the residence of the Proctor of St Andrew's who administered the church on behalf of its owners, the abbey of Vercelli near Milan.

William de Eyton, had finished work on Lichfield Cathedral in 1331. There are stylistic similarities between his work there and work carried out at Northborough. De Eyton died in 1337, when work at Northborough had been completed. The house was also used by Bishop Roger's protégé, Michael, Bishop of London. As well as the imposing gatehouse, the house was surrounded by a wall, fragments of which survive, but there is no certainty that it was moated. The village, too, was surrounded by a bank, probably topped by a palisade, and a ditch, and when the manor house was built up against the western edge of these defences, it appears that the highway was diverted around to the west of the manorial enclosure, creating the kink which is prominent today.

    The second example is quite different. The parish church of St Andrew, in Chesterton on the outskirts of Cambridge, was owned by the abbey of St Andrew at Vercelli, near Milan, to whose founder, Cardinal Guala (serving in England as papal legate in 1218) it had been given by Henry III. When the church was rebuilt in 1330, it was decided to provide a suitable residence for their proctor, who oversaw the abbey's interests in the property. Chesterton Tower (**16**) is an unusual building in that it combines the look of a monastic gatehouse without a gateway, with the features of a pele tower. The tower was entered at first-floor level, above the vaulted basement, by an external wooden stair. Rising higher than the tower's two storeys, are two polygonal corner-turrets, one containing a spiral stair, and the other corbelled out to create an enlarged octagonal chamber, originally vaulted. It would appear that a hall adjoined the tower.

The Peasants' Revolt

Whilst Essex remained the epicentre of the 1381 attempt to push Richard II into reforming the tax-gathering system which had produced the hated poll-tax, the action was in London. However, the commons in most of East Anglia had been drawn into the affair and afterwards, Bury-St-Edmunds, Norwich and Cambridge were singled out for harsher condemnation than many places. Bury had been the scene of the murder of Sir John Cavendish, Chief Justice and Chancellor of Cambridge University. In Norwich the townsfolk had enlisted the aid of knights to expel the ruling caste, and John Wrawe, a renegade priest, had brought a wave of lawlessness to the area between Bury, Ely and Cambridge. Henry Despencer, Bishop of Norwich had been forced to flee the city, retreating to his manor of Burley, outside Oakham (Rutland). Despencer had been raised to high office by a pope who looked for military training in his prelates, and he was spoiling for a fight with the rebels. With a small force he set out for Peterborough where he found an attack on the abbey in progress. On the bishop's unheralded arrival, some of the rebels had taken refuge inside the church, and they were dragged out by Despencer's men-at-arms and summarily despatched. He then moved on to Huntingdon where the townsfolk, possibly informed of the fighting bishop's progress, had barred the bridge, dispersing the rebel bands. Next he marched on Ramsey Abbey and besieged a band of rebels, who were routed in a dawn attack, with any who escaped being hunted down and killed. By the time he reached Cambridge, where the mayor had been instrumental in inciting the townsfolk to exploit the prevailing anarchy in paying off old scores against the university, the local land-owners and the church, the violence had begun to subside. It was only the fear of a total break-down of order that prevented Despencer from giving the mayor more than a verbal roasting. Setting out on his way to restore peace to Norfolk, he left enough signs of his displeasure, in the form of rebel heads on poles, to keep the chastened towns-folk on their best civic behaviour.

The Wars of the Roses

Cambridgeshire was spared much of the action in the campaigns which claimed the lives of over half the nobility of England and a significantly large proportion of the gentry. They died in battle, in the culling of the vanquished after the battle, and on the scaffold. When aggregated, actual incidents of warfare barely exceeded a few months in total during the thirty years of the conflict, but their savagery left few manors untouched.

On the few occasions that armies marched through territory they considered to be 'enemy', towns were sacked. This is what happened to towns on the Great North Road when the Lancastrians marched down to London in 1461 after their success at Wakefield. Considering the river Trent to be the line below which they had licence to pillage, these were some of the few occasions in the Wars that 'civilians' suffered directly through collateral damage, but Huntingdon was in such a depressed state anyway at this time, that the decision was taken not to resist. In mediaeval warfare it was expected that the common soldiers on the losing side would have their throats cut after a battle, whilst their lords were salvaged from the field for future ransom, but in this conflict it was the nobles who died in droves.

Several of the central figures in the conflict had strong connections to this county. Margaret Beaufort was descended, if illegitimately, from John of Gaunt, Duke of Lancaster and was closely connected to the Earl of Warwick. Many believed that, in the absence of an heir to Henry VI's throne, Margaret had the strongest claim. She had been brought up at Maxey, the castle belonging to her mother, Margaret Beauchamp, and it was to here in 1470, that her third husband, Sir Henry Stafford, brought the news of the Lancastrian defeat at Loosecoat Field near Stamford. Her mother had married Lionel, Lord Welles, who was killed at Towton, and his son, as leader of the rebel army, had been executed before the battle had even begun, and then *his* son at the end of it. Stafford himself was to die in October the next year, of wounds sustained at the Battle of Barnet, five months previously. Margaret's second husband (her betrothal to the Duke of Suffolk had been dissolved before either party was 10 years old) Edmund Tudor, Earl of Richmond, had died in 1455 of plague whilst a prisoner in Wales, leaving the 13-year-old pregnant with the future Henry VII. Before she was 30, she had lost: two husbands, her step-father, her step-brother, two former fathers-in-law at Northampton and Mortimers Cross, an uncle and a brother-in-law at St Albans. Her son was somewhere, probably overseas, in protective custody, but completely out of her control, and she married her fourth husband, Thomas, Lord Stanley in 1472. From these traumatic circumstances she would go on to broker the Lancastrian revival which would topple Richard III and place her son on the throne, the final victory helped by her husband's sudden change of allegiance on the battlefield of Bosworth. She lived, as England's richest woman, until 1509, outliving her husband by five years, endowing churches and founding colleges, including St John's and Christ's at Cambridge.

Dr John Morton was a churchman, serving in Henry VI's bureaucracy as Lord Privy Seal. Surviving plots, battles and sieges, he spent time in exile with Queen Margaret, and as a prisoner in the Tower. Pragmatic as any politician, after his capture at Tewkesbury he changed sides, becoming a Yorkist because, as he pointed out, God was clearly backing the fortunes of Edward IV. By 1472 he was Master of the Rolls and a Privy Councillor, advising the king in the secret meetings held in the Star Chamber, and carrying out diplomatic missions in France, receiving a French pension for his efforts. In 1479, Morton was consecrated as Bishop of Ely, a reward for his civil service. Here he embarked on an ambitious scheme to drain the Fens, and to improve river access to Wisbech with Morton's Leam, a 12 mile (19km) long cut, linking Guyhirn, Whittlesey and Stanground. By 1483 he was still prominent on the national stage as a member of the Council, seeking to safeguard the interests of the young Edward V, but in the end, he was powerless to resist Richard III's coup. Though under house arrest, he conspired with Margaret Beaufort and the Duke of Buckingham to arrange a marriage between Elizabeth of York and her son Henry Tudor. Acting as go-between for the plotters was Dr Christopher Urswick, Margaret Beaufort's confessor. Whilst Richard could not prove Morton's involvement, he engineered a smear campaign, accusing Morton of consorting with known necromancers and warlocks such as Thomas Nandyke of Cambridge but, in the meantime Morton had made good his escape to Flanders. After Richard's defeat at Bosworth (Leicestershire), Henry VII was delighted to employ Morton, from 1486 as Archbishop of Canterbury and, the next year as Lord Chancellor. Urswick became confessor to the king and Master of King's Hall in Cambridge, the precursor to Trinity College, and Dean of Windsor. In 1493 Morton became a cardinal, but is best remembered for ensnaring the rich in his cleft stick, known as 'Morton's Fork', probably the most obscure pub-name in Whittlesey, if not the world. This cunning maxim ordained that those nobles who lived frugally clearly had the resources from which to pay the high taxes demanded of them, whilst those revelling in conspicuous consumption could temper their extravagance by contributing more of their obviously inflated income to the Exchequer. Morton died in 1500 in his eighties, having served three monarchs efficiently if not entirely faithfully.

During such a turbulent period it might be expected that a spate of fortified dwellings would have been built, but the Wars of the Roses produced no sieges, or even sustained campaigns aimed at capturing territory and occupying castles and towns. Cambridgeshire boasts only the one fortified manor from the fifteenth century; Elton Hall is a courtyard house built by the Sapcotes after the wars were essentially over. One of the two vanished ranges

17 ELTON HALL: the fortified gatehouse of this manor house built in the second half of the fifteenth century. (Photo courtesy of Elton Estates)

contained the great hall, but the chapel survives over an undercroft and now serves as a drawing-room. The major remaining mediaeval feature is the machicolated three-storey gatehouse (**17**) with higher, octagonal stair-turret. The house was largely rebuilt in the seventeenth century and again in Victorian times, when the tower was built and lots of gothic detail added.

Moats were still being dug into the next century, but a good example, from the late fifteenth century, is Leighton Bromswold, a manor house with the gatehouse added in 1616. To the catalogue of reasons for digging moats listed above, another one can be added – the garden feature. Ancient moats were adapted, and new ones dug to create attractive gardens which might be viewed from the house itself or from vantage points specially raised for the purpose. The need for fortifications was disappearing, and by the middle of the century, Cambridge Castle was virtually derelict with repairs being made only to the curtain walls and to the gaol in the Great Gatehouse. Stone from the roof-less hall was taken by Henry VI in 1441 for his new King's College.

Bishops Building in Brick

By the mid-fifteenth century brick was gaining respectability as a building material. Ever keen to appear as trendsetters, a coterie of officers of state, most of them also bishops, built a number of semi-fortified palaces, four of which were in Cambridgeshire. Bishop Rotherham, of Ely until 1468 and then of Lincoln, built at Buckden, his work being completed from 1480 by Bishop Russell of Lincoln, Lord Chancellor to Richard III. Bishop Morton, of Ely from 1471, better-known for his work at Lambeth, built at Wisbech. Bishop Alcock who succeeded Morton at Ely in 1486, built at Ely, at Little Downham, and added to Morton's work at Wisbech. All these churchmen were closely associated with other secular and ecclesiastical posts. Morton, Rotherham, and Fisher were all Archbishops of Canterbury and Rotherham and Alcock were joint Lords Chancellor for some months in 1474, a post also held by Morton and Russell. The university adds a further dimension. Alcock was influenced by Rotherham's home-town Jesus College for his own foundation in Cambridge from 1490. Rotherham and Fisher were both Chancellors of Cambridge University, and it was Fisher who completed Margaret Beaufort's foundations at St John's and Christ's Colleges, shortly after her death in 1509.

Buckden Palace had been held by the bishops of Lincoln since the 1100s. Until 1836 the diocese extended much further south than it does now, so lodgings were required for the bishop when visiting his far-flung parishes. It was conveniently located on the Great North Road to provide a stopping-place for the bishop himself and also for royal parties travelling around the country. In its reconstructed form it included a three-storey great tower (**18**) with polygonal corner-turrets containing spiral stairs. The tower has domestic windows and a single gun-loop, but straddles a crenellated wall with wall-walk, forming an inner enclosure, formerly moated, and entered through a three-storey gate-tower (**19**). Adjoining one corner of the tower were the great hall, kitchen, chapel and great chamber. An outer enclosure, entered

18 BUCKDEN: the Great Tower of this palace of the bishops of Lincoln, completed during the last quarter of the fifteenth century alongside the Great North Road.

19 BUCKDEN: the gatehouse into the inner courtyard.

through a gatehouse, contained barns and stables. The initial impression is one of a
fortress, but grandeur was probably the major influence in its design, and it is closely
modelled on Tattershall (Lincolnshire), itself intended to project an image of power
and wealth. Buckden's great tower is overlooked by the contemporary church-tower,
so it must be inferred that defence would not have been the primary consideration,
but the vocabulary of fortification is exploited to the full. Most of the domestic buildings have been replaced, but the great tower, gatehouses and walls remain. The palace
is occupied by the Claretians, a Roman Catholic Order, which generously invites
free access to the grounds.

In Ely, the Bishop's Palace, a brick house of 1490 and later, was built by Bishop
Alcock (1486–1500). Despite several later re-modellings, the lower stages of the buttressed West Tower and the whole of the East Tower, formerly a gatehouse (**20**), are
essentially Alcock's work in red brick with blue diaper-work, and now joined by a
later range. At Little Downham, Alcock rebuilt an existing palace in brick with stone
facings. Two ranges remain linked by a wall; one of which, with an imposing doorway
and the arms of the See of Ely above, has been suggested as a chapel, while the other,
an oven being earlier reported, is thought to have served as a kitchen.

Like its contemporary in Cambridge, by the mid-1400s the castle at Wisbech (the
chapel still being in use) had fallen into such a state of disrepair that Bishop Morton

decided to build anew. From
1478–83, using bricks measuring 11 inches (27.5cm) in
length and 2.5 inches (6.5cm)
thick, with dressings of Ketton
stone, he constructed a mansion
whose cellars and foundations
can still be seen. This palace
was extended by Bishop Alcock
who died there in 1500. Morton
was also responsible for building Guyhirn Tower to mark
the eastern end of his drainage/
navigation channel or leam.
Its form is now unknown so it
could have been simply an out-
look tower as at Clifton House,
Kings Lynn, or it could have
been an episcopal residence.

20 ELY: Bishop Alcock's palace
showing the former gate-tower.

Citadels of Learning

After 1500 there was still little inclination on the part of masons or patrons to abandon the language of chivalry. In many new builds the gatehouse front was designed to promote an image of power and majesty. Although never remotely approaching the continuous insecurities of continental Europe, England nevertheless faced conflict in the form of both internal rebellions, and the threat of foreign invasions. Royal troops were mustered in Huntingdon, for instance, in 1536 to put down the Lincolnshire Rising, itself the curtain-raiser to the Pilgrimage of Grace. In Cambridge, the colleges adopted the monastic tradition of enclosed courts entered through imposing gatehouses. At Queens' College, the gatehouse opening onto Queens' Lane was a nominal collaboration between Margaret of Anjou, consort to Henry VI, and Elisabeth Woodville, Edward IV's queen. It was probably designed by the master-mason Reginald Ely during the 1450s, is of brick and is three-storeys in height with a polygonal angle-turret at each corner. Bishop Alcock's Jesus College is slightly later, dating from 1496. Here the gatehouses are square towers. The first, opening onto Jesus Lane, may have been the original entrance to the existing nunnery, but re-built in brick with castellations, those present now being eighteenth-century additions. The more substantial gatehouse in the Cloister Court is of three storeys, again with later stepped battlements. Next chronologically come the two foundations of Lady Margaret Beaufort, Christ's, begun around 1505 before her death, and St John's in 1511, both being completed by Chancellor Fisher. At both colleges the great gatehouses share certain similarities despite later tinkering. Over the ogival gate-arch are the Beaufort arms, with their yales, mythical beasts. There are two storeys over the gate, and polygonal angle-turrets. The main difference is that Christ's, originally of brick has been faced in stone since 1714, while St John's retains its original brick (**21**). What is now Trinity College was being rebuilt as King's Hall in 1519, part of that project being

21 CAMBRIDGE: the gate of St John's College showing the Beaufort arms over the signature ogival arch of the entrance.

the Great Gate (**22**). When Henry VIII re-founded the college in 1546, unsurprisingly, the monumental gatehouse was retained, even though it was a free-standing structure until ranges were added ten years later. At Magdalene the college founded by Henry VI can still be seen in its First Court much of which dates from 1430. When, after the Dissolution, it was re-founded by Lord Chancellor Audley in 1542, he referred to it as 'Magdalene *Castle*'. This may have been to dissociate the college from its monastic origins and to stress its modern secular character, but in a century during which nobles were executed for maintaining castles and liveried retainers, it would appear a little risky.

Tudor Houses

Kimbolton had been rebuilt as a manor house in 1522–5, and the RCHM(E) records only fragments of part of this Tudor fabric present in the rebuild of 1615. There would, no doubt, have been some discreet security arrangements made during the stay of Katherine of Aragon from 1534–6, but the house would have lacked overt defensive features. Hinchingbrooke House, a conversion of a nunnery, was built after 1541 and incorporated much of the mediaeval gatehouse from Ramsey Abbey. The tall gatehouse at Kirtling Tower (**23**), built around 1530 by the lawyer Edward North, underlines the shift from defence to display. North was Chancellor of the Court of Augmentations, the body responsible for disposing of monastic properties after the Dissolution. His new house occupied the moated platform of an earlier castle, and was quadrangular

22 (top left) CAMBRIDGE: the gate of Trinity College with separate carriage and pedestrian archways. (Photo: Pam Osborne)

23 (bottom left) KIRTLING TOWER: the double-height oriel window betrays the predominantly domestic nature of this Tudor gatehouse standing within the moat of a mediaeval castle.

with a gatehouse in the middle of the south range. Standing some 55 feet (16.75m) high and provided with the usual defensive motifs of polygonal turrets and battlements, its military credentials are undermined by the showy, but wholly domestic, double-height oriel window projecting over the gate-arch. With the reign of Henry VIII, any need for fortification was shifted away from the private castle to the public fortress, situated on the coast, and intended to prevent foreign invasion.

Citizen Soldiers

Anglo-Saxon kings could mobilise a body known as the *fyrd* for military service in times of danger. Based on hundreds, tythings and shires, these forces were assembled under local leaders, remaining embodied for as long as the campaign might last. There had existed a close correspondence between the size of individual *burhs* and the number of men available to man their defences. All this changed with the coming of the feudal system, but as early as the mid-1300s kings were not above invoking these ancient customs in order to make up the numbers, often for foreign expeditions. Only after Henry VII's disbandment of the nobility's private armies did the Constitutional Force come back to prominence. From the time of Henry VIII, when foreign invasion was a distinct possibility, a succession of Acts of Parliament was passed requiring Lords Lieutenant to ensure that the quotas set for their shires were achieved and maintained; that suitable horses were available; that stocks of arms, armour and munitions were kept in good order; and that men spent regular time in training.

The Spanish Armada

The threat posed by the Spanish against Elizabeth I in 1587, prompted a direction to leaders of these militias that they should especially form and train bodies of cavalry, presumably as their mobility would produce a speedier reaction to an enemy landing on the coast. They were already responsible for ensuring that the fire beacons, which would signal that enemy landings had taken place, were kept ready and manned at appropriate times of national emergency. The current system of fire-beacons had been established by Henry VIII in 1545. Each position consisted of three beacons, iron braziers anchored by clamps or brackets to a firm base. One fire meant that the enemy had been sighted. A second fire was intended to mobilise the militia, and three fires burning simultaneously indicated that the enemy had landed. The three baskets, raised up on poles, were filled with pitch-soaked grass, firewood, scrap timber and lumps of animal fat. They were maintained in this condition throughout the summer of 1588, but a number of panics and malicious firings had prompted a directive that beacons could only be lit on the orders of a JP. In Huntingdonshire the Lord Lieutenant, Lord St John of Bletsoe commanded that the beacons 'may be put in a proper state', and watched by men of 'good discretion and substance'. This directive was issued on 17 June 1588 but, away from the coast, watchers were only paid from 24 July. In the southern counties and the invasion coast, there were high cliffs and down-lands to ensure inter-visibility between beacons, but in the flatter landscape of East Anglia and the Midlands there were few naturally prominent sites. One site which appears on a map of 1633 apparently topped with a beacon lies between Swaffham Bulbeck and Swaffham Prior, to the south of the Burwell road. Here were two pre-historic barrows known as the 'Beacons', marking the end of a race-course, a name echoed by the nearby Beacon Farm. Generally, however, church-towers were employed, although replica beacons have been installed in many places, including Huntingdon Castle (**24**), in 1988, and in Ely Cathedral precinct near Cherry Hill.

As fears of the impending Armada had intensified, then a muster of the militia was ordered, along with a roll-call of available troops and an inventory of their weapons. Cambridge was to field 1,000 able-bodied men, half of whom were to be already trained, with the Shire producing a similar number in the same proportions. Additionally, 170 horsemen were required consisting of 50 lancers, 40 light-horsemen, presumably for piquets and scouting, and 80 armed with petronelles, large pistols generally fired from the saddle, braced against the horseman's chest (poitrine). The Marshall of Huntingdonshire, Sir Henry Cromwell of Hinchingbrooke and Ramsey commanded some 104 horsemen, whilst his two captains each fielded 450 infantry. Weapons included a high proportion of firearms – 250 Qualivers and 40 muskets, and the horse wore light armour. This total would appear to exceed the county's previous assessment. Northamptonshire, assessed at over 1,600 men, would have included some from Peterborough and the Soke. Most of these militia-men, theoretically over 111,000 across the country, were to muster at West Tilbury with its ferry across the Thames, where they were inspected and addressed by their lion-hearted Queen. They would then be in a position to repel the coming Spanish invasion wherever the enemy might make land-fall.

24 HUNTINGDON CASTLE: the Norman rampart overlooking the bridge, now with a modern commemorative replica, but occupying the site of a possibly original Armada beacon.

four

Stuart and Georgian Cambridgeshire

Towards the end of the mediaeval period the houses of the nobility and the gentry were shedding the last vestiges of defensibility, and taking on a no less grand, but notably un-warlike aspect. This is reflected in the buildings of the early part of the Stuart century. Kimbolton was rebuilt by the earls of Manchester from 1617 as a Jacobean house completely encasing earlier work. At Leighton Bromswold (**25**), the gatehouse of 1616, a rectangular block with four higher, square angle turrets within the moated area, is clearly intended to impress but not to repel. The 80 foot (24m) diameter circular bastions at each corner of the moat are unlikely to have had any defensive purpose. Nevertheless, however unfashionable surviving fortified buildings might have been regarded, many a family would be grateful for the strong walls and moat which might save them from at least roaming bands of soldiers in the coming Civil Wars. Others, thrown out by a garrison which needed a base from which to raid, forage, scout, or patrol lines of communication, would have wished that their ancestors had rebuilt their home as a pretty, but insubstantial Tudor mansion.

25 LEIGHTON BROMSWOLD CASTLE: this gatehouse of 1616 stands inside a mediaeval moat landscaped as a water feature.

Warfare in Europe in the Seventeenth Century

Mainland Europe had been a battleground for several hundred years. The advent of gun-powder artillery and of disciplined and trained infantry had transformed the battlefield. The increasing application of technological developments, and the concomitant growth of professionalism in the military widened the scope of war, but greatly increased both casualties, especially amongst civilians, and material damage to property. Consequently the conduct of warfare was radically altered. Generals sought to avoid pitched battles since the commitment of their troops was often suspect, and the strength of town defences turned sieges into marathon tests of endurance. Armies lived off the land so scorched earth could be a very effective counter, regardless of those whose land it was. 'Hearts and minds' was not, apparently, a notion inviting much credibility. Britain, as diarists in the Civil Wars commented, had missed all this. A number of Britons had fought abroad, notably Ireland's 'Wild Geese', many professional mercenaries escaping Scotland's lochs and glens, and a few English gentlemen in search of adventure, but since the Wars of the Roses most martial activity involving Britons had happened at sea. When Charles I raised his standard at Nottingham and started the First Civil War, there was a marked contrast between those for whom military leadership was an unfamiliar and unwelcome duty, attempting to stay one page ahead of their men in the drill-books, and those who had learned their trade abroad and may have had some inkling of what it was all about, who now had to impart that experience to their un-blooded colleagues.

Fortification in Europe in the Seventeenth Century

In response to the development of gunpowder, the art of fortification, influenced by such as Durer, da Vinci and Michelangelo, had undergone a transformation. The walls of fortresses became ever lower and thicker, to both mount and resist artillery. The Italian invention of the bastion, designed to flank the curtain wall by providing a projecting platform for muskets and cannon, had led to all sorts of sophisticated refinements. One example is the invention of the occupation of military engineer, a student of geology and geometry, who planned the defences of a town and then went off to conduct the siege of somebody-else's. Battering with cannon, undermining and starvation were the main means of attack, and it was the defenders' duty to resist for as long as possible, but to surrender as soon as an assault was inevitable. If a town were stormed, the defenders were entitled to little mercy as their final resistance was regarded as futile and expensive in attackers' lives. Distinct national schools of fortification emerged. The Dutch, for instance, exploited water defences in their flooded terrain, and the French and Italians created extensive concentric layouts, either on green-field sites or pushed out beyond the suburbs of an existing town with its mediaeval walled core, where towers would be lowered and filled with earth, and curtain walls thickened and backed with earth banks. Although all this had been witnessed by Britons, fighting in the Thirty Years War for instance, and many of the principles would be adhered to, these levels of sophistication were not going to be the pattern in the Civil Wars in the British Isles.

Fortification in England in the Civil Wars

In contrast to the geometrical exactitude of continental fortresses, only achieved through the expenditure of colossal amounts of materials, labour and treasure, almost all those fortifications raised in England were little more than field-works. Only the King's capital of Oxford, designed by the Dutch engineer de Gomme, had greater pretensions as an exemplar of classical fortification theory. Where town walls already existed they were strengthened; castles and mansions were given outworks of earthen bastions; even churches had musket-loops knocked through their walls. Many defences consisted simply of hastily dug ditches with palisades, sharpened stakes, gabions filled with pebbles and bundles of whatever material was available be it brushwood or wool. Streets in towns were obstructed by chains which would impede the horsemen who might otherwise descend in the night to pillage and burn. Even the 11 mile (18km) circuit of London's defences, built by a work-force of up to 20,000 citizens at a time, consisted of earth banks and ditches strengthened by a dozen redoubts, only some of which were revetted in brick. As the war unfolded, a pattern of skirmishes and minor sieges evolved. The mobility offered by the availability of light cannon, some even made of leather, and the standardisation of cavalry tactics and training, ensured that nowhere could feel very safe from sudden attack, and it was therefore necessary to maintain one's defences, however rudimentary they might be.

Cambridgeshire, a Vulnerable Frontier

East Anglia was the Parliamentarian heart-land. It provided recruits, horses, food and forage. It was where the core of the New Model Army was raised and trained, and it supplied much of the political and religious backbone for the Parliamentarian cause. Prominent local worthies like Oliver Cromwell found themselves not only representing their constituents in parliament, but also leading them into battle. But their first task was to secure the Eastern Association's northern border. Though isolated in a sea of Parliamentarians, Kings Lynn had nevertheless declared for the King in August 1643. Despite being strongly defended, there was little chance of relief when it was blockaded by land and sea. To ensure that no help could come by land, Wisbech Castle was re-fortified with out-posts at Leverington and at the Horseshoe. Lt Col Dodson commanded the garrison at Wisbech and also skirmished in the surrounding fenland. Back at Kings Lynn, a token bombardment and a threat of assault brought a speedy capitulation and, shortly afterwards, Peterborough was occupied, becoming a spring-board for taking Crowland (Lincolnshire), which then spent long periods of time in Parliamentarian occupation. The River Nene had thus been established as a secure frontier, but the threats to the Eastern Association had not yet been eliminated. Newark-upon-Trent (Nottinghamshire) was a vitally important Royalist centre acting as a key stronghold on the road linking Oxford to Yorkshire. Although it spent much of the war under siege, forces in the town, protected by extensive earthwork forts and a ring of outlying garrisons such as Belvoir Castle (Leicestershire), were able to carry out raids. In August 1643 a force of several hundred cavalry descended on Peterborough. They were quickly ejected by Cromwell, about to be appointed governor of the Isle of Ely, and retreated into Burghley House. Here, after a short demonstration of the effects of artillery, they surrendered and were transported as prisoners to Cambridge. Garrisons on both sides could hold out against local raiding parties but were vulnerable to the attentions of field armies with artillery. The disputed territory in north Cambridgeshire, south Lincolnshire and Rutland changed hands regularly as armies moved through it. In 1644, for instance, whilst the Parliamentarian army was in the north, a 500-strong force from Belvoir Castle attempted to garrison Wothorpe House (**26**) overlooking the Great North Road near Stamford, but were thwarted by local troops from Leicestershire under Lord Grey. In June 1645, in the run-up to the decisive Battle of Naseby, when Royalist forces were on the offensive, seizing Leicester and its surrounding garrisons, efforts were again made to secure the approaches to the Isle of Ely. Cromwell was given troops from Cambridgeshire, cannon and supplies of powder and shot, and permission to impress labour as necessary to ensure that all the forts were manned, armed and ready for action. In anticipation of a Royalist advance from the north, Colonel Vermuyden assembled a force at Stamford, and then at Deeping Gate, south of the Welland, to control the crossing.

26 WOTHORPE: the Elizabethan dower-house of Burghley, briefly occupied by Royalists in the Civil War, and later partly demolished and allowed to decay.

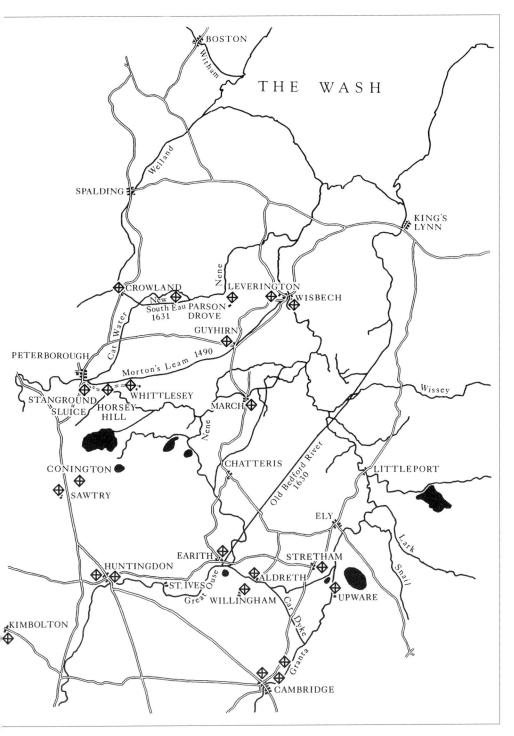

Fig. 3 Sketch map to show Civil War fortifications in Cambridgeshire. (By kind permission of John Goldsmith)

Cromwell's defences consisted of a number of layers (**Fig. 3**). For the odd times, as during Prince Rupert's campaign in 1644, when Crowland became untenable, redoubts – each garrisoned by fifty men and provisioned by boat – were built at Dowesdale Bank near Whaplode Drove Common, at Barrow Bank, Clough's Cross near Parson Drove and in the Guyhirn area. Another, even more isolated, redoubt site was Brotherhouse Bar on Queens Bank, north of Crowland, which must have been exposed in every way. The road north from Peterborough was defended by Northborough Manor, later to become the home of one of Cromwell's daughters when she married into the Claypoles. The approach to Ely via the Fen Causeway, running along the strip of land between Morton's Leam and Whittlesea Mere, was defended by a small work at Stanground Sluice and the much larger pentagonal fort at Horsey Hill, with a garrison in Whittlesey itself. March was an important depot with an arsenal and stabling, still known as 'Cavalry Barns', and a crossing of the Old Nene, all defended by a bastioned fort, which may have been placed to operate in conjunction with a work at Stonea Camp, where a cannon-ball of the period has been found. The road from Chatteris to Mepal, known as 'Ireton's Way' after the general who became another of Cromwell's sons-in-law, was protected by small works at Chatteris Ferry, and at Thompson's Coate, Witcham. The line of the Great Ouse was more heavily defended still. The castle and town of Huntingdon were re-fortified and here, and at St Ives, an arch of the town bridge was removed, and drawbridges inserted. At Earith where the Ouse met the Old Bedford River, dug in 1630, a large earthwork bastioned fort was built, and there were permanent piquets, in small redoubts, at Wivelingham (probably Willingham and possibly a re-fortified Belsar's Hill), and at Aldreth High Bridge. At Elford Closes, where the Cambridge–Ely road crosses the Old West River below Stretham, there appears to have been a flanked redoubt, now destroyed by gravel workings. These last three works protected the southern approaches to Ely. A moat at Upware, formerly looking very much like another bastioned fort, would have secured the Cam above Cambridge, and other smaller works are known north of Cambridge Castle which was re-fortified in 1643. On the west, the Great North Road was guarded by a gun-battery at Sawtry and two other sites cannot be discarded as possible contemporary forts. Kimbolton Castle, home of Edward Montagu, Earl of Manchester, a Parliamentarian general, may have been garrisoned since it occupied a position of such strategic importance. The other possibility is the enigmatic Conington Round Hill, which could have been a mediaeval moat, an earthwork artillery fort, a later garden feature, or all three.

Parliamentarian Fortifications in Cambridgeshire

By 1642 Cambridge Castle had undergone systematic demolition with the only remaining masonry representing the gaol, formerly Edward I's gatehouse. Its commanding location above the bridge, however, still made it a fine defensive position, and it was important that Cambridge with its symbolic importance to the Parliamentarian

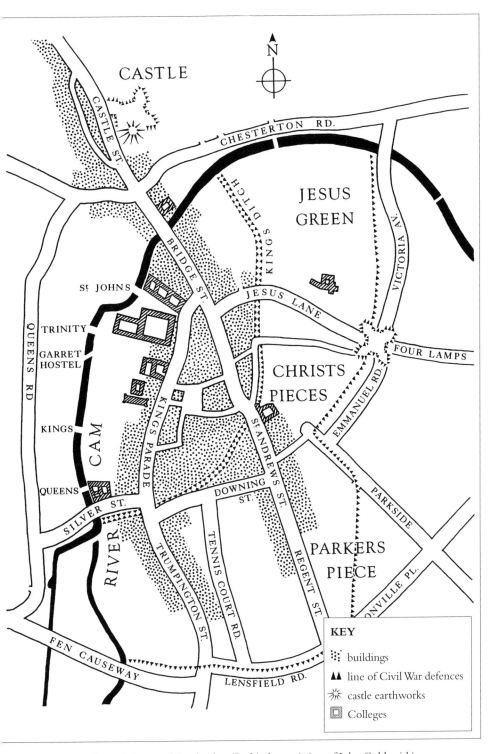

Fig. 4 The Civil War defences of Cambridge. (By kind permission of John Goldsmith)

cause was adequately defended (**Fig. 4**). Large, pointed earthen bastions were constructed at the north-east and north-west corners, with smaller ones on the other
sides. The work was well-advanced by the middle of 1643, it being reported by the
Governor that 'our town and castle are now very strongly fortified, being encompassed
with breastworks and bulwarks', and completed by the end of 1644. These works cost
over £2,000 and necessitated the demolition of fifteen houses near the castle, in order
to accommodate the new bastions and to improve fields of fire. Building materials,
including £400-worth intended for work at Clare Hall, were requisitioned for the
construction of barracks within the castle. The defences were never tested, and were
ordered by the House of Commons to be slighted in July 1647, but the north-east and
eastern bastions are still visible in the grounds of Shire Hall. The ditch of the western
bastion has recently been excavated revealing that it appears to have had an irregular
trace with a step in its northern flank. Surveys over the centuries would suggest that
the main ditch was 13 feet (4m) deep and 42 feet (13m) wide, with a height of around
30 feet (9.3m) from the bottom of the ditch to the top of the rampart. The town,
too, was provided with defences at the same time as the castle. A bank and ditch ran
from the river near Fen Causeway along Lensfield Road, across Parker's Piece, Christ's
Pieces, and Jesus Green, to regain the river opposite Chesterton Road, and a small
fort, or sconce, was built at Four Lamps at the east end of Jesus Lane where a grove of
trees had to be cut down. To complete the circuit of defences, the six footbridges on
the 'Backs', at Garrett Hostel, St John's, Trinity, King's and the two at Queens', were
removed, to be replaced in 1647. The town was also defended by outlying works. At
Chesterton, about a mile east of the castle, stood a flanked redoubt called Mount
Ararat, now destroyed, (TL470600). Further out, road-building operations in the 1970s
uncovered what appeared to be a seventeenth-century gun position on the Devil's
Ditch, a linear earth-work dating at least from Anglo-Saxon times.

At Huntingdon, the mediaeval castle was only ever composed of earthworks enclosing
timber buildings and commanded the bridge over the Great Ouse (**Fig. 5**). It was briefly
re-fortified in 1644, when the rampart nearest the bridge was widened and heightened
to accommodate cannon. A ramp was carved up the side of the motte in order to wheel
cannon to the top, and depressions in the summit may indicate where the trail of a gun
was dug in to obtain greater elevation. The town also was fortified at this time. A small
battery overlooking the river survives off the Hartford road, and the inner town was
defended by a ditch, with barricades where major roads entered. Later maps of the town
show a bowling green on the Brampton road in the unmistakeable shape of a sconce, and
a bastion-shaped hedge-line on the north-east side. This latter site was, incidentally, cited
as a reason for delaying the planned development of Spring Common, but was dismissed.
Mr Christian, the engineer who was probably responsible for the re-fortification of Kings
Lynn after the Royalists had been ejected, was paid for work carried out on the defences
of Huntingdon in November 1643, and again a year later for repairs to bulwarks.

There were at least three rare examples of authentic earth-work bastioned forts
in the county. Earith Bulwark is a well-preserved example of a detached fort, dating
from around 1643 or 1644, both years when the protection of the crossing of the

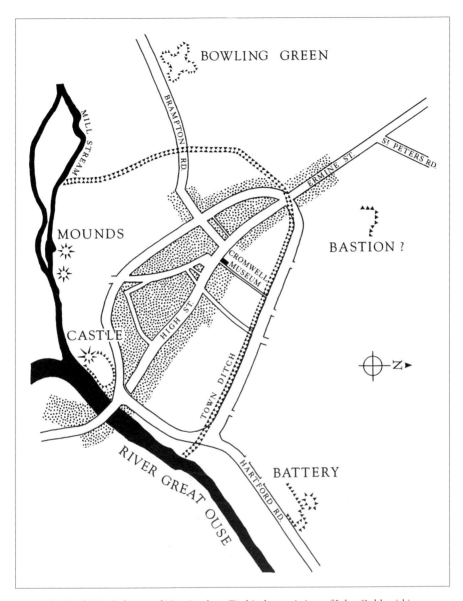

Fig. 5 The Civil War defences of Huntingdon. (By kind permission of John Goldsmith)

Old Bedford River/Great Ouse became a priority. It is built entirely of earth, excavations having revealed a total absence of masonry or brickwork. It is square with
a bastion at each corner, linked by curtains 50 yards long. The whole work is surrounded by continuous banks and ditches, incorporating a covered-way below the
level of the rampart enabling the defenders to move around unseen, and place d'armes
where they would mass to sally forth for a counter-attack. On the west side a possible entrance is protected by a further outwork, and two horn-works project from
the main fort. In places the top of the rampart stands over 10 feet (3m) above the

bottom of the ditch, a significant height in such a flat landscape. The fort was clearly designed by experienced engineers, who were familiar with both the principles and the details of contemporary military engineering (**Fig. 6**). It has been suggested that Richard Clampe and/or Captain John Hopes, may have been responsible. After the Battle of Dunbar (1650) Scottish prisoners were quartered in the fort whilst digging the New Bedford River. Horsey Hill Fort, in a commanding position on the road from Peterborough to Whittlesea, and close to the River Old Nene, was built around 1643. It is a pentagonal detached fort with a bastion at each corner, joined by curtains of about 50 yards, and the top of the rampart is up to 15 feet (4.5m) above the bottom of the ditch. There was a supporting work on Morton's Leam at Stanground Sluice, and a garrison in Whittlesea. The sconce at March is a rectangular earthwork with bastions

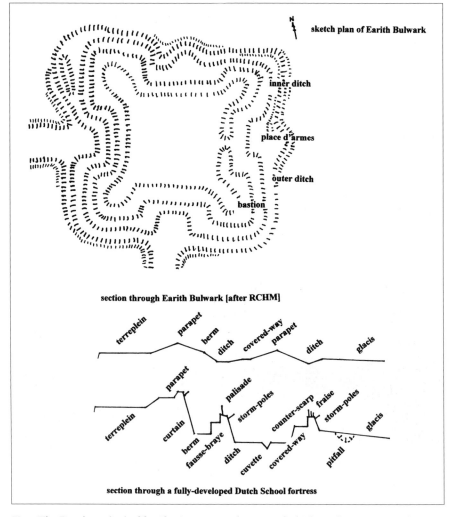

Fig. 6 The Dutch method of fortification c.1630, elements of which can be seen at Earith, Horsey Hill, March and elsewhere. (Not to scale)

surviving at three corners, but the south-west bastion was clearly never completed. The excavators suggest that the work could have been a training exercise overtaken by events which obviated the need ever to bring it into a state of full defensibility. Traditionally known as 'Battery Hills', this sconce would have defended the crossing of the Old River Nene, and the main magazine of the Isle of Ely. From the evidence of old maps, notably the 25 inch:mile edition of 1886, there was a square bastioned fort, generally mistaken for a mediaeval moated site, at Upware, commanding the Great Ouse above Cambridge.

As well as these larger bastioned forts there were several smaller batteries or redoubts. Leverington consists of a large mound, half a mile (0.8km) south of the church, with a ramp up one side, and a depression in the top. It may be a raised battery, representing part of the Wisbech/River Nene frontier defences. Tort Hill, Sawtry had been mistaken for a Roman signal station but was actually found to be a small rectangular gun platform, with one square and one rounded end, which was put up here, inside an earlier square earth-work enclosure, to command the Great North Road.

Several existing mediaeval fortifications were re-fortified to take their places in the Parliamentarian defence system. In 1643, Wisbech was brought back into a state of defence to secure the River Nene frontier of the Eastern Association, and block any attempt by the Newark garrison to relieve the Royalists besieged in Kings Lynn. The castle was armed with cannon, referred to as 'Great Guns', and money was spent on the iron-work necessary to repair the drawbridge. Northborough Manor was also made defensible. Around 1610, a wing had been added to the west side of the gatehouse, and six

27 NORTHBOROUGH MANOR: the mediaeval gatehouse with a later seventeenth-century wing provided with six loop-holes to command the road north from Peterborough towards Lincoln.

gun-loops were inserted into its north wall during the Civil War period. This was probably done in autumn 1643, when attempts were being made to tighten up the defences of the frontier. These loops (**27**) face due north up the main Lincoln road, the anticipated route of any Royalist incursion into the lands of the Eastern Association. Woodcroft Castle was deemed defensible in 1648 when it was involved in a desperate skirmish.

Cromwell and the New Model Army

Throughout the Thirty Years War both weapons and tactics forced a departure from the often serendipitous conduct of previous campaigns. The development of muskets, pikes and cannon produced a new approach to discipline and training. Soldiers became specialists, their skills honed by drill and by following the instructions set down in the many training manuals produced by English officers who had been fighting on the Continent. Cromwell was one of those who quickly realised that part-time, semi-trained soldiers would never win the war and, building on those he had led at Edgehill in 1642, he set about forming a corps of trained, professional troops who would still be there at the end of a campaign. He led his Ironsides, the embryonic New Model Army, in much of the fighting on the Eastern Association's frontier during 1643, and by early 1644 he had expanded this force to a double-regiment of fourteen 100-strong troops of cavalry. The majority of these recruits were mainly farmers from around Cambridge, Ely and Huntingdon. Beyond religion and politics some of them may have been motivated by the King's enthusiasm for draining the Fens and allocating the lion's share of the newly drained land to the Adventurers, a process which led to many locals losing their livelihoods. Ultimately these men would ensure, by their victory in the two major battles of Marston Moor (Yorkshire) and Naseby (Northamptonshire), that the King's fate would be sealed.

Local Actions during the Civil Wars

Given the enormous, and for the most part successful, efforts to maintain the county behind a secure frontier, little happened in the way of military action during the First Civil War (1642–46). Two raids were made from Newark-on-Trent, one on Peterborough in July 1643, ending with defeat for the Royalist force at Burghley. The second raid, in August 1645, was aimed at Huntingdon probably, given the strong Cromwell connection, as a propaganda exercise. The Royalists came down the Great North Road from Newark, and the defenders held out in the churches of St Mary's and All Saints, where the tower was damaged. The town was briefly taken but just as quickly abandoned.

In the Second Civil War in 1648, there were a number of actions involving Royalist forces prior to their final defeat at Colchester. Woodcroft Castle (**28**) is said to have been the scene of a fierce and bloody skirmish. Dr Michael Hudson was rector of

28 WOODCROFT CASTLE: this castle of the late thirteenth century was the scene of a desperate and bloody skirmish in the Second Civil War.

nearby West Deeping and previously of Uffington, an ex-royal chaplain at Oxford and, however improbably, also a veteran of Edgehill and former scoutmaster to the Duke of Newcastle's army of the north. Now he was on the run. Having conducted the King to Newark and thence into captivity, he had escaped but had been re-captured attempting to take ship for France. Following a further escape, this time in disguise from the Tower of London, he resumed his rank of Colonel and rallied a band of fellow fugitives. They occupied Woodcroft but were cornered there by Colonel Waite and a strong force of Parliamentarian troops. Hudson and his fifteen or so companions barred the gate, but Waite's men used fascines (bundles of branches) to cross the wet moat and force their way in. Tradition has it that Hudson fled to the roof and hung over the battlements by grasping a corbel but, his hands being severed, dropped to the moat and was then dragged out onto the bank by Waite's men to be despatched, at his own last request, on dry land.

The Linton Uprising of 1648 was an attempt, led by a Captain Reynolds from Castle Camps, to raise a relieving force for the Royalist army besieged at Colchester. Drawing support from an area stretching from Newmarket to Saffron Walden, the force of around 500 men was centred on Linton, where stores were assembled by a quartermaster. Realising that unless nipped in the bud, this uprising could gather momentum and threaten his forces blockading Colchester, Fairfax sent a detachment along with some local militia to capture the rebels. Despite attempts to delay this force by barricading Linton High Street, the rebels were quickly overcome by superior Parliamentarian numbers attacking at dawn, and most of the Royalists were captured, or fled the scene. Also happening at the same time as the siege of Colchester, but in July, a month after the Linton affair and a month before the surrender of Colchester, a Royalist rising in Surrey failed to attract support, and the leaders fled north through St Albans with 300 men. Colonel Scrope caught up with the force in St Neots and attacked early in the morning with 100 cavalry, scattering the guards on the bridge, and catching the rest unawares. Some dozen Royalists were killed whilst over 200 were taken prisoner. These included some of the leaders who were then taken to London to await execution. The Earl of Holland was taken to Warwick where he was executed, and the Earl of Peterborough was captured while on the run. The rest of the rebels, led by the Duke of Buckingham, scattered.

The Militia after 1700

With the Restoration of Charles II, the military resumed its previous status as a few regiments kept up as royal guards but there was no official standing army. In 1697, the militia returned, for Cambridgeshire and the Isle of Ely recorded an establishment of five companies of foot and three troops of horse, a total of 828 men under the Lord Lieutenant, the Duke of Bedford. Huntingdon, led by the Earl of Manchester numbered 462 men in five companies of foot and 72 cavalry troopers. In 1757 an Act of George II established the Cambridgeshire Militia as a regiment, available for service, but with a reputation for falling short of their required quorum. Like many other county militias, it was embodied in 1778–83, not to serve abroad itself but to release regular troops for foreign service, being stationed in Great Yarmouth for some months, protecting the harbour from American privateers. It was accepted that the Militia had always been raised exclusively for service at home, but a parcel of new legislation in 1798–99 permitted militia units to serve in Ireland, and allowed for any surplus recruits to enrol in the regular army. Compulsory training was initially set at twenty-one days and then raised to twenty-eight. The Cambridgeshire Militia also served in support of the civil power. The Gordon Riots of 1780 were aimed at continuing a policy of keeping Roman Catholics out of public life, and it was necessary for the Government to draft 10,000 militiamen into London to restore public order. One of the targets of the mob was the Lord Chief Justice, the Earl of Mansfield, suspected of catholic sympathies, and a detachment of 100 men of the Cambridgeshire Militia was detailed to guard his home, Kenwood House. The rest of the regiment, under canvas on Hampstead Heath, carried out patrols around Highgate and Kentish Town. During the French Wars, the Cambridgeshire Militia were embodied from 1793–1802, volunteering for service in Ireland in 1798 under their colonel, the Earl of Hardwicke, and serving in Dublin. After the collapse of the Peace of Amiens, they were again embodied from 1803–16. In 1810 they were back in London on duties in support of the civil power, and then to Dublin again where revolution was feared to be about to break out. In 1814, five officers and 160 other ranks volunteered to serve in the Militia Brigade as part of Wellington's army in France.

The Volunteers and Yeomanry in the French Wars

Even when the Militia was fully embodied to augment the regular army, it was felt that Britain was vulnerable to invasion by Napoleon's forces, and that with most of the nation's forces fighting abroad or stationed in Ireland there were few troops left for home defence. In 1745 a public meeting was held in Peterborough to form a volunteer force to protect the city from the Jacobites who were streaming southwards. Underwritten by Earl Fitzwilliam, who promised arms, equipment and £100 towards the cost of uniforms, a body of sixty men was formed to operate within 10 miles of the city, under the leadership of Matthew Wyldbore. Fortunately the rampaging Scots were halted at Derby. The years after the French Revolution had seen the establishment of volunteer military associations, primarily formed to guard the middle classes and their property against anticipated revolutionary activities in Britain, but the impact of a global war against Napoleon broadened the focus to safeguarding the nation as a whole. In Wisbech a Corps of Volunteer Infantry was formed in 1797. Initially the make-up of the volunteer units barely changed, only four of the eighty members of the Ely Volunteers being agricultural labourers, for instance, but those units formed in the early years of the conflict were disbanded after the Peace of Amiens in 1802. With the renewal of the war, the volunteers re-formed but their character had changed. Many officers took their men into the Militia, but not all were free to take this option. This meant that many units, now receiving pay and continuing to be exempt from service in the Militia, recruited new members of a different social background from amongst labourers and servants. Although the citizens of Cambridge formed a unit of volunteer infantry in 1803, they actually put £1,500 into the Yeomanry, and a further £500 to the Militia. This may imply that they were reluctant to support what may have been perceived as an unreliable, even subversive force, despite the fact that volunteer units in towns were thought to be more cohesive and controllable. A Light Infantry company was added to the Wisbech corps in 1807. The Ely Volunteers were now composed of 42 per cent labourers (110 of 262), whilst those of Wisbech (151 out of 231) and of Whittlesea (86 out of 132), both approached 66 per cent. Peterborough also set up a volunteer infantry unit at this time, mainly recruited from artisans and tradesmen, and led by Captain Tonge, an ironmonger with a shop in the Market Square. In Cambridge the university first allocated funds to the volunteer movement generally, and then formed its own unit, under the instruction of a regular officer from the 30th Foot (the Cambridgeshires). The university decided that this body, though showered with plaudits from inspecting officers, would not be registered under the Volunteer Act, in order to be able to maintain its eccentric pattern of drilling only during term-time. In fact it was more useful than most units in that it offered officer training, feeding its members as they graduated into regular Militia and volunteer units across the land.

Training was carried out, amongst other places, in the fields around Madingley, with drills and parades on Parkhurst [*sic*] Piece. The Cambridge University Volunteers, with 180 members in 1803, were drilled as Light Infantry or Rangers and equipped with the new Baker Carbine, but may not have been in existence for more than a couple of years. The government was much happier with Militia units over which they exercised some control, on which they could impose proper military discipline, and whose deployment they could determine. They feared that volunteer units, particularly if they were not well-led, or were scattered across rural parishes, might channel their

energies into acts of insubordination, and armed insubordination at that. It was felt
that having caches of arms and ammunition, distributed around the country, would
create opportunities for armed insurrection. The lack of a spirit of communal enter-
prise was blamed for a failure within the Ely United Volunteers, whose dispersed
nature led to its Sutton Company being disbanded in 1804 due to a breakdown of
discipline apparently caused by poor leadership. Similar disbanding, due to mutinous
behaviour, occurred at West Wratting and Little Swaffham, one officer being threatened with a bayonet. Notwithstanding the odd failure, the Cambridgeshire Volunteer
Corps under the Duke of Manchester managed to keep 30 per cent of the eligible
male population under arms for considerable periods of time. In order that volunteer
units might quickly take up arms in the event of an invasion, stores of weapons and
gunpowder were established in safe but convenient locations. One such store was that
in Magazine Lane, March, and the existence of another Magazine Lane, on the north
bank of the Nene near the brewery in Wisbech, is backed up by local oral tradition as
the likely site of another one.

The Yeomanry Cavalry, composed mainly of tenant farmers and gentry, and led by
wealthy landed aristocrats, had always seen themselves as a cut above the rest. They
provided their own mounts and raised funds through subscriptions, supplemented by
balls and concerts or their officers' deep pockets, to provide the spectacular uniforms
and beautifully turned-out horses which gave them their cachet. A Cambridgeshire
troop of volunteer yeomanry had been formed in 1796, with two more troops by 1803.
Earl Spencer of Althorp raised the Northamptonshire Yeomanry Cavalry in 1794,
whose Peterborough Troop operated throughout the wars. Its re-formation in 1803

29 BURGHLEY HOUSE: this great Elizabethan house was the scene of a skirmish in the Civil
War, the formation of a Yeomanry unit in 1803, and a military hospital in the two world wars.

took place at Burghley House (**29**) where the subscriptions were collected and the officers were sworn in. For some, service in the volunteers was a step to greater things. Having joined the Whittlesea Troop in 1804, within a year the young Harry Smith had been given a commission in the 95th Foot (The Rifles) and went on to be a distinguished general in India and acclaimed 'Hero of Aliwal', another obscure Whittlesey pub-name.

Measures against Invasion

Although the Battle of Trafalgar in 1805 effectively destroyed Napoleon's plans for invading Britain, preparations to repel such an assault continued unabated for most of the remaining ten years of the wars. Although there was an established brickyard in Stanground, bought by Thomas White in 1785, it is not known whether it produced any of the 13.5 million bricks needed for the Martello Tower programme, those on the east coast reaching as far as Aldeburgh (Suffolk). It would have been perfectly feasible to transport them there by barge, perhaps trans-shipping them at Kings Lynn. If the transport of bricks and mortar was straightforward if slow, the rapid communication of urgent information was a problem, and the Admiralty set up chains of stations to relay messages. These employed a variety of methods including visual telegraphs or semaphores of shutters, lights, rotating pointers, flags and black-balls and jointed or pivoted arms. Although the main effort went into coastal installations involving the recording of both our own and the enemy's ships, there were chains connecting potential invasion beaches to the Admiralty, and from the Admiralty to its dock-yards. In 1798, one such chain had been planned to connect London to Norwich with a spur to the port of Great Yarmouth. It probably used portable equipment, and was reported operational in 1803. An alternative route had been proposed in 1802 but not completed until 1808. This consisted of permanent, or at least static, stations with a new system using different combinations of six shutters in open or closed positions to produce seventeen letters. This line ran from London to Dunstable Downs, and then north-east through Baldock and Royston to the station at Telegraph Clump on the Gog Magog Hills. From there it ran on to Newmarket, and Norwich. A crew consisting of a naval Lieutenant on half-pay, a petty-officer, and two trusty seamen, were accommodated in a hut with rudimentary facilities. Their task, using a telescope bought at a cost of two guineas from Messrs P & J Dolland, was to look out for signals from the stations adjacent to theirs, copy them down, and then relay them on to the next one.

French Prisoners of War

Norman Cross Depot, also referred to as Yaxley or Stilton Barracks, was one of the largest of the twenty-five camps and depots set up to hold French prisoners of war.

Begun in 1796, the depot accommodated an average of around 6,000 prisoners during the eighteen years of its operation, who arrived by barge from Kings Lynn at Yaxley Wharf. The depot was a squashed octagon in shape, surrounded by inner and outer timber fences, three-quarters of a mile (2.8km) round, and divided into four compounds. Three of these compounds held four long, timber, two-storey huts, each capable of holding 500 prisoners in hammocks a few inches apart, and hung three-high downstairs, and two-high on the upper floor. The fourth compound held similar barracks but was used for accommodating officer prisoners and the two battalions of militiamen who guarded the prisoners. There were also a hospital, tailors' shop, cookeries and, of course, a black hole, in later wars to become infamous as the 'cooler'. The depot represented a community the size of a small town and was virtually self-sufficient. Rations could be supplemented at the market which was regularly held outside the gate, where inmates could exchange their amazingly intricate models made from salvaged materials such as bone and straw, for vegetables. For many, particularly those who might be spending up to ten years confined to this tedious existence, this contact with the normal world saved their sanity. Some 1,700 prisoners died from wounds sustained in the war or from disease and are buried in the adjacent graveyard. Around 1,000 prisoners died in one particular outbreak in 1800–01, and medical provision was increased over the years with some barrack-blocks being converted into hospital accommodation. Officers were usually allowed to live relatively freely in parole towns such as Wansford, but those who either refused to give undertakings, or subsequently broke their parole, were locked up in a special officers' block.

The guards were perceived by the prisoners as 'ever-wakeful sentinels, constantly passing and re-passing, who were constantly changing'. The Militia units which, over time, included regiments from East Norfolk, Hertfordshire, Westminster and Shropshire amongst others, were themselves constantly rotated in order not to be drawn into compromising situations by the prisoners who were always looking out for ways to escape. In October 1804 there was an attempted mass-breakout, when 500 prisoners pushed down a section of the inner fence. Though held in check by guards with fixed bayonets, help was urgently needed to prevent this volatile situation from escalating out of control. A request for aid was sent to Peterborough and it so happened that one troop of the Whittlesea Yeomanry had not yet been dismissed after a Field Day. They raced up the Stilton road and restored order in the nick of time. It was on this occasion that a diminutive Harry Smith was told to 'go 'ome to your mama, leetle man'. In the centre of the whole depot, where the paths separating the compounds met, there was an octagonal timber block-house with a shingled pointed roof. The upper floor projected out over the lower and had eight cannon mounted. These would have fired grape-shot indiscriminately and were surely there only for deterrent purposes. Other cannon were mounted on the perimeter, the fence having been rebuilt as a brick wall in 1807, and there was a guardhouse in the middle of each side and sentry-boxes at regular intervals in between.

Norman Cross Depot closed in 1814 and was quickly demolished, the timber being sold locally. Until well into the second half of the twentieth century there was a hut in

St Leonard's Street, now under Peterborough's Queensgate shopping centre, which was built of some of this timber. At Norman Cross itself there now remains little evidence of the depot which had covered 22 acres (9 ha). The three-storey Barrack-master's house (**30**), its stables (**31**), and two other officers' houses survive as private dwellings on the A15, along with a memorial pillar surmounted by a Napoleonic eagle. Peterborough Museum displays the finest collection anywhere of prisoner-of-war work of the time.

30 NORMAN CROSS: the Governor's House, home of the commandant of the Napoleonic prisoner-of-war camp.

31 NORMAN CROSS: the stables alongside the Governor's House.

five

The Victorian Period 1815-1914

The years following the Congress of Vienna in 1815, which signalled the end of the French Wars, were marked by a general lack of interest in martial endeavour, and serious attempts at social and political reform. By the middle of the century a number of wars had begun to highlight the army's shortcomings and major reorganisations were eventually pushed through. Again, at the century's end, perceptions of poor leadership and performance in the South African wars prompted more reforms, with significant military development taking place in the years leading up to the First World War. Events in Cambridgeshire can be seen to reflect what was happening on the national scene during these periods of change.

The general run-down of the military after the long and costly French Wars meant that it was a scratch force of Militia from Ely, a troop of regular Dragoons, and the Royston Troop of the Hertfordshire Yeomanry which was sent to Littleport in 1816 to put down a riot caused by the rising costs of food and rents. Within days, another force of three troops of cavalry, and three companies of the 79th Foot with two field guns had arrived to reinforce them. Only one rioter was killed but over eighty people were arraigned before the magistrates in Ely. Of those found guilty, five were hanged, nine transported, and many more imprisoned.

The Army in the Victorian Period

Following a prolonged period of peace, two events in the 1850s were seen to highlight the shortcomings of the army – the Indian Mutiny, and the Crimean War. Leadership, logistics, training, tactics, weapons and equipment were all found to be wanting, and the next three decades saw strenuous efforts made for improvement.

The Regular Army
One of the factors which affected the army's performance was its dislocation from wider society. Regiments had no fixed home base and could serve abroad for ten years or more at a stretch. When they were at home, soldiers were billeted in inns and private houses, alienating hosts and neighbours alike. Regiments had only notional ties to specific communities and recruited wherever they happened to be. Officers were able to buy their commissions, as they could subsequent promotions. Logistical support,

particularly medical provision, was haphazard or non-existent. A series of reforms tackled these problems by providing regiments with fixed depots, the so-called 'localisation programme'. The 30th Foot, established in 1702, had carried 'Cambridgeshire' in its title, but so tenuous was this connection that the 1881 re-organisation saw it become the 1st Battalion, East Lancashire Regiment, based at Preston. Left with no county regiment of its own, Cambridgeshire was lumped in with Suffolk, Regimental District No. 12, whose infantry and Yeomanry were based at Bury-St-Edmunds. The barracks of the Suffolk Regiment, with its great vaulted, red-brick, mediaeval-style armoury can still be seen, as can the 1857 barracks in King Street, now converted to housing and, though now named 'Yeomanry Close', more likely to have housed the West Suffolk Militia.

The Militia

The Militia, though officially remaining in existence after 1815, was shamefully neglected by the government, suffering from a reaction against the war and a general public contempt for the army. After a revival in 1833 and the allocation of a new order of precedence, Cambridgeshire and Huntingdonshire each had its own regiment of Militia, respectively re-numbered the 2nd with HQ in Huntingdon, and the 68th in Ely. The Cambridgeshire Militia spent the duration of the 1854–56 Crimean War in Ireland, releasing regular troops to fight at Alma and Sevastopol. The Childers reforms of 1887 saw them absorbed into the Suffolk Regiment as its Fourth Battalion, serving as such in the South African War, but being disbanded in 1908 when the Territorial Force was launched. The 1887 re-organisation placed the Huntingdonshire Militia

32 HUNTINGDON MILITIA BARRACKS: the main front of the barracks built around 1852 for the 2nd Huntingdonshire Regiment of Militia. Sadly, the building was demolished in 2012.

in the Kings Royal Rifle Corps along with a number of other similar rifle units with inadequate recruiting bases, and no obvious alternative home.

Both these county Militias had been given permanent barracks. Mr Hutchinson of Huntingdon designed a quadrangular building in Cowper Road (**32**), which opened some time after 1852. It was of yellow brick with contrasting detail, a central tower and rusticated decoration. It originally held the magazine and armoury, stores and offices, a mess, and living accommodation for the permanent staff. There was a drill-square sufficient for 400 men, stables and sheds for storing transport. The front-range

33 ELY MILITIA BARRACKS: the barracks of the 68th Cambridgeshire Regiment of Militia was built around 1855; here the block containing the Adjutant's house, armoury and orderly room is now the Masonic Hall.

34 ELY MILITIA BARRACKS: the Hospital standing at the end of The Range, which comprises a terrace of staff NCOs' cottages.

35 ELY MILITIA BARRACKS: a terrace of cottages for permanent staff on Parade Lane, formerly Mill Alley.

survived until very recently as a care-home. At Ely, built around 1855, the buildings were more scattered, with the Adjutant's house, armoury and orderly room in one building now the Masonic Hall (33), and stores and stables in others along Silver Street, where several WD boundary markers may still be seen. There is a Hospital (34), latterly the RBL Club, of three storeys and T-shaped with gables; it is at the top of The Range, past a row of Permanent Staff-sergeants' cottages, with a second terrace of staff cottages (35) standing on Parade Lane, formerly Mill Alley. A further block of double-pile stables, with a single-storey cellblock behind it is now named Militia House on Silver Street. On the basis of other Militia barracks it is probably reasonable to assume that the Prince Albert PH started life as the wet canteen. The parade-ground itself is now the car-park on Barton Road, alongside the later drill hall.

The Rifle Volunteers

One immediate popular response to the criticism of soldiers' recent performance, particularly of their marksmanship, was to set up rifle clubs. Queen Victoria fired the first shot of the newly formed National Rifle Association on Wimbledon Common in 1859, but local clubs, such as the Cambridge Rifle Club, sprang up simultaneously.

There was a feeling amongst the urban professional and artisan classes that they should emulate their country cousins in the Yeomanry. In 1860, therefore, building on the momentum created by the rifle clubs, the Rifle Volunteer movement was launched across the country. The Cambridge Rifle Club volunteered en masse to become the 1st Cambridgeshire Rifle Volunteers. In December 1859 the Vice-Chancellor of the University sanctioned a 3rd Corps of five, soon to be six, companies, each being recruited from one or more colleges. Across the county other corps were formed in Ely, Wisbech, Whittlesea, March, Upwell and Soham. There was some debate about who should be allowed to join, with Lord Hardwicke, the Lord Lieutenant, arguing against arming those who had nothing to protect, but who might use their weapon in the interests of acquisition.

Appropriately it was at Newmarket that a unit of Mounted Rifles was formed in August 1860, with a second unit at Cambridge. This development was either a prescient anticipation of the need for such troops in the Boer War, still forty years ahead, or a looking-back to the old dragoons of the two previous centuries. It might, of course, simply have fulfilled a need to parade on horse-back wearing a splendid uniform, a poorer man's version of the Yeomanry. Neither unit survived past 1865, by which time the remnants had transferred to the Huntingdonshire Light Horse.

A corps of rifle volunteers was raised in Huntingdon in April 1860 but, finding itself competing for recruits with the Light Horse, the HQ was eventually moved to St Neots where it was absorbed into a Cambridgeshire administrative battalion. In 1859 the Duke of Manchester had raised the 1st Huntingdonshire Mounted Rifles, a body of mounted infantry, at Kimbolton (**36**). In January 1861 he took in the Bedford and Sharnbrook Troops and changed their name to the 1st Huntingdonshire Light Horse Volunteers. It would appear that the Light Horse became socially superior, with the Prince of Wales, a frequent visitor to Kimbolton, as Honorary Colonel, and officers who had previously served in fashionable cavalry regiments. The Light Horse was disbanded in 1882, one of the reasons most likely being cost. Even if the

36 KIMBOLTON CASTLE: successively the base for the Huntingdonshire Light Horse, and a troop of 'D' Squadron of the Bedfordshire Yeomanry based in Godmanchester, and then a prisoner-of-war camp in the First World War. (Photo: Pam Osborne)

37 PETERBOROUGH SESSIONS HOUSE: this building, opened in 1842 on Thorpe Road as a gaol, provided a secure armoury for the 6th Corps of Northamptonshire Rifle Volunteers from 1860.

Duke could put in the initial investment of £300 per troop, and pay the estimated £100 per annum maintenance costs, each volunteer needed £50 per year to keep a suitable horse for drill, and was required to pay an annual subscription of up to five guineas. Membership, fluctuating between fifty and ninety actives, with eighty honorary sponsors, tended to be composed of farmers and their sons, a few professionals and gentry, and a very few craftsmen and tradesmen, mainly from horse-related occupations. Drills, held at 11 a.m. on Tuesdays, were rotated around different locations within the regiment's catchment area.

In Peterborough, as the result of a public meeting held in March 1860, fifty men with their elected officers, formed the 6th Corps of the Northamptonshire Rifle Volunteers under the patronage of the Fitzwilliams of Milton Hall. They drilled in the open air on the bowling green of the Royal Hotel, probably in Westgate, and in the fields alongside St Mark's Church in 1862. Shooting was practised at Castor Fields, and then at more regular butts at Milton Ferry, where annual shooting competitions were staged. Arms were stored in the Sessions House (37) on Thorpe Road, and by 1885 new butts had been built in Thorpe Meadows. An Orderly room to handle the Corps' business and to provide some administrative space for its officers, was set up in Cumbergate, and by 1862, the Wentworth Hotel was providing space for some indoor drill.

As well as regular weekly drill and arms training, the Rifle Volunteers also participated in longer summer camps. From 1875, the Cambridgeshire battalion, for instance, joined with the Harwich Volunteer Infantry Brigade for camps at Lowestoft and Great Yarmouth.

Drill Halls

As the Rifle Volunteers developed they needed specialist, secure, dedicated premises beyond the hotels and public halls they had hitherto used. To qualify for a grant from the War Office they had to field trained 'effectives', but also had to demonstrate that they had a secure store for their rifles and ammunition. As the bureaucracy increased, then the CO needed somewhere to store the paperwork and, unless he was a solicitor with an office or a doctor with a big house, an Orderly room was vital. The University Corps had a base from the start in Grange Road. This consisted of an armoury, magazine and forge, an office and a house for the regular army sergeant-major, serving as the permanent staff instructor. The Orderly room was at no. 19 Rose Crescent until 1888 when Gonville & Caius College reclaimed the property and a move was made to new premises at no. 2 Wheeler Street. This soon proved inadequate and, in 1891 a property on four floors at no. 22 Market Street was leased with a ground-floor room for drill and sword exercise, an office for the CO and Adjutant, a room for band-practice, and a Corps Stores. Initially a range in Cherry Hinton chalk-pit had been used, followed by the Rifle Club's new 480 yard range in Mill Road in August 1859, and then a 1,250 yard range at Grange Road from Christmas 1860. By the 1880s land in Grange Road had been handed over to the Football Club, limiting the length of the range, but the 3rd Volunteer Battalion allowed the University Volunteers to use their longer range on Coldham's Common, conveniently served by a regular tram-service.

It was not until 1868 that a dedicated drill hall was built, by public subscription, in Queen Street, Peterborough. Its opening was marked by a concert and it stood

38 ELY SHIRE HALL: built in 1820, by the 1880s one wing housed the Armoury and Orderly room of 'H' Company, 3rd Volunteer Battalion of the Suffolk Regiment, whilst the other housed the city's police station.

on the eastern side of the street, opposite Perkins works, on a site now lost under Queensgate. In the previous year, a specialist corps of railway engineers had been formed, the Northamptonshire Volunteer Royal Engineers (NVRE), one of only three such units in the country, recruited mainly from Great Northern Railway employees. Finding the Wentworth Hotel and the Corn Exchange unsuitable for its very practical curriculum, its first task was to construct its own Orderly room, workshop and model-making studio, which it did in St Leonard's Street. These buildings were demolished in 1911 when Crescent Bridge was built. The unit attended annual camps with the Royal Engineers at Chatham and, by then two companies strong, sent a section to the South African War to work on the block-houses which guarded the railway system against raids by the Boer commandos.

The old Napoleonic armoury in Magazine Lane, now Gas Road, was used by the 5th Cambridgeshire Corps in March, whilst in Ely, a wing of the Shire Hall (**38**) built in 1820, served as the Armoury for the 6th Cambridgeshire Corps. In Wisbech the Orderly room of the 2nd Cambridgeshire Corps was in Great Church Street, but had moved to the Corn Exchange by 1888. At some date after 1893, a drill hall was built at no. 4 North Terrace. The Soham Corps had fallen by the wayside by 1865, and that at Upwell lasted not much longer. By 1885, the Wesleyan Chapel (**39**), built around 1825 on Gas Road in March, had been converted into a new drill hall, with an Orderly room in the High Street. In Whittlesea there had been an Orderly room at Inhams End, but by 1912, 'F' Company of the Cambridgeshires was meeting in the Public Hall (**40**).

39 MARCH: the Wesleyan chapel of *c*.1825 in Gas Road which, by the 1880s, had been converted into the drill hall of 'G' Coy of the 1st Battalion of the Cambridgeshire Regiment.

40 WHITTLESEY: the Public Hall on Station Road, built in 1880 and now a club, was used as their drill hall by 'F' Company, 1st Battalion the Cambridgeshire Regiment, from at least 1908 until a purpose-built drill hall was opened in 1914.

The Yeomanry

Some Yeomanry units suffered from financial embarrassment, but the Peterborough Troop of Northamptonshire Yeomanry Cavalry finished the French Wars with a healthy surplus, which they elected to be used to fund a public dispensary in a rented house in Cowgate. This eventually led to the setting up of the hospital in Priestgate, now the Museum, but once the home of Thomas Cooke, the Yeomanry Troop's commander. Not all of the Yeomanry disbanded, partly as an insurance policy against agrarian unrest characterised by rick-burning and the smashing of machinery by the Luddites and, later on, against the Chartists. The Whittlesea and Cambridgeshire Troop recorded in the 1850 Army List, with a reference to its officers in 1831, appears to have been either one of those units with an extended life, or one of the several reformed as the Chartist movement gathered momentum but, whatever its earlier history, it had gone by the late 1850s.

There would be no Cambridgeshire Yeomanry which is probably one of the reasons why the Huntingdonshire Light Horse lasted as long as it did. The Loyal Suffolk Yeomanry had remained in being for most of the nineteenth century and, at least as early as 1885, maintained a squadron in Cambridge, using the University Rifle Volunteers' range in Grange Road. Their HQ, possibly the home of one of their senior NCOs, was in Norwich Street, at no. 82 in 1904, and no. 50 by 1912, both these properties being Victorian terraced houses. On the outbreak of war with the Boers, companies of Imperial Yeomanry were formed for service in South Africa, and in 1902 the Northamptonshire Yeomanry were re-formed, 'B' Squadron, under Captain Wickham of Barnwell, late of the 2nd Dragoons (Royal Scots Greys), being based in Peterborough with one troop in St Ives. Squadron HQ was in The Saracen's Head PH, and its horses were stabled in Hodgson's Repositories. Its first mounted drill took place in Milton Park on 24 April 1902, where annual camps were often subsequently located, along with Althorp, Boughton and Rockingham (all Northamptonshire), giving some indication of the Yeomanry's social standing. Following the disbandment of the NVRE in 1908, the squadron moved into their drill hall in St Leonard's Street, and in 1911, into Queen Street with the artillery.

Reorganisations 1881–1908

The changes which affected the regular army and the Militia were reflected by the volunteers. In 1887 the new-look Suffolk Regiment had two regular battalions, a third battalion drawn from the West Suffolk Militia, a fourth from the Cambridgeshire Militia, and two Volunteer Battalions composed of corps of the Suffolk Rifle Volunteers. The Cambridgeshire Rifle Volunteers became the 3rd Volunteer Battalion of the Suffolk Regiment, and the Cambridge University Volunteer Rifle Corps became the 4th.

With the loss of the Mounted Rifles and the disbandment of the St Neots company of the Cambridgeshire Volunteer Battalion in 1889, there were no volunteer units left in Huntingdonshire, until 1900 when a 4th (Huntingdonshire) Volunteer Battalion of the Bedfordshire Regiment was recruited in the county, comprising six companies based in Huntingdon, St Neots, St Ives and Fletton. There was a drill hall, a long, low timber building, in Bull Lane, St Ives, and in St Neots, the Corn Exchange was used. The vacant Militia barracks in Huntingdon was available, and in Fletton, south of the river in Peterborough, the Coffee Palace in London Road, provided for its employees in 1898 by the London Brick Company, was acquired, remaining in use until 1917. Peterborough was the base for two companies of the 1st Volunteer Battalion of the Northamptonshire Regiment.

During the South African wars volunteers were allowed to enrol in units specially raised for the conflict – the Imperial Yeomanry and the Imperial Volunteers – so a number of men from Cambridgeshire fought against the Boers but under the aegis of these umbrella organisations. Regular training took place with field days attempting to replicate wartime situations, drills and lectures, shooting competitions, parades and inspections. At times of national emergency enrolments went up, and the increasing professionalism of the volunteers led to the next, more radical re-structuring, which for the very first time defined a real role for the force.

The Territorial Force 1908–1914

The South African War had alerted the nation to the fact that when the regular army was engaged in fighting overseas, Britain itself was well-nigh defenceless, particularly when many of the volunteers were themselves off abroad on voluntary service with the regulars. Viscount Haldane, Secretary-of-State for War, initiated plans for a government-funded Home Defence Army. This was embodied in 1908 as The Territorial Force composed of fourteen self-contained divisions administered by County Territorial Associations, each consisting of an infantry division, a mounted brigade and artillery batteries, with supporting supply, transport and medical services. The major development for Cambridgeshire was that the Cambridgeshire Regiment was re-instated as one of several all-volunteer units. Its HQ was moved to Corn Exchange Street, four of its eight companies were based in Cambridge with outlying drill-stations, and the other companies were centred on Wisbech, Whittlesea, March and Ely. Camps were held at West Fen Camp, Ely and at Ashridge Park (Hertfordshire). The Bedfordshire Regiment continued to run its 5th (Huntingdonshire) Battalion with 'G' Company at Fletton and a drill-station in Yaxley, where a drill hall with indoor rifle-range in Chapel Street, lasted until 1963 when it burnt down. 'H' Company was in Huntingdon with drill-stations in St Ives and Ramsey. There were now three squadrons of Yeomanry in the county, all attached to the Eastern Mounted Brigade. Cambridge remained home to 'A' Squadron of the Loyal Suffolk Hussars, as did Peterborough for 'B' Squadron of the Northamptonshire Yeomanry, but 'D' Squadron of the Bedfordshire Yeomanry gained a new base at Godmanchester with drill-stations at St Neots, Kimbolton, Ramsey, Somersham, Sutton and Chatteris. In addition to these, one troop of the Norfolk Yeomanry's 'D' Squadron, based in Kings Lynn, had a drill station in Wisbech. Many of these drill stations were probably inns with stabling and tack-rooms, but in 1911 Ramsey, also used by the infantry, acquired a brand-new drill hall that was only recently demolished for housing. Peterborough lost its old connection to the Northamptonshire Regiment, but gained a Northamptonshire battery of the 4th East Anglian Brigade of Field Artillery whose HQ was in Hertford, with its other batteries in St Albans and Watford (both Hertfordshire). This unit took over the

41 HUNTINGDON: the St Mary's Street drill hall, converted from a Brewery, for use by 'H' Company 5th (Huntingdonshire) Battalion, Bedfordshire Regiment, from 1908, and as HQ Huntingdonshire Cyclist Battalion, 1914–18.

Queen Street drill hall, supplemented by a new gun-shed and harness-room, built in the yard of Messrs. Sexton, Grimwade and Beck's repository on Boroughbury. Annual camps were held on the ranges at Lydd (Kent) or Shoeburyness (Essex) in order to advance specialist training. In 1914, an entirely new unit, the Huntingdonshire Cyclists' Battalion was formed, and many of the members of the Bedfordshire Regiment's 5th Battalion transferred into it *en bloc* under their second-in-command, Major Herbert, who became the Cyclists' first CO. Its HQ was at St Mary's drill hall in Huntingdon, a converted brewery (**41**), and its eight companies were based at Huntingdon and Godmanchester, St Ives, St Neots, Ramsey, Fletton and Yaxley. When rifles were issued in June 1914, they were test-fired at the Grafham range. The cyclist unit was designated as Corps troops, for general duties such as reconnaissance or courier work, and was affiliated to the Northamptonshire Regiment.

In re-organising the volunteer forces, Haldane had recognised the problem of a deficiency across the board in trained officers. He therefore established the Officer Training Corps, senior units in universities, and junior ones in schools. The Senior OTCs were to be equipped to provide the appropriate training for potential officers in all arms of the service. The CUOTC therefore received a battery of 18-pounder guns, bridging and signalling equipment for the engineers, a traction engine and motorcycles for the service corps. The Junior OTC included contingents at The Leys, Cambridge County and Perse Schools. Cadet companies, affiliated to infantry regiments, were formed at grammar schools in March, Huntingdon, Kimbolton, Ramsey and Wisbech, and King's School, Peterborough. There were two companies of Boys Brigade Cadets in Cambridge, and two of the Church Lads Brigade (St Luke's and Linton, and St Andrew's, Chesterton) with a further three of the latter in Peterborough (St John's).

The Annual Army Manoeuvres and the use of Flight

By 1910 the British Army had begun to embrace the notion of flying, bringing a new dimension to warfare. Balloons had been in regular use for twenty years when Bleriot made his flight across the Channel in a powered aircraft. Consequently it was decided that the annual military manoeuvres of 1911 would involve aerial observation of the forces on the ground. The manoeuvres were scheduled for Cambridgeshire, and the newly formed Air Battalion would have a chance to make a long-distance flight from their Farnborough (Hampshire) base. Hardwick Farm, one mile north-west of Comberton, was chosen as a landing-ground for the army's seven aircraft. As it happened, the manoeuvres were cancelled but the fliers decided to go ahead with what became known as the Cambridge Odyssey. Unfortunately only two made it to Hardwick Farm, and one of those crashed on the return journey, but swift progress was nevertheless being made, as would be demonstrated within a year.

The 1912 event, the last full-scale such manoeuvres to be held before the outbreak of the First World War, did go ahead, and was held on the Gog Magog hills. Lt Gen Haig, aided by his regular staff from Aldershot (Hampshire), led the Red Army of two regular infantry divisions and a brigade of regular cavalry. The Blue Army, led by Lt Gen Grierson, GOC Eastern Command, was made up of two regular infantry divisions, a brigade of yeomanry cavalry, Territorial Force cyclists as reconnaissance troops, and a scratch staff. The two armies together numbered at least 100,000 men. In attendance was JEB Seely, Asquith's Secretary of State for War, himself a decorated yeomanry officer who would go on to command a cavalry brigade in the coming war. He had invited a distinguished group of observers, which included King George V, Grand Duke Nicholas of Russia, the French General Foch and defence ministers from Canada and South Africa. The King stayed at Trinity College where sentry-boxes and a guard-of-honour had been installed. Both armies were provided with aircraft, but the Blue Army quickly used theirs to locate the 'enemy', whilst keeping hidden from view, before carrying out an unexpected and devastating attack, resulting in an overwhelming defeat for Haig's force. The Blue Army then bivouacked in Linton, the Red Army on Midsummer Common, and the umpires conducted their debrief at Trinity Hall. The airships *Beta II* and *Gamma* were both present, operating from Jesus College grounds, along with aircraft flown by pioneer military aviators including Cody, who landed in Cambridge in order to do some shopping. When *Beta II* made a forced landing with engine failure, it was repaired by mechanics from the nearby Marshall's Garage in Jesus Lane. Both Haig and Grierson started the First World War as corps commanders but, whilst Haig went on to greater things, Grierson died suddenly of an aneurism two weeks into the war. The manoeuvres had misleadingly reinforced the notion that mobility would win wars, but had also demonstrated the potential of the intelligent use of air-power.

six

Cambridgeshire in the First World War

The declaration of war in August 1914 prompted an immediate mobilisation of regulars and Territorials alike. As the British Expeditionary Force retreated from Mons, efforts went into raising fresh troops, Kitchener's New Armies. A major focus of the county's military efforts was the training of officers for the army and pilots for the Royal Flying Corps. All the while, large forces were maintained to counter the ever-present perception of the imminence of invasion. Although enemy aircraft over-flew the county, bound for juicier targets, actual bombings were rare. On one occasion, for instance, a Zeppelin was seen to circle Burghley House before dropping a bomb near the Blackstone's engineering works in neighbouring Stamford.

Mobilisation

The Cambridgeshire Regiment's first battalion, at the end of their annual camp at Ashridge Park near Tring (Hertfordshire), was mobilised from their HQ at no. 14 Corn Exchange Street and their other assembly points across the county, and sent straight away to join the East Anglian Division in Suffolk, leaving the way clear to recruit extra battalions. There were so many recruits coming forward in Cambridge that the organisation of the Suffolk Regiment, at their depot in Bury-St-Edmunds, was unable to cope and a separate battalion was formed in Cambridge itself, billeted initially in the Corn Exchange and then in the Girls' County School. Recruits also came forward in the town of March, where a meeting had been held in the Public Hall in November. In May 1915 it was designated the 11th Battalion of the Suffolk Regiment, gathered together at Stowlangtoft Hall (Suffolk) and then posted for intensive training to the enormous infantry camp at Ripon (North Yorkshire). Between September 1914 and November 1915, three further battalions of the Cambridgeshire Regiment, the 2/1st, 3/1st and 4/1st were recruited, along with the 13th (Reserve) Battalion of the Suffolks, formed in Cambridge in September 1915. All these four units stayed in Britain serving with Home Defence divisions, but supplying a constant stream of replacement drafts to the 1st Battalion. The Huntingdonshire Cyclists were mobilised at their local drill halls immediately after war broke out. For instance, 'F' and 'G' Companies at the Fletton drill hall on hearing the fire siren, and 'H' Company, at the Girls' School in Yaxley. They proceeded directly to their war station at Grimsby, to guard a coast with which they had been familiarised during recent summer camps. On 27 October, the Earl of Sandwich, the regiment's Honorary Colonel, addressed a recruitment meeting in the Old Fletton Council School, producing a further 40 recruits to add to the 300+ already committed to forming a reserve unit, the 2/1st Battalion. A 3/1st Battalion was also recruited the next year, recruits enlisting at the St Mary's drill hall HQ in Huntingdon. There were Recruiting Offices for men bound for Kitchener's New Armies at no. 5 Ermine Street, Huntingdon, and in the Prudential Insurance Company offices on the corner of Long Causeway and Cathedral Square in Peterborough (42). In August 1914 prior to joining up with the rest of the regiment to be shipped from Southampton to France as divisional cavalry, 'B' Squadron of the Northamptonshire Yeomanry was quartered in the Corn Exchange in Peterborough's Church Street. The Huntingdon squadron of the Bedfordshire Yeomanry drilled by Bridge House, now the Old Bridge Hotel (43), which was also used as their mess by the officers of the Huntingdonshire Cyclists. The Cyclists' sergeants had their mess in the Black Bull in Godmanchester, and their other ranks were billeted in the Corn Mill Maltings. The Northamptonshire Battery of the 4th East Anglian Brigade RFA was at camp in Northumberland when war broke out, and hurried back to Peterborough by train in order to mobilise on the 5 and 6 August. Sexton's repository on Lincoln Road was requisitioned and the Bedford Coffee House provided messing facilities, with some officers accommodated in the Angel Hotel in Narrow Bridge Street. The Battery's ammunition was delivered to Peterborough by train, and moved under armed guard to the gun-park which had been built on the repository site in 1909 when the Queen Street drill hall had proved inaccessible for the field-guns. Some eighty-nine recruits enlisted at Queen Street, where the artillery continued to maintain an Orderly room.

42 PETERBOROUGH CATHEDRAL SQUARE: the Prudential offices which housed the Army Recruiting Office in the First World War.

43 HUNTINGDON BRIDGE HOUSE: this was the location for the weekly drills of the Huntingdon squadron of the Bedfordshire Yeomanry, and the officers mess of the Huntingdonshire Cyclists Battalion. It is now the Old Bridge Hotel. (Photo: Pam Osborne)

Cambridge witnessed a headlong rush to enlist, particularly from the student body. These were handled by the Board of Military Studies using the CUOTC offices in Market Street, but such was the crush that Corpus Christi College was prevailed upon to provide extra office accommodation. The majority of recruits were sent for temporary commissions in the New Armies and the Territorial Force. Pembroke College's Old Library became a new Orderly room for the CUOTC in 1915. Two-thirds of those former members of the CUOTC who had graduated between 1908 and 1915 were commissioned into the army, whilst others had joined up in other services. Over 13,000 recent graduates of the university served in the British armed forces, 97 per cent of them as junior infantry officers, the most at-risk group of all. Over 2,000 of these died, representing a proportion well above the war-average of one in eight and, for several colleges, their war-dead exceeded this average by a factor of two. However, a significant number of deaths (16 per cent) were of older men who had graduated by 1900.

Some individuals were able to offer particular talents. Charles Inglis (1875–1952), for instance, was a Fellow of King's College from 1901 and had been instrumental, along with the university's Department of Engineering, in promoting a RE Section in the CUOTC. In 1913 he had designed a light-weight portable bridge for enabling infantry to cross ditches and in 1915 he joined the staff of the School of Military Engineering in Chatham (Kent), finishing the war as a Lt Col and being awarded the DSO. He was later knighted, awarded a Chair at Cambridge and became a FRS. Others, involved through the CUOTC in pioneering experiments with communications equipment, took their expertise to RE Signals units. At another level, academics were co-opted onto the myriad of groups formulating policy or running the war economy. Thus, Sir T. Clifford Albutt, the Regius Professor of Medicine, served on the Central Medical War Committee, whose task it was to provide sufficient medical officers for the services whilst maintaining a barely adequate coverage at home.

Defence against Invasion

Fears of a German invasion fleet, sailing across the North Sea to land on the vulnerable beaches of East Anglia, had featured in popular literature since the perceived threat from Germany first appeared in the early 1900s. When war was declared, troops were consequently deployed along the East Coast. The Huntingdonshire Cyclists had already had an opportunity to reconnoitre their sector in the Skegness-Grimsby area, and they were joined by other units. By 1915 they had been issued with ten automobiles but their 615 bicycles remained their basic means of patrolling the coast. The 2/1st Battalion of the Cambridgeshires spent some time in 1915–16 digging trenches near Rayleigh (Essex) as part of the London defences. From June 1915, elements of the 4/1st Battalion of the Cambridgeshires were deployed on the Norfolk coast constructing and manning anti-invasion defences. Likewise, the Suffolk Yeomanry, along with the Bedfordshire Yeomanry, joined with the Eastern Mounted Brigade to spend the next year on the Suffolk coast on anti-invasion duties. Many of the second and third-line Territorial units which formed the Reserve Divisions were employed on similar duties. The 208th Brigade of the 69th (East Anglian Reserve) Division had its HQ at Peterborough's Great Northern Hotel (44), and in December 1914, it included the 2/4th and 2/5th Battalions of the Suffolk Regiment, one of which was based around the Barnack area with its HQ in Walcot Hall (45) with extra billets in Barnack Grange. They moved to Cambridge in May of the next year, into one of the big tented encampments set up on any available green space. The 207th Brigade, also based in the Peterborough and Cambridge areas, included two of the new battalions of the Cambridgeshire Regiment. The 69th Division was one of nine territorial divisions which, along with two yeomanry cavalry divisions and attached cyclist units, made up the Central Force (CF) tasked with countering an invasion in the eastern counties. The South Wales Mounted Brigade was based in Cambridge with its HQ at the University Arms Hotel. Cambridge was regarded as a key communications centre with rail-links to London and Bedford, one of the CF's other HQs, as well as to the important east coast ports of Great Yarmouth, Kings Lynn, Lowestoft and Harwich. The Highland Mounted Brigade was based at Godmanchester and Huntingdon, benefiting from that same rail mobility. Huts were built for the troopers on Mill Common, and their horses were kept in paddocks near Castle Hill House. The officers' mess of the Fife and Forfar Yeomanry, one of the three regiments in the Brigade, was in Wych House (46) in the Broadway, St Ives. The invasion threat persisted throughout the war, as it was thought even as late as 1917 that the Germans might seek to break the stalemate of the Western Front by despatching a force to invade Britain.

44 PETERBOROUGH GREAT NORTHERN HOTEL: HQ of the 208th Brigade of the 69th East Anglian (Reserve) Division. In December 1914, it included the two second-line TF battalions of the Suffolk Regiment.

45 WALCOT HALL: this Carolean mansion near Barnack housed the HQ of a battalion of the Suffolk Regiment in 1914. At the beginning of the Second World War it was the remote Operations Room for RAF Wittering, and from 1942 it was HQ of the 67th Fighter Wing of the 8th USAAF.

46 ST IVES, Wych House: situated in The Broadway, this served as the officers' mess of the Fife and Forfar Yeomanry, one of the three regiments in the Highland Mounted Brigade. During the Second World War it housed the HQ of the 2nd Huntingdonshire Battalion, Home Guard.

Despite the extreme unlikelihood of this happening, large numbers of troops were tied up on these garrison and patrolling duties. Second-line territorial artillery units of the Central Force were based in Huntingdon where the gun-park was in the Market Square, and in St Neots. Here their HQ was in Priory Hill House, but bad weather turned the park, still known as 'Artillery Field', into a quagmire and the 15-pounder guns were moved to a new gun-park, again in the Market Square.

The Northamptonshire Battery from Peterborough joined with its sister batteries and was posted to the Norfolk coast, under their CO Lt Col Lord Exeter. The Zeppelins had begun their bombing raids in January 1915, generally crossing the North Norfolk coast at night. Although AA defence was in the hands of the Royal Naval Air Service, any artillery unit nearby was pressed into service. The trails of the 15-pounder guns were dug into the ground in an attempt to elevate their barrels skywards.

Local Defence

From the very first day, a detail of the 1st Battalion the Cambridgeshire Regiment was despatched to guard the Ipswich wireless station, but as the first troops were sent to France these duties were picked up from other sources as, in order to free troops for training, volunteers were recruited to take on these local guard duties. Those few members of the CUOTC not yet old enough to enlist guarded railway bridges and telegraph lines. The Volunteer Training Corps was set up for this very purpose, much like the Home Guard of the next war, with three companies being recruited in Cambridgeshire over the course of the war. Youngsters were taught to drill and to shoot in preparation for their call-up to the forces, and men in reserved occupations were enabled to make their contribution to the nation's defence, by guarding vulnerable points or escorting prisoners of war. The National Motor Volunteers were civilians who provided vehicles and drivers for military use, usually ferrying wounded servicemen between hospitals, or providing staff cars for senior officers or politicians. Initially the government wanted nothing to do with the VTC, even forbidding the wearing of uniforms, fearing it would reduce the numbers available for conscription, but once it was established that its members were extra to the main effort, views softened and some VTC units were even affiliated to their local regiment to the extent of being allowed to wear their cap-badges. The St Neots and District Drill Club formed in November 1914 with members who were able-bodied men over 38 years of age. They carried out route marches and underwent inspections, presumably carried out by officers stationed in the town, at the Corn Exchange. In Huntingdon a range was set up in premises in the High Street and volunteers drilled in the Grammar School's new assembly hall. Over 700 were inspected by Sir John French at Hinchingbrooke in 1918.

Air Defence

The aerial attacks on British targets, by firstly Zeppelins and then Gotha bombers, prompted the provision of AA weapons. Although Krupp had developed a Balloon Gun, the allies had lagged behind, relying on a hotch-potch of light 1-, 3- and 6-pounder naval guns, and improvisations involving machine guns on posts, or field guns ramped up to the near vertical. Both the purpose-designed French 75mm Auto-cannon and the British 3-inch 20cwt AA gun were eventually deployed in large numbers around London, but second-string provincial targets made do with alternative models. Peterborough was protected by two 18-pounder guns. These were standard field guns which had been re-sleeved to fire a 13-pound shell with the 18-pounder cartridge, thus increasing their effective ceiling. The gun was mounted on a static pedestal mount bolted to a hold-fast set in concrete, and was accompanied by a searchlight powered by a petrol generator. The two gun-sites were at Paston Hall and Garton End on the north-east edge of the city. Each site consisted of a sectional, match-board-lined timber living hut 50 feet by 15 (15 x 4.5m), a kitchen/store 40 feet by 15 (12 x 4.5m), a magazine with dwarf-brick walls and corrugated-iron superstructure, a telephone hut, sentry-boxes and an engine-house with petrol store. The complex was completed by the Home and Distant Height Finding Station at Dogsthorpe with two further huts, and a fourth site at Ham Farm, Werrington where there was a Boarden Hut, 47 feet by 16 (14 x 5m) containing a cooking-range. The four sites were shut down and the buildings sold at auction on 18 October 1919, with no trace remaining on the ground.

Airfields

The two major components of the air war over Cambridgeshire were training and home defence. Home Defence fighter squadrons operated throughout the war as a defence against Zeppelins coming in over the Norfolk coast. Wyton operated the

BE2cs and BE2ds of No. 46 Squadron from April 1916 when it was sent to the Western Front, being replaced by No. 65 (Home Defence) Squadron. Stamford, later called Wittering, opened in September 1916, housing the FE2bs of one of No. 38 Home Defence Squadron's three flights. It was also HQ of No. 35 Wing RFC which included No. 1 Training Depot Station (TDS) from August 1917 through to May 1919. To allow fighters to spend the maximum time aloft in order to intercept enemy bombing sorties, networks of day and night landing-grounds were established. Hill Farm, Bury, near Ramsey, was requisitioned by the War Department in 1917 as an Emergency Landing Ground. It subsequently became a fully fledged aerodrome for the Be2 aircraft of 7 Squadron RFC. By April 1918 it had five large hangars, measuring 100 feet by 170 feet (30 x 50m), possibly GS hangars (568/18) and permanent hutting. Renamed Upwood, it had become part of the 6th Midland Brigade of No. 47 Home Defence Wing, RAF. Molesworth had been established for use by 75 Squadron, and remained in use until late 1917. Huts were then dispersed to neighbouring farms, and the airfield abandoned. Yelling also operated as a Home Defence airfield. Other basic landing-grounds with little more than a hut for a ground party, and some fuel tanks, were at Cottenham and Horseheath. Hardwick Farm, which had been identified as a landing-ground in 1911, operated as a private flying-school. At Ely was No. 4 Stores Distribution Park, RFC, and it is possible that Brooklands House in Cambridge, used by the RAF in the Second World War, also served as an administrative centre for the RFC, perhaps at the time that Fowlmere and Duxford were being built. Rudimentary bombing practice was carried out over The Wash.

47 DUXFORD AIRFIELD: the Watch Office for the duty pilot, and the Squadron Offices, built around 1918 to a local design (DX698).

48 DUXFORD AIRFIELD: a double GS flight shed to design 332/17, often referred to as 'Belfast Truss Hangars' owing to their timber roofs. This is one of three such double hangars which stood along with a single Aircraft Repair Shed, which was destroyed in the 1960s during the filming of 'The Battle of Britain'.

49 DUXFORD AIRFIELD: Building No. 80 comprising workshops, Parachute Store and Oil and Dope store (286/17).

In 1916 Wyton switched its emphasis to become primarily a training station supplying pilots for the RFC, with No. 31 Training Squadron in residence until 1918, and other units spending shorter periods of time there. The site chosen was on the western side of the present airfield, opposite the row of cottages near the later bomb-dump. All the buildings were timber, and were removed after the war. Bury also had a training role as the base of No. 191 Night Training Squadron in July 1918, and of No. 190 Night Training Squadron which moved in from Newmarket later in the year. Portholme Meadow, on the outskirts of Godmanchester was the initial location for No. 211 Training Depot Station in April 1918 which moved to Scopwick (RAF Digby, Lincolnshire) as No. 50 TDS three months later.

Towards the end of the war, Fowlmere was established as No. 31 TDS, one of a network set up to train British and US pilots on the new de Havilland 0/400 four-engined bomber, designed to operate over Germany. The airfield had the characteristic layout of three double-GS Hangars, and an Aircraft Repair Shed. Building began at Duxford for No. 35 TDS, replicating the set-up at Fowlmere, whose satellite it was. A number of buildings from the period survive at Duxford, including the Flight Office (**47**), GS hangars (**48**), workshops (**49**) and a barrack-block (**50**) with its distinctive clerestory roof. Fowlmere was soon demolished, but Duxford continued in use. No. 1 TDS at Stamford, to be re-named as Wittering after the war, shared a similar layout with two double aircraft sheds to a design of 1917, and hutting.

50 DUXFORD AIRFIELD: a rare survival of a First World War barrack hut (481/18), this one built as Single Officers' Quarters. Located behind the officers' mess, it was refurbished in 1935 (421/35).

Deployments of Local Units

In the face of overwhelming enemy numbers, after the Retreat from Mons, the regular units in the British Expeditionary Force were so depleted that first-line territorial units were thrown into the line as fast as they could be mobilised. The 1st Cambridgeshires went to France on 15 February 1915 as part of 27th Division, serving in the trenches, with only a single short break from front-line duties, as the Third Army training battalion. They stayed in France for the duration, returning home in May 1919. Over the four years of war, during which time the battalion won twenty-seven battle honours, some 10,000 men served, of whom nearly half were either killed or wounded. They were followed out a year later by the 11th (Cambridgeshire) Battalion of the Suffolk Regiment which joined 61st Division in France, staying until November 1918.

After a year on the East Coast, the Northamptonshire Battery spent October 1915 in their home area, carrying out recruiting marches through Peterborough, Oundle, Kettering, Stamford and Huntingdon. Having handed over their 15-pounder guns to their second-line unit with 69th Division, they were re-equipped with new 18-pounder guns and sailed for France. Next they were shipped from Marseilles to Cairo, where they fought under Allenby against the Turks. Their base at Gaza was named 'Milton Park' as a reminder of home. At the end of the war the artillery brigade was broken up, the last two men returning to Peterborough in early Autumn 1919.

After a spell in Essex on home defence duties, the 1/1st Bedfordshire Yeomanry served as divisional cavalry in France right up until early 1918 when they were briefly re-organised as a machine-gun unit, but soon regained their horses. Their second and third-line units served as divisional cavalry at home and in Ireland. The Loyal Suffolk Hussars lost their horses in the first year of the war, sailing for Egypt via Gallipoli and in 1917 being re-formed as a battalion of the Suffolk Regiment guarding the Suez Canal. The 2/1st joined the Reserve Eastern Mounted Brigade at Ely in January 1915, and served as cyclists in Suffolk before being re-deployed to Ireland in 1918. The Northamptonshire Yeomanry served as divisional cavalry in France from November 1914, and then in Italy during 1917. The 2/1st served as divisional cavalry at home, but in 1917 one squadron was absorbed into the new Tank Corps.

Training

Early in the war it was realised that all the new young officers, most of whom were destined to command infantry platoons, would need some induction into their new duties, something that their regiments, undergoing massive expansion or in action abroad, would not be able to provide. Schools of Instruction for new junior officers were therefore organised around Cambridge using the almost-empty colleges as billets. However this ad hoc effort could only be a stop-gap, and so from February 1916 a new system of Officer Cadet Battalions was set up. Each of the twenty-two battalions, spread across the British Isles, had an establishment of around 400 cadets. These had to be over eighteen and a half years of age, must have been on active service and been recommended by their COs, or must have served in an OTC. Three of these battalions were located in Cambridge colleges: No. 2 OCB in Pembroke, No. 5 OCB in Trinity, and the Garrison Battalion, later No. 22 OCB, in Jesus. Other colleges were used as billets. In 1916 for instance, Christ's was accommodating 50 cadets, and the next year, the 100 cadets of 'F' Coy No. 2 OCB, whilst 'E' Company of No. 5 OCB was in St John's College in 1917, with further billets in Sidney Sussex College. The deployment of huge armies in difficult circumstances demanded detailed staff-work but, after the first years of war, the majority of staff-officers were amateur soldiers. The army's Staff College at Camberley was therefore replicated in France as well as in Cambridge in 1917, running short courses.

Premises for the Army

At the beginning of the war the Cambridgeshires continued to use no. 14 Corn Exchange Street as their administrative centre but had to establish a temporary depot in the Girls' County School, built in 1900 in Collier Road. But in November 1914, the TF units based in Cambridge were given a brand-new drill hall, converted from the Technical School on East Road, into which they moved in February 1915, along with the Yeomanry and the administration of the 1st Eastern General Hospital. The front of the two-storey building entered through two separate entrances contained orderly rooms, offices, armoury, clothing and saddlery stores, a band-room, a lecture-room, messes for officers and sergeants, and a canteen and servery for the men. Passages led from the road to the drill hall itself, and to the miniature range behind it. The hall measured 100 feet (30m) in length by 30 feet (9m) wide with a gallery at one end. Finally, a separate building in the yard housed the Maxim guns. In contrast to this comfortable and functional building, the majority of new accommodation consisted of hutted camps, of which there were many around Cambridge, Stretham and Ely. As well as the infantry camps, there was an artillery camp at Ely, and ASC camps at Teversham and in Cambridge, servicing some of the larger formations of the Central Force. Soldiers from these camps were employed in 1917 in building a new road between Stretham and Wicken to ease the movement of men and materiel.

Munitions Production

Marshalls Garage in Jesus Lane, Cambridge, serviced vehicles for the army including Rolls Royce armoured cars and the ambulances which ferried wounded servicemen between rail-head and hospital, but the major contribution of Cambridge to the war effort was intellectual and scientific. Horace Darwin, son of Charles, ran the Cambridge Scientific Instrument Company and had been a founder member of the Advisory Committee for Aeronautics, set up in 1909. During the war his company acted as a focus for those scientists who sought to address the practical problems of the war. The first of these related to manufacturing industry which was deprived of imports from Germany. Pyrometers were particularly missed, and Darwin set up a factory to make them in a skating rink in Magrath Avenue near his company's works in Chesterton Road. Porcelain sheaths were sourced from Royal Worcester. The work-force was recruited largely from women, working a fifty-three and a half hour week, and forbidden to wear corsets containing steel ribs. This latter injunction was caused by the work being conducted on submarine detection devices consisting of magnetic wire loops laid on the seabed. Darwin's colleagues, particularly F.E. Smith, in response to urgent requests from the Admiralty, also developed magnetic mines which greatly improved the hit-rate against submarines and surface vessels. The factory was adopted as one that could only handle work of national importance. Royal Engineers were seconded to the company to initiate work on gas detection on the battle-field, achieving apparatus which could discern one part of chlorine in 10,000 parts of air, but unfortunately the time-lag involved was too long to make it practicable. More successful was an alarm for detecting escaping hydrogen in airship hangars. Work was also carried out to develop accurate, gyroscopically controlled bomb-sights for aircraft, and sound-ranging equipment for locating enemy artillery. In 1917 a Trade School was established at no. 24 Carlyle Road for apprentices, including lads from W.G. Pye. After the war the skating-rink was returned to recreational use, ultimately becoming the Rex Cinema and Ball-room. Horace Darwin was knighted in 1919 for services to the Munitions Inventions Department Panel. Paul's, the north London firm with which Darwin amalgamated after the war, had invented the standard AA height-finding equipment adopted by the army in 1915. W.G. Pye, a former foreman at Darwin's company, had set up his own factory in Cambridge producing gun-sights, Aldis signalling lamps, aero-compasses and the Hartree Height-Finder.

Although the information gained was not always disseminated as widely as it might have been in order to protect the source, Sir Alfred Ewing, another Cambridge scientist, had pioneered the listening, or 'Y' stations, which enabled the movements of German warships to be collated in Room 40 in the Admiralty's Old Building.

Frederick Sage and Co. was already a long-established joinery and shop-fitting firm, when it commissioned first one, and then a second new factory with its distinctive water-tower, beside the railway in Walton, Peterborough, both completed by 1911. In 1915 it won contracts to assemble aircraft for the expanding RFC and RNAS. The factory, which had to be extended several times, produced over 80 Short 184 Seaplanes, and over 300 BE2cs and Avro 504Ks. The Short 184s were employed on anti-submarine patrols, attacking and sinking U-boats with air-launched torpedoes. Simultaneously, Sages design team was building prototypes of their own aircraft, including a bomber and a sea-plane, none of which was successfully developed, despite one Sage 2 being tested to destruction at Cranwell. By the time a viable design had been achieved, the war was over and contracts had been cancelled. Sage's Aircraft Design Department was shut down in 1920. The aircraft sheds added in 1915 and extended in 1916, have recently (2011) been demolished, leaving only the solitary water-tower as a reminder. The sheds (**51**) shared many of the features of the RFC's hangars with their wooden roofs, usually described as 'Belfast Trusses'. Sages also produced cabs for airships, and these were stored in a workshop in Princes Street (**52**).

51 PETERBOROUGH, SAGES LANE: aircraft factory sheds built to a similar design to hangars on operational airfields; they have recently been demolished.

52 PETERBOROUGH, PRINCES STREET: sheds used for the storage of the cabs for airships which Sages manufactured.

Two flying enthusiasts, Radley and Moorhouse, had promoted flying events on Portholme Meadow at Huntingdon and begun trading as the Portholme Aerodrome Company. Their aircraft, however, proved accident-prone and the business was acquired in 1912 by Handley Page, who took over the factory at no. 26 St John's Street to make coachwork for automobiles. Moorhouse would later win a posthumous VC in the RFC over Belgium. In 1915 the company won contracts to build Wright 840 seaplanes for the RNAS, along with Sopwith Camels and Snipes. Only four of the seaplanes were completed and the contract was apparently cancelled.

Baker Perkins Westwood Works in Peterborough had produced mobile steam ovens, known to the soldiers as 'Polly Perkins', for the British army since 1866. Production and supply of these mobile bakeries continued throughout the First World War, being particularly important in the conditions of the Western Front, where constant shelling made mobility essential, and hot food a life-saver.

Hospitals and Welfare

When the TF was established in 1908 it included a network of regional general hospitals staffed by part-time volunteer members of the RAMC. Cambridge was the location for the 1st Eastern General Hospital (TF) with its HQ at no. 39 Green Street. On the outbreak of war the hospital mobilised, moving its HQ to Trinity College, and on the opening of the new drill hall, its stores to East Road. Its CO was Lt Col Joseph Griffiths, a surgeon at Addenbrookes, and the hospital was established in temporary hutted accommodation on Clare and King's Colleges' cricket grounds, with space for 1,500 beds. Officially there were 151 beds for officers and a further 1,191 for ORs. If the need arose, there were overflow facilities at Addenbrookes and the Leys School. The hospital was staffed by RAMC officers, nurses and orderlies, assisted by voluntary workers, and by those students who had progressed beyond the first stages of their medical degree and were permitted to work as dressers. Across the county there was widespread provision for the wounded and the sick, as well as convalescent and rehabilitation facilities. Some of this provision, such as the VD hospitals at Cherry Hinton and Barnwell, was under the direct control of the army through the RAMC, but most of the established hospitals opened their doors to war casualties, either by designating a number of 'military beds' or by helping out as necessary. During the course of the war some 80,000 casualties arrived at Cambridge by train. Local cottage hospitals such as the North Cambridgeshire at Wisbech or the Huntingdon County

53 PETERBOROUGH, MILTON HALL: the North Front of this Fitzwilliam seat dates from *circa* 1600 with the upper storey added in 1770. The hall served as a base for volunteer forces from Napoleonic times onwards; as a hospital in the First World War; and in the Second World War as the HQ of an AA Division, as a Czech army depot, and as an SOE/SAS training school.

Hospital all made themselves available in these ways. Many of the new hospitals were run either by established organisations such as the Red Cross as at Wordsworth Grove in Cambridge, or Brunswick Villas in Huntingdon which, proving inadequate for the demand, was moved into Walden House as an eighty-five-bed hospital. Others were run by groups of volunteers who would nurse patients under the medical supervision of GPs. These were the Voluntary Aid Detachments (VADs) set up in numerous large houses ranging from stately homes such as Burghley House, affiliated to the 5th Northern General Hospital, RAMC (TF) in Leicester, Kimbolton Castle, Milton Hall (**53**), and Wimpole Park, to the humbler Fordham Manse or Mrs Butler's house in Eaton Socon, a convalescent home for wounded soldiers. In Fulbourn the school and church hall were both taken over.

Apart from offering medical aid to soldiers home from the war, another way of helping those still at the Front was to provide recreational facilities. The YMCA and the other church missions all provided huts where soldiers could try to relax, be entertained and enjoy non-alcoholic beverages in a peaceful ambience. The university as a whole, as well as individual colleges such as Christ's, for instance, raised sums of money to pay for such huts.

Prisoner-of-War Camps

Although some POWs were kept in secure camps and guarded by garrison troops, the majority were organised into work-parties and billeted in large houses or on individual farms. Camps listed in Cambridgeshire include the Hardwick Arms at Arrington, the stables at Kimbolton Castle, the military hospital in Cambridge, alongside apparently conventional camps on Newmarket Road, Cambridge, in Littleport and in Huntingdon.

seven

The Interwar Years

At the end of the First World War, there was an immediate reduction in all the armed forces. The army demobilised all but the core cadres of its numerous regiments, and many former soldiers found difficulty getting work, some of the more badly disabled being cared for in hostels like those established in outbuildings behind Castle Hill House in Huntingdon, where they received skills training. The RAF, newly created in 1918, almost disappeared.

The Army 1920–1939

The Territorial Army

Two of the Cambridgeshire Regiment's four battalions had been disbanded even before the end of the war, and a third absorbed into a composite unit, leaving only the 1st Battalion in existence when the Territorial Army was re-formed in 1920. Its HQ was in the East Road drill hall in Cambridge, and companies were maintained in Ely, March, Newmarket, Whittlesea and Wisbech. The Huntingdonshire Cyclists had been disbanded in 1918, many of their number joining the 5th (Huntingdonshire) Battalion of the Northamptonshire Regiment, whose battalion HQ was in Huntingdon until 1927 when it moved to Peterborough. Here it joined the battalion's 'D' Company in Yaxley, where there was a drill hut with an indoor range, and at Fletton. Other companies were based in St Neots and Oundle (Northamptonshire).

Experiences on the battlefield had emphasised the lack of any real role for horsed cavalry in modern war. Both the Bedfordshire and the Suffolk Yeomanry, who had largely relinquished their mounts some time previously, were converted to artillery field regiments in 1920. The Hertfordshire batteries of the 4th East Anglian Brigade, RFA combined with the Hertfordshire Yeomanry to form the 86th Field Regiment, RA, TA, and the Northamptonshire battery of the 4th East Anglian Brigade, RFA, from Peterborough, joined with three existing Norfolk batteries to form the 84th Field Regiment. Field-guns, the 18-pounders and 4.5-inch Howitzers used in the First World War, could still be horse-drawn into the late 1920s, but mechanisation was gradually taking over as Morris six-wheeled tractors were introduced around 1923. In 1920 the responsibility for AA defence at home was handed to the newly formed TA but without the resources to do very much about it.

54 RAMSEY MILITIA CAMP: put up to accommodate conscripts under the Militia Act of May 1939.

By 1937, however, it had become apparent that war was inevitable and there was going to be a need for specialist AA defences, so a number of TA infantry units underwent conversion. One such unit was the Northamptonshires' 4th Battalion which, joined by 'D' Company of the 5th Battalion from Fletton, became a searchlight regiment, 50th (Northants) AA Battalion, RE (TA), part of the 2nd AA Division with HQ in Hucknall (Nottinghamshire). Its No. 402 Company was based in Peterborough which, with its engineering industry, railway, and RAF airfield, was seen as a likely target for air attack. An attempt was made to align the control of the AA defences by integrating the AA guns with the fighters of the RAF. Duxford, a Fighter Command Sector Station, became HQ for 40th AA Brigade. In November 1938 a major reorganisation took place in the field artillery. The Northamptonshire No. 336 Battery was detached from its Norwich-based unit, which was to become the 78th HAA Regiment, and returned to the Hertfordshire-based 86th Field Regiment, becoming 'E' and 'F' Troops of No. 344 Battery, whose BHQ and 'D' Troop were in Hitchin.

As war approached a rapid expansion of the army became a priority. In May 1939, a Militia was formed providing a compulsory six months basic military training for all fit young men. Hutted camps were built at Huntingdon, Eaton Socon, Ramsey (54) and Yaxley, and the old TF camp at West Fen, Ely, was refurbished. The other measure was the duplication of TA units. Rather than simply recruiting whole second-line units, as had been the custom in the First World War, each TA unit was required to clone itself by forming a cadre of experienced officers and NCOs as a nucleus around which a duplicate unit might be formed. The two parts of the 86th Field Regiment which were based in Hitchin (Hertfordshire) and Peterborough, Nos 344 and 336 Batteries respectively, were hived off as the nucleus of the new 135 Field Regiment RA, TA, with HQ in Hitchin. In Peterborough, this operation was carried out from the Millfield drill hall using the adjacent Unity and PSA Halls as temporary canteen and instruction spaces. One must hope that the delights of the Pleasant Sunday Afternoon Hall mitigated some of the shock for the newly recruited gunners. In October 1939 duplication was complete, when the regiment gained the newly raised 499 Battery. Duplication also affected the infantry when Cambridge became the base for the new 55th Infantry Brigade composed of the 1st Battalion of the Cambridgeshire Regiment, its cloned 2nd Battalion, and 5th Battalion of the

Bedfordshire and Hertfordshire Regiment, as part of the 18th Division, itself a clone
of the 54th Division. The 86th Field Regiment was part of the 54th's divisional artillery, and the 135th Field Regiment of the 18th Division's. The duplicate unit of the
5th Battalion the Northamptonshire Regiment became a new 4th Battalion, replacing the one that had become an AA unit in 1937.

Drill Halls and other Premises

In Peterborough, a new drill hut was built opposite the football ground near the Peacock
PH, but it only lasted a few years, for a grand design was on the drawing-board. A brand-
new drill hall in Millfield (**55**) was built in 1927 for the infantry of the 5th Battalion and,
later on, the returning guns of the Northamptonshire Battery, RFA. This imposing structure, now the City Youth Centre in Lincoln Road, consists of a two-storey front block
with neo-Georgian detail, backed by extensive halls, garaging and office accommodation. Premises had also to be found for the new searchlight unit which would satisfy its
need for the storage of complex equipment, and specialist training space. 'Shortacres' on
London Road, an Edwardian double-fronted house (**56**) with ample room for expansion, was selected and acquired for TA use, opening for business in June 1939. Included in
the extension were three rooms and a garage specifically for a Sound Locator unit, soon
to be superseded by radar. A new drill hall opened in 1922 in Ware Road, St Neots, for a
company of the 5th (Huntingdonshire) Battalion of the Northamptonshire Regiment.
Mechanisation had implications for premises and the CUOTC was provided with
garaging for fourteen vehicles at Grange Road in 1938. In 1929, 'C' Company of the
Cambridgeshires at Wisbech was still listed as based at North Terrace, but by 1937 this
had been rebuilt as 'Sandylands'. In Barton Road, Ely, a new drill hall opened in 1939

55 PETERBOROUGH, MILLFIELD: the drill hall built in 1927 for the field gunners and the
infantry.

56 PETERBOROUGH, London Road: 'Shortacres', the house purchased as the basis for a drill hall for AA units of the TA, and still (2013) in use.

57 ELY, BARTON ROAD: the drill hall which opened in 1939 for 'B' Company, 1st Battalion the Cambridgeshire Regiment. It stands alongside the parade-ground of the former Militia Barracks. (Photo: Pam Osborne)

58 CAXTON: the Mobilisation Centre which held AA guns and equipment for issue to the TA on the outbreak of war. It later served as a RASC Command depot.

for 'B' Company, 1st Battalion the Cambridgeshires (**57**). A number of Mobilisation Stores were built across the country to hold vehicles and equipment ready for issue to the TA and to new units in the event of war breaking out. One of these standardised complexes can be seen at Caxton, consisting of a large vehicle shed with a saw-tooth roof with hipped ends (**58**), fuel store, garaging and caretaker's bungalow. It began life as a specialist AA ordnance store, was listed in 1941 as a RASC Command Depot, and is now a Karting rink. In 1937 the War Office had acquired Sage's former aircraft factory in Walton, Peterborough, as a RAOC depot and in February 1939 submitted plans to the local authority for extending it in order to be able to stockpile more of the weapons needed for the coming conflict.

The RAF between the Wars

At the end of the First World War, the RAF had three substantial TDSs in the county at Fowlmere, Duxford and Wittering, with further training provision at Bury (Upwood) and at Wyton. Within a short while, however, the very existence of the RAF was called into question, and thousands of their aircraft were scrapped and the vast majority of their airfields returned to agriculture. A combination of lack of funds, a return to the traditional policy of the Royal Navy as the nation's first line of defence, and a perception that an air force was only good for carrying out imperial policing duties, meant that these cuts threatened the very survival of a Home Air Force. By the early 1920s there were barely two dozen RAF establishments across the whole country, and in Cambridgeshire only Duxford and Wittering survived the cull.

Reorganisation and Consolidation

The Ten Year Rule justified keeping defence spending to a minimum on the basis that it would take foreign nations, specifically Germany, ten years to re-arm, thus affording Britain sufficient time in which to respond. However, there was anxiety that Britain would be defenceless against any unexpected aerial attack from the Continent and, ironically, it was from France that the source of this threat was anticipated. The Steel-Bartholomew Plan of 1923 and the 52-Squadron Plan of 1925 were intended to address this problem by fixing parity of numbers with the French air force as the yard-stick. These plans were based on a screen of fighter airfields protecting London, and a cluster of bomber airfields, located to the west of London, poised for retaliation. Duxford, until then home to a Flying Training School, was selected as one of these fighter airfields, equipped with two squadrons of bi-planes. Although Duxford had retained many of its buildings from its 1918–19 beginnings, such as the GS hangars, flight office, workshops and barrack-blocks, more buildings from the Home Defence period were added. At first these were mainly functional utilitarian structures such as the Operations Block, a pump-house, aviation fuel storage and WT masts, but by 1930 new domestic buildings were appearing. The Sergeants' Mess is to a design of 1929, and the Station Offices (**59**), of 1930. In 1926 the Cambridge University Air Squadron was started with its HQ in the Engineering Laboratories on Cam Causeway, and using Duxford's facilities for flying training.

Wittering, still known as Stamford, served as No. 1 TDS from August 1917 through to May 1919, with two double aircraft sheds to a design of 1917, after which the airfield became a storage depot, prior to being put under Care and Maintenance in 1920. In 1926, on the basis that it was well away from any likely action, it was renamed Wittering,

59 RAF DUXFORD: the Station Offices (352-3/30) of this fighter airfield.

60 RAF WITTERING: the water
tower (1178/25) holding 30,000
gallons (135,000 litres).

61 RAF WITTERING: the
parachute-store (2355/26).

and reopened as the Central Flying School, training the RAF's flying instructors, and some of its infrastructure dates from this period. The guardhouse (84/24), power-house (1380/24), water-tank to hold 30,000 gallons (135,000 litres) (1178/25) (**60**), parachute-store (2355/26) (**61**) and station office (1799/25) all still survive, as do three 'C' type barrack-blocks (242/23) (**62**), built in 1925, next to the Institute or canteen.

62 RAF WITTERING: one of three surviving 'C' type barrack-blocks (242/23) built in 1925.

63 PETERBOROUGH, RAF WESTWOOD FARM: the storage sheds with railway platform to their left, belonging to No. 1 Aircraft Storage Unit which opened in 1932. Parts of aircraft and other items of equipment came in by rail to be stored and issued to airfields.

Re-orientation and Expansion

By 1930 it was becoming obvious that the nation must be better prepared for a future conflict than it had been in the past. Although the Ten Year Rule would not be abandoned until 1932, the nadir of defence budgets, a tentative start was made on re-arming. Much effort was now channelled into producing reserves of aircraft and the pilots to fly them. Peterborough (Westwood Farm) had been proposed as the site for a municipal aerodrome but, in 1928 the Air Ministry stepped in, purchasing the land as an Aircraft Storage Park which opened in 1931. Situated conveniently close to the railway, it was served by a branch line along which aircraft fuselages, wings and engines could be delivered by train to be assembled and stored in hangars, to be flown off from the grass-field as necessary. It is still possible to see the platforms onto which aircraft were unloaded and the warehouse in which they were initially stored, in the yard of BT alongside Saville Road (63). Within a short time, the need for pilots over-rode that for aircraft, and the site was converted into a flying training school, No. 7 SFTS opening in 1935. Added to the existing 'A' Type hangar (19a/24), were the elegant Officers' Mess (7035/30) (64), Sergeants' Mess (325/30) and a Station HQ (714/30), all still standing. Ironically, while the RAF had been cutting back there had been an enormous upsurge in interest in flying and, at the other end of the county, Marshalls had opened a private flying school in 1930, on the family farm at Whitehill, Fen Ditton. This school trained many who would play important roles both in the RAF and the aircraft industry. When the new Cambridge Aerodrome opened in 1937 on Newmarket Road, Marshalls continued to operate No. 22 E&RFTS along

64 PETERBOROUGH, RAF WESTWOOD FARM: the officers' mess to design number 7035/30 and dated 1931 over the door.

65 CAMBRIDGE: the Flying Control Building of Marshalls aerodrome and flying school at Teversham, opened in 1937.

66 CAMBRIDGE: Hangar No. 1 at Marshalls aerodrome, with the Control Building beyond.

with No. 26 E&RFTS at Kidlington (Oxfordshire). Marshalls also ran its own Flying Instructor Training Scheme so was able to staff its flying schools without drawing on Air Ministry resources. All this military activity continued against the romantic back-drop of the aerodrome's Control Building (65), Hotel and No. 1 Hangar (66), all designed in the *moderne* style of the period. At this time the AA were publishing lists of landing-grounds for use by private pilots and such are included at Ely (TL530813) and at Peterborough (Horsey Toll at TL220968). At Wittering, No. 11 FTS formed in 1935, but had to move out within a couple of years due to the station's radically altered role. The private airfield of Peterborough Flying Club at Horsey Toll on the Whittlesey road provided some training for members of the Civil Air Guard from 1938, using Aeronca aircraft built at Sages. Cambridge University established a gliding club at Caxton Gibbet in 1935, many of whose members would go on to fly powered aircraft in the coming war.

As it became clearer that the threat of war was coming once more from Germany, the orientation of the RAF's airfields had to be shifted to face the east. The bomber force would need to be located to strike across the North Sea, and fighters would need to be positioned to intercept bombing raids. Duxford was now joined by Wittering as a Fighter Command Sector Station. East Anglia became home to 2 Group Bomber Command, with the heavy bombers based in Norfolk (Marham) and Suffolk (Honington, Mildenhall and Stradishall). The light bombers were based in Watton and West Raynham (Norfolk), Wattisham (Suffolk), and on two Cambridgeshire airfields. In July 1936 Wyton opened, becoming 2 Group's HQ in 1938, flying light bombers along with Upwood which had opened in January 1937. At Bassingbourn, opened in March 1938, were based the Operational Training Units which would

67 RAF BASSINGBOURN: one of the airfield's four 'C' type hangars, built in concrete with protected roofs.

68 RAF BASSINGBOURN: parachute store to design 175/36.

69 RAF WATERBEACH: guard-house to design 469/38.

70 RAF UPWOOD: officers' mess to design 570-2/37.

serve these light bomber squadrons. All these airfields were designed by the Air Ministry's architect, A. Bullock FRIBA, overseen by both the Council for the Protection of Rural England, and the Royal Fine Arts Commission with Sir Edwin Lutyens. Consequently a neo-Georgian style was chosen which might be expected to have a similar impact on the landscape as the country-houses among which these airfields were interspersed. They all followed a similar layout and used the same combination of buildings to the same drawings. An arc of four or five 'C' Type hangars (**67**) skirted one side of the grass flying-field with a watch office and fire station in front. Behind, built on a regular grid of roads, were main workshops and stores; parachute store (**68**), armoury and sick-bay; MT compound and station HQ; central-heating station and works department; and synthetic training buildings. At the gate was a Guard-house (**69**), and nearby were officers' (**70**) and sergeants' messes. The airmen lived in H-shaped barrack-blocks and were fed in the Institute and dining-room (**71**). On the periphery were married quarters, sports facilities and utilities. Much of this universal layout may still be seen at Bassingbourn, Wyton (**Fig. 7**), Upwood and, probably for not much longer, at Waterbeach.

It was intended that each station would have a satellite station providing alternative dispersals for the aircraft and crew whilst not actually on operations. Alconbury, the very first of these, opened in 1938 as Upwood's satellite, but then transferred to Wyton. Serving a different purpose to the parent airfields, Alconbury was given generally temporary buildings, a war-time-pattern watch office, and used a local manor house for the officers' mess. Right up until the beginning of the war, airfield construction was continuing. Oakington, Waterbeach and Molesworth were all planned in peace-time, but completed in the first eighteen months of the war, and owing to this urgency, some compromises were necessary on building quality. All three were given 'J' Type hangars (**72**)

71 RAF UPWOOD: dining room, being a flat-roofed version of design 1680/39.

instead of the much sturdier 'C' Type, but otherwise, many of the buildings at the first two were identical to those at the earlier airfields. Waterbeach and Oakington, like Wyton, both had 'Villa' type watch offices (5845/39) (**73**) with features more likely to be found in a 1930s beach-house, which had taken over from Bassingbourn's earlier 'Fort' type (207/36) (**74**) watch office. Molesworth just missed out, being given a tb watch office (518/40). Commenced on the very eve of war, Castle Camps, a satellite for the fighter Sector Station at Debden (Essex) was given entirely temporary buildings, and this would become the pattern throughout the war. During the summer of 1939, part of the old Collyweston airfield, named 'K3', became an emergency landing-ground for Wittering, but its runway could only extend to 4,500 feet (1385m), and it would be a further two years before it would be extended again.

Sage's old aircraft factory in Peterborough had gained a new, but very brief, lease of life in 1936, when it was bought by the Aeronautical Corporation of Great Britain Ltd. Although, in the Aeronca 100 they had a well-proven model from the USA, new airworthiness standards and poor marketing prevented its success in the British market, and after building just twenty-five aircraft in Peterborough, the company closed down after a year.

Preparing for the Bombers: ARP and (R)OC

In the year before war broke out some local authorities had run exercises to test the resilience of their fire-fighting, first aid and administrative services in an emergency situation such as a bombing attack. One element of the official preparations had been in place for a while, however. A lesson of the First World War had been the value of running an integrated air defence system involving early warning and joint centralised control of AA guns and fighter aircraft. Although the technology had moved on, the principle had not changed. In the First World War special constables had been enrolled to act as spotters, reporting the arrival and, if possible, the likely destination, of hostile aircraft. This had proved so valuable that despite the suggestion that the exciting developments in RDF (later Radar) might be about to render such low-tech activity redundant, it was decided in 1934 that membership of the Observer Corps, re-formed in 1925, should be

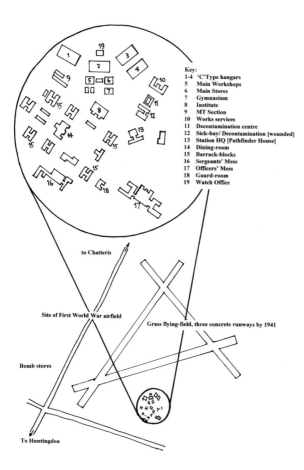

Fig. 7 Raf Wyton, 1936: a
typical Expansion Period
airfield lay-out.

Key:
1-4   'C'Type hangars
5   Main Workshops
6   Main Stores
7   Gymnasium
8   Institute
9   MT Section
10   Works services
11   Decontamination centre
12   Sick-bay/ Decontamination [wounded]
13   Station HQ [Pathfinder House]
14   Dining-room
15   Barrack-blocks
16   Sergeants' Mess
17   Officers' Mess
18   Guard-room
19   Watch Office

to Chatteris

Site of First World War airfield

Grass flying-field, three concrete runways by 1941

Bomb stores

To Huntingdon

72 RAF OAKINGTON:
a 'J' type hangar to design
5836/39. The site has now
been cleared for a new
township.

greatly increased as part of the expansion of the RAF. In 1935 the Corps Commandant made his annual inspection in 15 Group's area containing Cambridgeshire, the Isle of Ely and Huntingdonshire. Group HQ, reporting to Duxford, was at the GPO in Cambridge, where a room was set aside exclusively for Observer Corps use. There was also an emergency stand-by centre at the University Arms Hotel in Regent Street. By 1938 eighteen aircraft-spotting posts had been opened in Cambridgeshire and the Isle of Ely, with another at Ramsey in Huntingdonshire. Each post was either a timber, semi-covered 'rabbit-hutch' or an

73 RAF WATERBEACH: the watch office to design 5845/39 often referred to as the 'Villa' type for obvious reasons.

improvised structure on a vantage point, either natural as at the Cherry Hinton post on Gog-Magog hills, or man-made as at Stretham's windmill (75), and Sutton's brewery roof. Rudimentary plotting instruments were used to chart an aircraft's direction of flight which, coupled with visual recognition of aircraft type, was sent to control for onward transmission to the Fighter Command Sector Station at Duxford. The nation might not have been totally prepared for the onslaught to come, but much of the necessary infrastructure was in place.

74 RAF BASSINGBOURN: the 'Fort' type watch office, this example built in concrete to design 207/36 but later modified by the addition of an extra storey, wrapped around the tower which itself has also been heightened.

75 STRETHAM: the tower windmill (TL512749) was adopted by the Observer Corps as an aircraft-spotting post.

eight

The Second World War

Cambridgeshire was in the thick of the Battle of Britain, and potentially in the front line from mid-1940 until the threat of invasion dissipated towards the end of 1941. After that the local regiments were sent off on catastrophic adventures abroad whilst, at home, the RAF, later joined by the USAAF, carried out a bombing offensive against continental targets. Whilst the landscape was transformed by new airfields, army camps, defences and intensive farming, two sites never achieved their potential. Burghley House, out of all Britain's stately homes, had been awarded the honour of being selected as his official British residence by Hermann Goering, the over-promoted former fighter-pilot and architect of the Luftwaffe's operational failure. There was also an active role envisaged for the athletic Sixth Marquess, according to his daughter, in the Aryan breeding programme. At the other end of the scale was the charming, but insignificant Willow Hall, between Thorney and Eye. Through aerial reconnaissance for the 1940 invasion of Britain, the Operation Sealion planners had spotted the existence of a Fenland farm with a 2-mile-long (3km), obstacle-free landing-field, screened from view by woodland, representing the ideal site for their airborne force's forward HQ. As it turned out, this level of attention to detail at such an early stage in the planning was always to prove disappointingly premature.

Mobilisation and Recruitment

On the outbreak of war, the Northamptonshire Regiment's 5th Battalion vacated their Millfield drill hall in Peterborough, and set up a new HQ and HQ Company at St Peter's (76), the teacher training college next to the cathedral (now Peterscourt). Its four companies assembled at Ramsey, Oundle, Huntingdon and St Neots, and then joined up with 11th Infantry Brigade, prior to becoming part of the BEF and sailing for Flanders. The army established a recruiting office in Rothesay Villas, Lincoln Road.

It was only after Dunkirk that the main effort to build defences got under way, but Cambridgeshire County Council was quick off the mark in 1939, building the pillbox which still stands, if a little drunkenly, at Dog-in-a-Doublet, and borrowing airmen from RAF Westwood Farm to camouflage it (77). Such actions must have underlined the need to enlist. In June 1940, ATS recruits in Cambridgeshire's Militia camps found themselves caring for the troops evacuated from Dunkirk, re-clothing, re-equipping,

76 PETERBOROUGH, CITY ROAD, PETERSCOURT: the teacher training college taken over by the 5th Bn Northamptonshire Regiment as their HQ and depot in September 1939.

77 DOG-IN-A-DOUBLET: the bridge and lock on the River Nene north of Whittlesey (TL274994) was defended by this pillbox, built in 1939 by the county council, and camouflaged by airmen from RAF Peterborough.

and re-humanising them. In late 1941, cadet companies for boys from 14 years of age with HQ at Swanspool House, Midgate, Peterborough, were raised by the Territorial Association of the Soke of Peterborough and Huntingdon in order for youngsters to commence training as soon as possible. Half the projected strength of 600 had been recruited by early 1942, and a Sea Cadet Corps was formed in July 1942, recruiting another 70–80 cadets in the 14–17 age-group, and meeting at Brook Street School (Peterborough College of Adult Education). A Sea Cadet unit was started in Wisbech in 1944 with two loans of £400 for equipment and premises. Although one of these loans was interest-free, a minimum of £100 had to be repaid annually. After a couple of years' service in the Home Guard, all these lads, already semi-trained, could be con-scripted into the regular services and were able to hit the ground marching.

Defence against Invasion, 1940

The Defensive Strategy

By the end of May 1940, a German invasion was perceived as both inevitable and imminent. Given that the army had been forced to abandon most of its transport, armour, artillery and equipment prior to its evacuation from Dunkirk, General Ironside, C-in-C Home Forces, had little option but to plan a static defence. The first element of his plan was the Coastal Crust, defences designed to hold up an inva-sion force on the beaches until the navy could arrive to sever the supply chain and isolate the invaders. The next key element was the GHQ Line, a linear anti-tank defence stretching from Somerset to the Medway, across the Thames, through Essex and Cambridgeshire to the Welland, and then on up the Trent to Yorkshire, even-tually ending up at Loch Tay. This would delay any invading force and give the GHQ Reserve a chance to deploy its armour. The Coastal Crust consisted of bat-teries of heavy guns defending the ports, and strings of pillboxes and lighter guns defending the most likely and vulnerable invasion beaches. Probable landing places were obstructed by minefields, wire entanglements, barriers of scaffolding, and iron stakes set below high-water to prevent the flat-bottomed barges beaching. Reports of experiments with flame warfare were allowed to filter out, and pamphlets pointing out the hazards of amphibious landings were dropped on the German troops assem-bling in the Channel ports.

The GHQ Line

The defensive strategy rested on a succession of delaying positions (**Fig. 8**) of which the GHQ Line was the most important and most robust. It consisted of a continuous anti-tank (AT) barrier based, where possible, on natural obstacles which, in the Fens of Cambridgeshire, were predominantly rivers and drainage dykes. It was supported by concrete pillboxes and AT emplacements, regularly spaced, with concentrations in particularly vulnerable spots, built as prepared positions only to be manned as and when the enemy approached. In the early days these troops would have been from

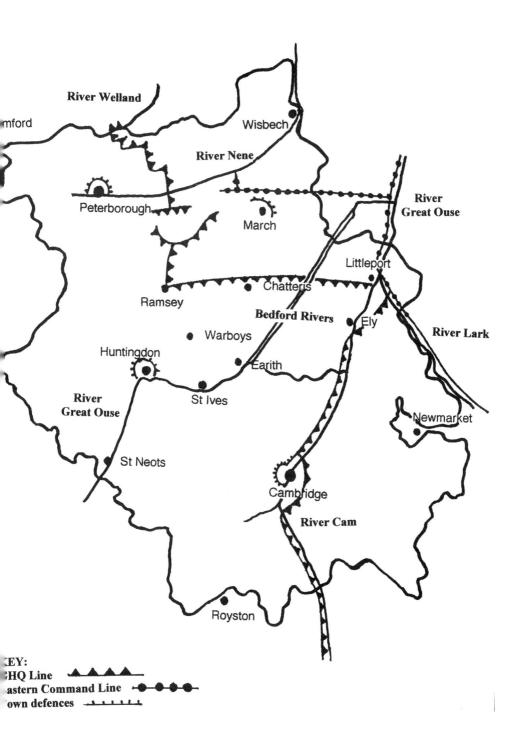

Fig. 8 The GHQ Line and other stop-lines in Cambridgeshire.

the 2nd London Infantry Division, whose 4th Infantry Brigade was based around Huntingdon, with a battalion of the Royal Fusiliers, for instance, in St Ives. The 18th or 55th Divisions would have fallen back from their forward positions and, *in extremis*, the GHQ Mobile Reserve would have been involved. Later, it would be the Home Guard and second-line home-garrison troops. The Line entered the county at Great Chesterford, ran up the River Cam to Cambridge, where an artificial AT ditch was dug to the east of the city, re-joining the river below Waterbeach. From here it followed the Cam, north to Ely and Littleport, before turning westwards for Chatteris and Ramsey and the crossing of the Nene at Dog-in-a-Doublet, east of Whittlesey. It then headed for the Welland, here marking the county boundary, by skirting the east side of Peterborough. The Eastern Command Line, originated in Colchester and ran across Essex and Suffolk, following the River Lark to join the Great Ouse at Padnal Fen, south of Littleport, then continued as far as Kings Lynn, with a spur running west from Downham Market to March. The report of the original reconnaissance for the construction of the GHQ Line, produced by RE officers on 14–15 June 1940, suggested taking the Line from Cambridge up an artificial AT ditch to Twenty Pence Ferry, and thence up the Great Ouse to Earith, later cutting an additional AT ditch in a straight line from Cambridge to Earith. This was clearly seen as impracticable and the Cam route was chosen. By the autumn, Ironside had been replaced by Brooke, who was able to modify the policy of static defence, and put a curb on the programme of constructing hardened defences. It would appear that the majority of the pillboxes planned for the Line between Cambridge and the Essex border, where only isolated examples can be seen, were never built.

The construction of the GHQ Line was supervised by RE officers who drew up detailed plans which were given to a local builder to carry out using sub-contractors. In Cambridgeshire, the building operations were overseen by the Federation of Master Builders in Tenison Road, Cambridge, with 130 members spread across the region. Their papers reveal that they were under constant pressure from the War Office Directorate of Fortifications and Works (DFW3) to economise on materials, even to the extent of doing without floors in pillboxes and including higher than normal amounts of aggregate in the concrete mix. Contractors were also encouraged to make the back walls of pillboxes thinner than the rest as the enemy was clearly not expected to attack from the rear. In fact, the peculiar circumstances of the Fens demanded more, not less, materials. At Welches Dam, Hugh Cave of Thorney, who held the contract for the Line north of Chatteris, found his workers needed to span dykes with great concrete platforms to carry the pillboxes, and then only after a narrow-gauge railway to get the materials there had first been laid, and the Drainage Board's stipulations over maintaining the free flow of run-off from the agriculturally vital fields had been met. Timber for shuttering was in very short supply so Flettons were used for many of the county's pillboxes; although this increased the thickness of the walls by 4.5 inches (11cm) it has ensured a more rapid degradation of the fabric. Both Cave's firm and Coulson's in Cambridge employed sub-contractors to carry out much of the work. Some three hundred or so pillboxes and AT emplacements

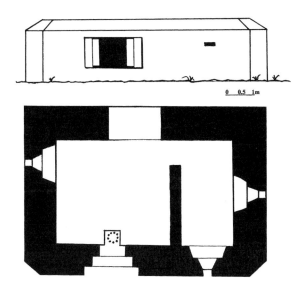

0   0.5   1m

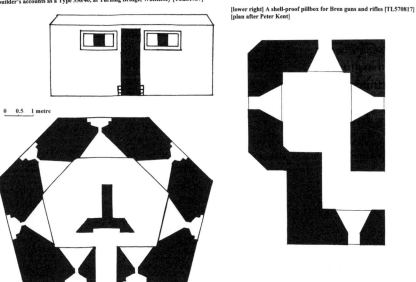

[top] An emplacement [DFW3/28a] for a 6-pounder Hotchkiss QF gun, showing the narrower embrasure, the pedestal for mounting the gun with its 9-bolt hold-fast, and the separate chamber for a Bren gun. [TL573869] [plan after Colin Alexander]

[lower left] A shell-proof pillbox for a section of infantry equipped with Bren guns and rifles, similar to the standard design [DFW3/24] but described in the builder's accounts as a Type 350/40, at Turning Bridge, Whittlesey [TL281957]

[lower right] A shell-proof pillbox for Bren guns and rifles [TL570817] [plan after Peter Kent]

0   0.5   1 metre

Fig. 9 Pillbox designs used on the GHQ Line in Cambridgeshire. Top: an emplacement (DFW3/28a) for a 6-pounder Hotchkiss QF gun, showing the narrower embrasure, the pedestal for mounting the gun with its 9-bolt hold-fast, and the separate chamber for a Bren gun (TL573869). (Plan after Colin Alexander) Lower left: a shell-proof pillbox for a section of infantry equipped with Bren guns and rifles, similar to the standard design (DFW3/24) but described in the builder's accounts as a Type 350/40, at Turning Bridge, Whittlesey (TL281957). Lower right: A shell-proof pillbox for Bren guns and rifles (TL570817). (Plan after Peter Kent)

were built in Cambridgeshire alone between May and Christmas 1940/41, some of
the larger ones weighing in at over 100 tons. It was a mammoth operation in terms
of transporting materials, recruiting labour when the armed services were con-
scripting all available manpower, and carrying out the actual construction in sites

78 RIVER CAM, north of Waterbeach: a shellproof DFW3/24 pillbox (TL495640) built in
the summer of 1940 as part of the GHQ Line.

79 NEWBOROUGH, south of Bukehorn Road: a bullet-proof DFW3/24 pillbox (TF235055)
built in the summer of 1940 as part of the second-line defences of the GHQ Line.

which were difficult of access. Cash flow was also a problem for the contractors as not only were expenses claims constantly being queried but, even when the contractors' invoices had been accepted, payment was delayed by the War Office for as long as possible.

The War Office's DFW3 provided a suite of drawings of defence works for the contractors to follow, whilst RE officers, who might have been designing houses up until very recently, advised on location, orientation, type of work to be built and fields of fire. Camouflage was often the responsibility of those who had been artists or theatre designers in civilian life. There were several main designs of pillbox and AT emplacement used on most of the GHQ Line (**Fig. 9**). There were shell-proof hexagonal pillboxes for a section of infantry armed with Bren guns and rifles (DFW3/24 or 350/40) (**78**), with a bullet and splinter-proof version (DFW3/24) (**79**) for infantry armed with rifles, both these versions having a longer rear face containing the entrance; next was a rectangular shell-proof pillbox with a rear, loop-holed blast-wall for three Bren guns (**80**); and finally, there was a large rectangular shell-proof emplacement for a 2-pounder AT gun (DFW3/28 or 28a), the Type 28a with

80 PYMORE: a rectangular shellproof pillbox (TL498847) built in the summer of 1940 as part of the GHQ Line.

81 HOBBS LOTS BRIDGE, at the junction of the A605 and A141: A DFW3/28a anti-tank emplacement (TF395014). The loophole for the Bren chamber can be seen to the right of the wide 2-pounder embrasure. The peeling bricks of the form-work are visible on the front and side.

82 EUXIMOOR HOUSE FARM: A DFW3/28 anti-tank emplacement (TF498002).

a second compartment alongside the gun-room for one or more Bren guns (**81, 82**). Because so many of the army's 2-pounder AT guns had been lost in France, and much of the new production was earmarked for mounting in Cruiser tanks, naval Hotchkiss 6-pounder QF guns were substituted. These guns had originally been mounted along the sides of pre-First World War Dreadnoughts, had then been adapted for mounting in First World War male tanks, and were once again being taken out of retirement for mounting in AT emplacements. Those type 28 and 28a emplacements built specifically for the 2-pounder gun had a pivot set in the floor and two slots in the front wall under the embrasure to hold the spade grips on the legs of the gun (**83**), whilst those for the 6-pounder gun had a concrete pedestal, with a nine-bolt holdfast for the gun, set below a narrower embrasure. In July 1940 six 6-pounders were supplied for mounting in emplacements in the II Corps area, but they were soon unbolted and despatched to 18th Division's coast defence positions. Eventually in 1941 these guns would be supplemented by a range of improvised weapons, referred to as sub-artillery, which had been developed for use by the Home Guard and the newly formed RAF Regiment. The three shell-proof models were generally built to fire across or along the AT ditch, with the weaker Type 24 set back in a supporting line. AT Blocks strung together with hawsers, AT Rails set vertically in concrete, coils of Dannert barbed-wire and minefields were all used to strengthen the defences, and points where the Line crossed roads were particularly heavily fortified. Railway lines were obstructed with AT blocks beside the tracks, and removable vertical rails inserted in the permanent way itself to prevent the movement of enemy tanks. Between Great Chesterford and Littleport there were twelve such blocks with more at Whittlesey, Chatteris Dock and Thorney.

83 THORNEY: interior of a DFW3/28 anti-tank emplacement (TF279050) showing the fittings for a 2-pounder AT gun, the central socket and the two forward slots for the trail legs.

84 RIVER WELLAND: a shellproof DFW3/24 pillbox built into the river-bank (TF202090), one of two effectively marking the northern end of the GHQ Line as built. These pillboxes were entered through a hatch in the roof.

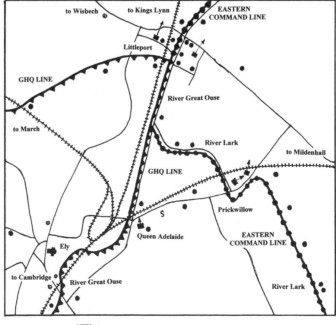

Fig. 10 The junction of 1940 stop-lines around Littleport and Ely.

The best-preserved part of the GHQ Line in Cambridgeshire is the section from the Dog-in-a-Doublet sluice-gates on the Nene, northwards to the Welland, which includes examples of all those different types of pillbox used in the Line. There are also variations such as the two built into the flood-bank of the Welland (**84**) with access hatches in the roof. At several points, the rear line of thin-walled pillboxes is visible, and at Thorney a spigot mortar has been emplaced.

The most complex part of the GHQ Line in Cambridgeshire is the junction with the Eastern Command Line in the Queen Adelaide/Prickwillow/Littleport area (**Fig. 10**). Here the GHQ Line defences leave the Great Ouse at Queen Adelaide, running to Prickwillow along the railway. Having effected the junction with the Eastern Command Line, the combined lines then ran north-west to meet the Great Ouse about 1¼ miles (2km) south of Littleport. The GHQ Line then left the Great Ouse at Littleport to run west across the top of Little Downham to Pymore, hitting the Bedford Rivers at Welches Dam, and heading for Chatteris. The Eastern Command Line continued north to Downham Market where it left the river, making for Salters Lode then along Pophams Eau and the Old Nene to March.

The GHQ Reserve

After Dunkirk the returning II Corps, by now responsible for the defence of much of East Anglia, established its HQ at Madingley Hall. The GHQ Reserve was divided into two concentrations of the best equipped and most mobile formations, one centred on Aldershot covering the south coast, and the other, initially Northampton but later Cambridge, covering the east. This eastern force consisted of what passed for two Armoured Divisions, the 2nd with its HQ at Madingley and the 6th which, within a short while, would be re-deployed to the south. The two armoured brigades of the 6th Armoured Division were the 26th with HQ at Ripley House, Great Shelford, and the 20th with HQ at Dullingham House, including the 1st and 2nd Northamptonshire Yeomanries. The 6th Support Group had its HQ at Anstey Hall, Trumpington. In the move south, the 20th Armoured Brigade took up its new station in the Tonbridge (Kent) area. The 2nd Armoured Division, remaining around Cambridge, consisted of the 1st Armoured Brigade centred on Swaffham Prior, the 22nd Armoured Brigade with its HQ in Babraham Hall, and the 2nd Support Group, a battalion of mechanised infantry and field artillery, at Newton Hall near Harston. Also attached was the 1st Armoured Brigade whose 3rd Royal Tank Regiment (RTR) had re-assembled at Bottisham after Dunkirk, later moving to Thornhaugh Hall, near Wittering. As the factories stepped up their production to turn out more and more tanks and guns, these units were steadily re-equipped. By the end of August 1940 3rd RTR had received 56 new Cruiser tanks with 2-pounder guns, but the rest of 1st Armoured Brigade still had only light tanks armed with machine-guns. In the event of an invasion, this mobile GHQ Reserve would be moved by rail to wherever it was needed, responding to coded orders: 'George' meant they would go to the Thetford and Brandon area on the Norfolk/Suffolk border, 'Percy' stood for the Fens around the Wash and 'William' indicated a position astride the GHQ Line in

Cambridgeshire and Essex. Later instructions designated 'Nancy' as the north Norfolk coast, whilst 'June' signified the Harwich/Clacton area.

Local Command and Control

For the army, Cambridge was a District, an Area and a sub-Area centre. Eastern Command's Cambridge District HQ was at St Regis House in Montague Road. The Area HQ (**85**) was at 'Binsted', no. 5 Herschel Road, and the sub-Area HQ was in King's College (later moved to no. 62 Grange Road), with the other sub-Area HQs at the St Mary's Street drill hall in Huntingdon, and at no. 27 The Embankment, Bedford. For the purposes of anti-invasion defences, as at 14 July 1940 for instance, Cambridge Area liaised closely with the HQ of the Officer Commanding the South Staffordshire Regiment at no. 12 Portland Street, Kings Lynn (Norfolk), with HQ 55th Infantry Division c/o GPO Diss (Norfolk) and with HQ 40th AA Brigade, Sawston Hall. Super-imposed on this infra-structure were the HQs of the Home Guard. A large number of Temporary Office Buildings (TOB) were erected at Brooklands to accommodate government offices evacuated from the London area.

The Home Guard

After Dunkirk it was quickly realised that the defeated regular army would need time to re-build, re-train, re-arm and re-equip, before even contemplating any reversal of the dire military situation. While this was going on it would be necessary to raise a force specifically for home defence and the Local Defence Volunteers, later the Home Guard, was born. Large numbers of men and youths came forward, willing to give their time even after long days working in the fields and the factories. As weapons became available, particularly US and Canadian rifles, Home Guard units took on the appearance of an efficient and effective force. In Peterborough, the first Home Guard unit established its HQ in Fox & Vergette's Horse Repository in Lincoln Road, and in May 1940 over 1,000 men were enrolled in the force. A month later nearly 3,000 men had signed up in Huntingdonshire. As the force became organised, boundaries and

85 CAMBRIDGE, 'Binsted', no. 5 Herschel Road: the Army's Cambridge Area HQ.

responsibilities were changed around, but the accent never shifted from what it said on members' shoulders. The Home Guard was a locally raised force, with local knowledge and an emphatic will to defend its members' homes and families. By Stand Down at the end of 1944, there were eight Cambridgeshire battalions, one of which spanned the Suffolk border from its HQ in Newmarket, another which comprised only GPO workers with HQ and one company in Cambridge, and the other two companies in Norwich and Bedford. Peterborough raised its own GPO unit in 1941. There were three battalions in the Isle of Ely, three more in Huntingdonshire, and two of the Northamptonshire Home Guard's fifteen battalions were recruited from, and based in Peterborough and the Soke. From 1942 the 10th Home Guard AA Regiment was based in Peterborough with its other batteries in Cambridge and Leicester, and 2007 MT Company was based at Cambridge, part of the Norfolk & Cambridge Home Guard Transport Column with HQ at Fordham.

Along with the patrols, training went on constantly. Much of it was on an individual basis, improving personal skills on particular weapons. Most training facilities had to be replicated at a local level as there was little time or fuel for travel. There were rifle-ranges all over, a grenade-range in a quarry at Helpston, a Lewis Gun range at Grafham and a spigot mortar range at Pondersbridge. Here the only effective shooting on one particular day was achieved by the man who shot last, having been in the pub all day. Often more adventurous training was attempted such as river-crossings at Hemingford Grey. All those towns large enough to warrant a Defence Plan underwent periodic trial runs. For an exercise in Peterborough in May 1941, a notional Keep was

86 LITTLEPORT: a spigot mortar pedestal, its surrounding pit and ammunition lockers long ago filled in (TL553873).

constructed close by East Station, consisting of three shelters surrounded by wire. The umpires were based at Farrow's factory and conducted the de-briefing at the Angel Hotel. If regular troops were involved then the stakes were raised. Home Guard who used their local knowledge to advantage could very often put one over on the professionals, and objections were raised in Peterborough when the locals outflanked a road-block by using a railway embankment, but that was the whole point of enjoying familiarity with the terrain. Some units such as the 8th Battalion in Cambridge even managed a camp at Longstowe in 1943, and the 2nd Battalion went to an un-named farm at Balsham, but very often their instruction consisted of a training film at the Doric in Newmarket.

'Sub-artillery' was the generic name given to the extemporised Heath-Robinson weapons, produced to increase the Home Guard's fire-power in the absence of proper ones. These included Northover Projectors which fired phosphorous bombs or Molotov Cocktails from a drain-pipe on a tripod; the Stokes mortar which was a left-over from the trenches of the Western Front; the 3-inch Smith gun, towed by an Austin 7; and the Blacker Bombard or spigot mortar. This last was invented by Major Blacker who worked at Winston Churchill's Toyshop in Buckinghamshire and would later come up with the PIAT, a sort of AT bazooka. The spigot mortar was mounted on a concrete pedestal the size of a dustbin. Embedded in the concrete was the 'spider', a framework of tubular steel on which, projecting from the pedestal's domed top, was a stainless steel pintle onto which was attached the spigot mortar (**86**). There was also a mobile version on a scaffold-pole frame with spade grips. The spigot mortar would be kept under cover and then mounted on a fixed position at action stations. It fired a 14lb anti-personnel, or a 20lb AT bomb, at an effective range of about 100 yards. A spigot mortar pedestal would stand in a pit with brick ready-use ammunition lockers built into its sides. Nowadays most of these pits have filled up with debris and the only thing visible will often be the pintle in a domed concrete slab. One such can be seen on the Green at Ramsey. Some counties adopted this weapon with more enthusiasm than others and many can be seen around Cambridgeshire. According to the Cambridge Defence Plan there were ninety-two spigot mortars available to the 5th Battalion, but a pedestal has never surfaced in Cambridge so they may all have been on field mountings. From its introduction in 1941 it was even installed on the GHQ Line, as at Thorney where one stands in for the 2-pounder AT gun which was never mounted in the purpose-built DFW3/28 emplacement provided there. For many units these improvised weapons were all they had and so they were forced both to train with them and to plan for their use in action. One fascinating account by a Home Guardsman in Grantchester reveals the detail which went into that planning. Alan Lawrie, in a RBL anthology, relates how he and the classics professor were given what he calls a Stokes Mortar, but sounds more like a Northover Projector, in order to defend the Mill Bridge. Everything was worked out. The first tank over the bridge would be allowed to proceed through two sharp bends where, hidden from view, it would be stopped by an AT mine in the road. The second tank would do the same, but the third tank would be blasted by Alan and the professor, sealing the bridge to further progress. The two stationary tanks, meanwhile, would be disposed of with sticky-bombs and Molotov Cocktails, and a large mine on a trolley would be trundled behind the third tank, now nicely ablaze. No mention, however, is made of the accompanying German infantry who would presumably have had some say in this production. But it is not quite as far-fetched as it might appear for, in the urban warfare of the Spanish Civil War, all sorts of methods were used to force tanks to stop, making them vulnerable to just those weapons which the Home Guard carried. Up-turned soup-plates in the middle of the road might be AT mines, and who knew what threat lay behind the blankets strung across the street on ropes? Tom Wintringham and others, formerly of the International Brigade, introduced these techniques and tricks into Home Guard training manuals, so it is likely that they influenced such planning.

The Home Guard were provided with Stores which appear to be particularly linked to the provision of spigot mortars. They would hold the more dangerous supplies and keep them out of the kitchen. Instructions dictated that these Stores were divided into two sections: one for explosives such as grenades or spigot mortar bombs, and the other for inflammables. Some of these Stores were rectangular brick buildings, some of which survive (**87**), whilst others were Elephant Shelters, huts made of curved sheets of corrugated-iron with bricked-in ends, similar to Nissen huts or large Anderson shelters, one such being installed at Quy. The brick Store in the garden of the Bull Inn at Newborough was used by No. 2 Platoon, 'D' Company of the 2nd (Soke of Peterborough) Battalion. At Stand Down they were required to return forty-five rifles, two light machine-guns, twenty-nine Sten guns and one spigot mortar. Apart from these

87 MARCH, Gas Road: the Explosives and Inflammables Store, built with two separate compartments, and used by the Home Guard. It stands beside the post-war drill hall.

secure stores, all types of premises were used for parades and training activities, including public halls such as the Badminton Hall in Ely or the tin tabernacle in Upton; public houses and farms; public buildings and private houses.

One branch of the Home Guard which remained secret long after the war was the British Resistance Organisation or Auxiliary Units. These were small independent cells known as 'patrols' of seven or eight men who, in the event of an invasion, would go to ground, emerging only to harass the enemy by sabotage, to kill isolated soldiers (particularly despatch riders), carry out attacks on the lines of communication, and generally disrupt supplies and transport. Each patrol was provided with two or three underground hides, known as Operational Bases (OBs), which were accessed by concealed trap-doors and had at least one escape tunnel. The OBs were equipped with two weeks' food, a means of purifying water, bunks, a weapons rack and ammunition storage, and a chemical toilet. Cells were unaware of neighbouring cells, receiving their orders from an area intelligence officer by dead-letter drop, or via a local radio operator, who had no idea whence came the transmissions she might receive. Auxiliary Units operated mainly in coastal areas, and it is known that there was a patrol in Elm, near Wisbech, and there almost certainly would have been others along the Norfolk and Lincolnshire borders. So vital was the secrecy surrounding the topic that surviving former members remain reluctant to talk about it to this day.

Defended Places and Nodal Points

Defensive policy changed as Brooke shifted the emphasis from the linear defences of the GHQ and Eastern Command Lines to the all-round defence of key locations. From the start, large towns like Chelmsford (Essex) and Cambridge had been regarded as 'defended places', capable of holding out independently with their own permanent garrisons against an invading force. Large industrial centres such as Peterborough with its munitions works, ordnance depot, railway junction and airfield were also seen as needing all-round defences. Other smaller towns were identified as communication hubs, and by June 1940 Ely, Chatteris, Littleport, all astride the GHQ Line, and Whittlesey, to its west, had been designated as 'nodal points'. Equally important in delaying an enemy attack were the river crossings at Huntingdon, St Ives and St Neots, and the key position of Earith on the crossing of the Bedford Rivers. All these places were intended to deny transit to the enemy.

The Cambridge Defence Plan

Although designated a 'defended place' from mid-1940, it was only well into 1941 that the Cambridge Defence Plan assumed its final form, integrating the military elements with those of passive and active air defence, and the responsibilities for safeguarding the civilian population in emergency situations. Appendices were still being added as late as September 1943. Cambridge had the AT ditch of the GHQ Line to its east, but was also almost completely surrounded by further AT ditches (**Fig. 11**), with road-blocks at all entry points and strong hardened defences. At the end of the war, a total of over fifty pillboxes were listed for demolition, a

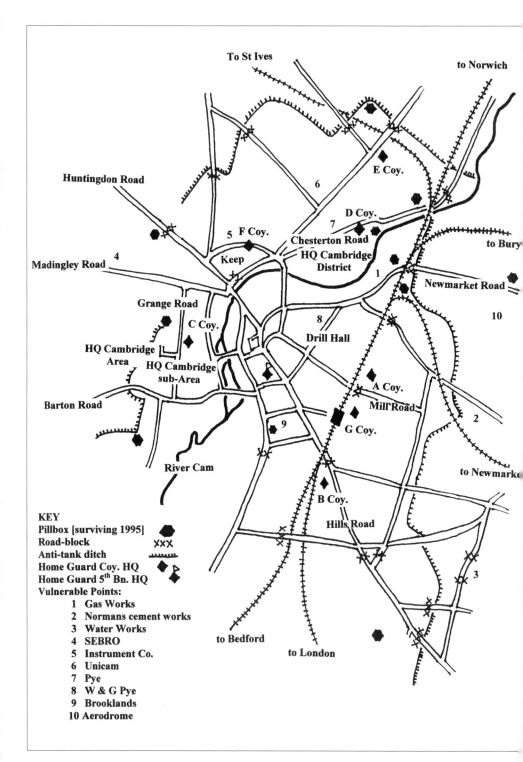

To St Ives

to Norwich

Huntingdon Road

E Coy.

6

D Coy.

7

5 F Coy.

Chesterton Road

HQ Cambridge
District

to Bury

Keep

Madingley Road   4

1

Newmarket Road

10

Grange Road

C Coy.

8

Drill Hall

HQ Cambridge
Area

HQ Cambridge
sub-Area

A Coy.

Mill Road

Barton Road

2

9

G Coy.

River Cam

to Newmarket

B Coy.

Hills Road

3

KEY
Pillbox [surviving 1995]
Road-block
Anti-tank ditch
Home Guard Coy. HQ
Home Guard 5ᵗʰ Bn. HQ
Vulnerable Points:
  1   Gas Works
  2   Normans cement works
  3   Water Works
  4   SEBRO
  5   Instrument Co.
  6   Unicam
  7   Pye
  8   W & G Pye
  9   Brooklands
  10 Aerodrome

to Bedford

to London

Fig. 11 The defences of Cambridge in 1941.

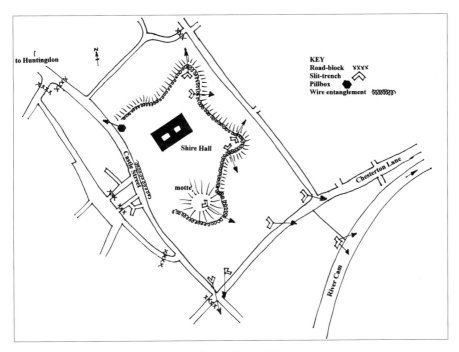

Fig. 12 The defences of the Cambridge Shire Hall 'Keep' in 1941.

similar number to the total represented on the map accompanying the Defence Plan. Over forty of these had formed a defensive ring surrounding the town, others had been built to defend important road junctions inside these outer defences, and more had been positioned to cover specific locations such as the railway adjacent to Newmarket Road. The Shire Hall complex on the castle and Civil War fort site became the Keep (**Fig. 12**), defended by slit trenches, wire and weapons pits with a pillbox outside the main entrance. There were two inner defence lines, one of which ran from a point on the railway between the station and the gasworks and along Brooklands Avenue where a pillbox still stands on the edge of the brook. The other ran down East Road and along Lensfield Road, the line, incidentally, of the Civil War defences. The town's garrison, controlled from the Home Guard Zone HQ in the Guildhall, consisted of the 5th Battalion of the Cambridgeshire Home Guard whose five rifle companies were each allocated a segment of the town and manned the road-blocks in their sectors. Each road-block, of which there were at least nine-teen, consisted of permanent obstacles which narrowed the street to one vehicle's width. This gap could itself be closed by placing either vertical, or V-shaped steel rails known as 'hairpins', into prepared concrete sockets covered by iron caps. The proto-col was very clear on the brinksmanship required for this to happen, specifying that as much friendly traffic must be allowed in before a last-minute closure, at which time any vehicles on the outside would be immobilised and petrol stocks destroyed. The LNER formed a sixth, 'G' Company, responsible for the blocks on the railway line. Individual platoons were responsible for developing the defences in their own

88 CAMBRIDGE, Science Park: a bullet-proof DFW3/24 pillbox in the angle of the anti-tank ditch dug to defend Cambridge in 1940 (TL465616).

89 CAMBRIDGE, Downing Street: the Music School served as the HQ, armoury and stores of the 5th Battalion of the Cambridgeshire Home Guard.

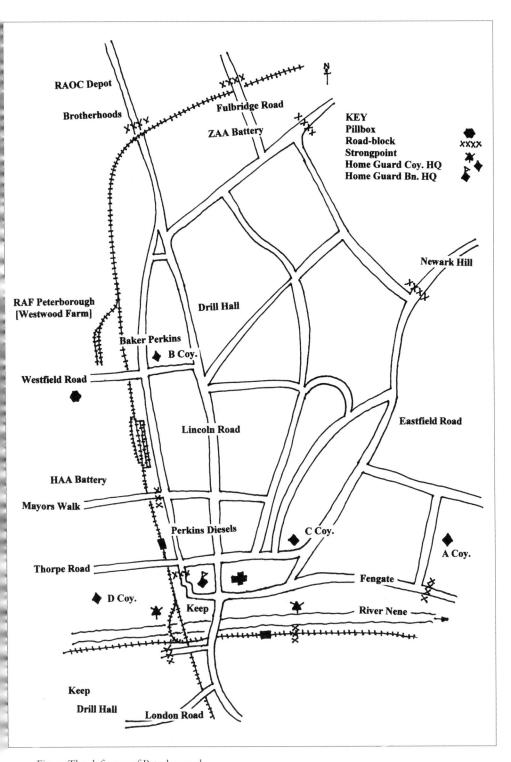

KEY
Pillbox
Road-block
Strongpoint
Home Guard Coy. HQ
Home Guard Bn. HQ

Fig. 13 The defences of Peterborough.

areas, and an account in the history of the Cambridgeshire Home Guard describes
how one particular such unit laid 1,000 yards of double-apron barbed-wire around
their pillboxes, forming part of the outer defences (**88**). Battalion HQ, armoury and
stores were in the Music School (**89**) in Downing Place, with unit HQs in each
company area. In addition to the 5th Battalion, there was part of a GPO battalion
and two raised by the university. The 8th (Senior Training Corps) Battalion, with
its HQ at Quayside, was structured as an officer training unit and consequently
equipped with armour, artillery, signals and transport, thus being able to function as
a mobile strike force. It had a tank and four armoured cars, four gun-tractors, four
18-pounders and four 75mm guns, as well as the usual infantry weapons. Composed
mainly of under-graduates, the 7th Battalion was armed with 500 rifles, each with
50 rounds of ammunition, with a further 40 rounds per gun in reserve. With its HQ
at Ferry House, on Midsummer Common, it was also designated as 'Mobile' and
nearly 100 trucks, cars and motorcycles were earmarked for requisition on 'action
stations'. However, problems were raised by absences from these two battalions outside term-time, often exacerbated by a lack of contact numbers and forwarding
addresses, a factor recognised in the Defence Plan. One unintended outcome of the
eastern AT ditch was that, dug out of the white chalk, it provided a perfect guide for
enemy bombers.

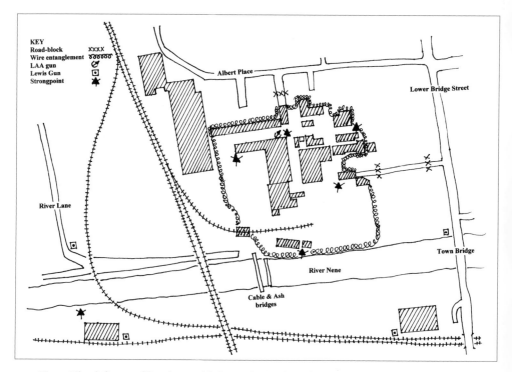

Fig. 14 The defences of Peterborough's Power Station 'Keep' in 1940–1941. (From plans held by
the Northamptonshire Record Office)

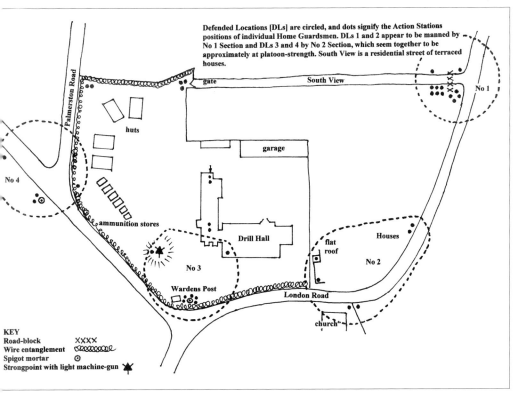

Fig. 15 The defences of Peterborough's London Road 'Keep' in March 1944. (From information and plan supplied by Bob Beales)

Peterborough's Defences

The city, so important from all viewpoints – military, industrial and communications – was given all-round defences (**Fig. 13**), consisting mainly of road-blocks reinforced by weapons pits. The Nene provided an effective AT barrier on the south, and railway embankments could be secured to do the same on the north. On the west was the airfield, and on the east, the Fens. The Keep was located in the Power Station near the river bridges (**Fig. 14**), and a second keep was established, south of the river, centred on the London Road drill hall (**Fig. 15**), the HQ of the 1st Huntingdonshire Battalion, Home Guard. At the power station, the manager was in charge of the Home Guard, and many of his work-force had enrolled in the works unit but, it was clearly pointed out in Council Minutes, under the overall control of the local commander. Two battalions of the Northamptonshire Home Guard provided the city's garrison, with the 1st (City of Peterborough) Battalion having responsibility for the city itself from the river and Thorpe Hall to the north at Paston. The 2nd (Soke of Peterborough) Battalion had its HQ at the Cock Inn, Werrington, later moving to Priestgate, and had oversight of the northern strip from the A1 viaduct and rail/river crossings at Wansford in the west, to the RAOC depot at Walton, and on to Newborough and the GHQ Line. Later, Stamford, Uffington and Tallington, all in

Lincolnshire, were attached. Very little of the city's fixed defences survives beyond a single AT block marking one of the Keep's outer strong-points on the southern river-bank. Peter Brotherhoods and Baker Perkins, two of the city's major munitions producers, had their own Works Home Guard platoons.

Huntingdonshire's Defences

Huntingdon was set up as an AT Island, roughly triangular in shape (**Fig. 16**), bounded by the river Great Ouse on one side, the railway on another, and the line of the town ditch on the third, but defended by only meagre resources. The defenders' primary objective was to hold the river-crossing so a third of the potential Home Guard garrison was stationed either side of the river, in the castle, in Mill House and in

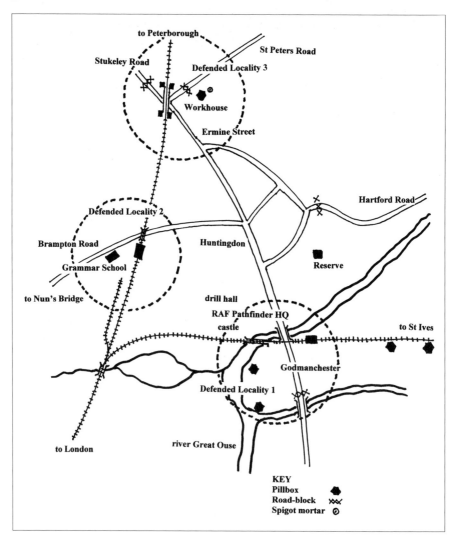

Fig. 16 The defences of Huntingdon in 1941.

90 EARITH BULWARK: an Allan Williams turret built on a bastion of the Civil War fort (TL393749) to defend the river-crossing. Nearby and across the road are two spigot mortar pedestals.

Godmanchester railway station, armed with spigot mortars and Lewis guns. A second concentration was out on the Brampton Road near North Station, based in the Grammar School, and armed with a couple of spigot mortars, some Lewis Guns and two Northover Projectors. The Brampton village platoon, with a strength that fluctuated between forty-five and seventy-five, held an outer post on this side of the town at Nun's Bridge, where a pillbox and machine-gun posts were established as an integral part of Huntingdon's defences. The third Defended Locality (DL) in Huntingdon itself was the old workhouse in St Peter's Road where AT blocks, a loop-holed wall, a pillbox and a spigot mortar pedestal were visible as lately as the 1990s. This position also took in the Iron Bridge which had four mini-pillboxes built into it at high level. All this, with a small reserve near the St Ives road, totalled a little over 300 men.

At St Ives the river-bridge was the focus of defence. The Home Guard HQ was in Wych House with the town's Battle HQ in the Dolphin Inn right by the bridge which had been prepared for demolition. This DL was defended by seventy-five men. There was a pillbox near the church and others along the railway line and one still stands in the Guided Bus terminal. At St Neots similar provision was made to protect its bridge, but the only surviving pillbox faces north on the edge of the common, which could suggest either a defensive perimeter or discrete DLs. At Earith there is an Allan Williams turret (90) on a bastion of the Civil War fort, supported by two spigot mortar pedestals covering the bridges.

Vulnerable Points and Local Defence

Dotted around Cambridge in particular were important industrial sites which were designated as 'vulnerable points' (VPs). These included SEBRO on the Madingley Road, the Unicam Instrument Co. on Arbury Road, the Pye factories on Chesterton and Newmarket Roads, the Norman Cement Co. Ltd on Coldhams Lane, and the Cambridge Scientific Instrument Company on Victoria Road. Each of these factories, along with utilities such as the water and gasworks, raised platoons of Home Guard specifically to safeguard their own places of work. The platoon at Pye's was also charged with guarding the Eastern Command Cambridge District HQ in Montague Road. All these units liaised closely with their parent companies and with units outside the 5th Battalion's orbit in adjoining areas, particularly over such VPs as the aerodrome which sat on the edge of the defended area. Regular patrols, especially at night, ensured that VPs such as telephone exchanges and petrol supplies were taken care of. At the RAOC Depot in the former Sages aircraft factory in Peterborough, two loop-holed guard-posts were constructed to defend the works in case of attack.

Apart from those locations, either part of the GHQ Line or designated as nodal points, there were other places deemed important enough to be given fixed defences. One such place was Guyhirn where the Birmingham-Norwich road and the March-Spalding railway-line crossed the River Nene. Here a pair of pillboxes, now adapted as bat-sanctuaries, sat either side of the railway-line, concrete sockets, recently dug up, were provided for a rail-block, and several spigot mortars were emplaced, one of them in a pit constructed of concrete sand-bags. Next to the old schoolhouse at Rings End is an air-raid shelter.

91 WARDY HILL: a DFW3/22 pillbox (TL476819) which was built to turn a searchlight site into a defensible strong-point.

Orders were constantly stressing the need to look out for airborne attack and to take prompt and effective action before the enemy might have time to consolidate his position. Measures had been taken to prevent enemy transports landing troops and equipment on the profusion of open spaces in the county. Anti-glider poles and trenches, many dug by secondary school-children in school-time, criss-crossed the water-meadows at Hemingford Grey. Playing-fields, parkland and pasture-land were all obstructed by old cars filled with rubble, scaffolding-poles linked together by taut wires, trenches and heaps of earth. Huntingdon race-course, and Portholme Meadow, once a flying-field, were similarly treated by 'volunteers' from the ATC and the schools. This aerial threat never went away, and in Peterborough, as late as 21–22 November 1942, Exercise 'Delta', organised and monitored by the City's Emergency and Invasion Committees, was carried out to test the response of the City's Home Guard and emergency services to a simulated aerial attack and airborne drop.

A number of examples of hardened defences remain across the county giving clues to the defensive strategy. Pillboxes, usually a bullet and splinter-proof regular hexagon (DFW 3/22) can be seen at a dozen isolated sites, probably all formerly searchlight sites. A number of DFW 3/22s including Beald Drove, Ely, Wardy Hill (**91**), Quy Common, Chalk Farm and Ramsey, all have the same pistol-loop to the left of the entrance, and appear to have been built as part of the same programme. Spigot mortars survive at Rampton Castle, Sutton Gault, Wisbech and Boots Bridge near Wimblington. A lone loophole in a wall near Kimbolton School and hairpin AT rails at Elm (**92**), inexplicable survivors, draw attention to what has been lost. Home Guard Explosives and Inflammables Stores can be seen at Long Stanton rail crossing, beside the Gas Road drill

92 ELM: two anti-tank rails, or 'hairpins' at (TF474075).

hall in March, and behind Peterborough's Millfield drill hall. When Brooke ordered that no more fixed defences be built on the GHQ Line, the emphasis shifted to demolitions on crossings of the AT ditch. Angle Bridge over the Whittlesey Dyke north of Benwick, and Speechleys Drove near Newborough, are both examples of such prepared demolitions, the latter worryingly retaining its charges in situ until long after the end of the war.

Airfield Defences

If any open space was seen as a potential landing-ground for enemy forces, then real airfields were even more vulnerable, and were given garrisons and fixed defences from the start. Cambridge, in the early days, was guarded by fifty permanent staff of the FTS, and the lads of No. 104 Squadron Air Defence Cadet Corps, prior to gaining a permanent Home Guard garrison. The trainee-pilots were also rostered to carry out regular security patrols. The 4th Battalion Northamptonshire Regiment provided garrisons of company strength at Wittering, Upwood, Wyton and Peterborough, later being replaced at Peterborough by a company of the Warwickshire Regiment. There was also back-up from an armoured unit, possibly 3RTR from Thornhaugh, part of 2nd Armoured Division based, at the time, in Corby (Northamptonshire). After these early *ad hoc* arrangements, in autumn 1940, the Air Ministry invited General Taylor, Director of Fortifications and Works at the War Office, to produce an official defence policy for airfields. Those airfields within 20 miles of a qualifying port were defined as Class I airfields and would receive the greatest level of protection. Included in Class IIa were all those airfields with a significant part to play in repelling an invasion. Airfields within 5 miles of important VPs were put in Class IIb, and the remainder were consigned to Class III. In land-locked Cambridgeshire there were unsurprisingly no Class I airfields, but the existing four fighter and six bomber airfields were all in Class IIa along with a further nine bomber fields under construction. Peterborough, so close to the industrial and military complex, was Class IIb, whilst Cambridge, Caxton Gibbet and Sibson were assigned to Class III.

Class II airfields were given between fifteen and twenty-four concrete pillboxes, some facing onto the flying-field to repel an airborne assault, and others around the outer perimeter to guard against an external attack launched by invasion forces. Eight defence posts with AA lmgs were recommended along with three armoured vehicles. These could be the products of local initiative, as at Cambridge where Marshalls converted a pair of Austin 12s into armoured cars by covering them in boiler plate and modifying their springs; or they could be mass-produced Beaverettes or Armadilloes; or later even light tanks which had been passed down by the army. One of Cambridge's two machine-guns was mounted on the Control Building whilst the other was fitted to a vehicle. The Armadillo was a three-ton flat-bed truck with an open chamber on the back made from boxes of gravel piled up to shoulder height. A Lewis gun was mounted on a post in the middle, providing a mobile AA platform, but one with no protection against aerial attack. Just as he set the complement of pillboxes, so Taylor prescribed the size of garrison. Ideally, a Class II airfield would have 225 regulars, assigned across all these various roles. Additionally, RAF personnel including cooks, clerks and drivers, would supplement this force, so that a total of nearer 400 men might be reached, and this garrison would be expected to hold out for the four or five hours it might take a mobile relief column to arrive. In 1941, the RAF Regiment was formed specifically for airfield defence, and the defensive layouts gradually changed from the linear model to inter-dependent DLs manned by regular troops, RAF ground personnel, RAF Regiment squadrons, AA and Searchlight

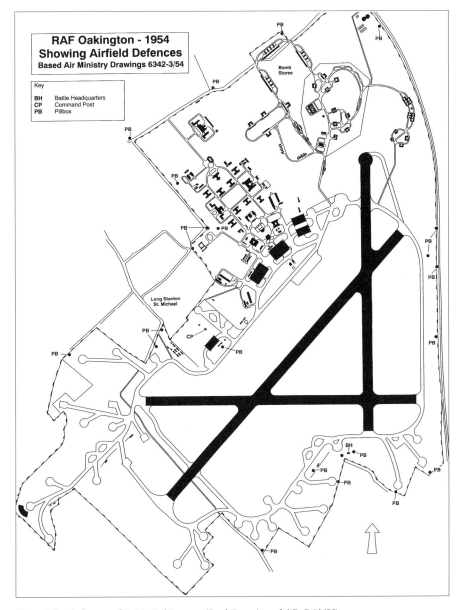

Fig. 17 The defences of RAF Oakington. (Paul Francis and ARG/AiX)

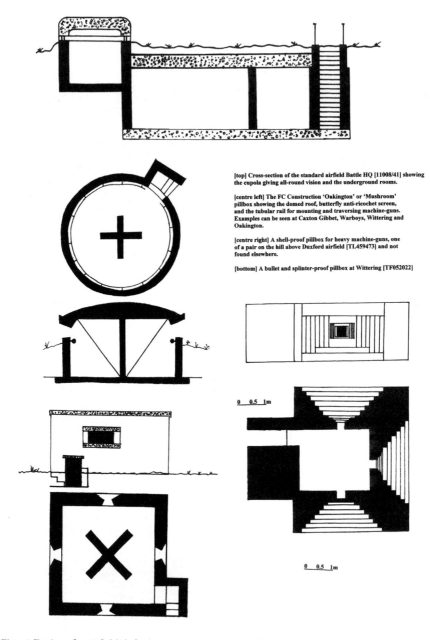

[top] Cross-section of the standard airfield Battle HQ [11008/41] showing the cupola giving all-round vision and the underground rooms.

[centre left] The FC Construction 'Oakington' or 'Mushroom' pillbox showing the domed roof, butterfly anti-ricochet screen, and the tubular rail for mounting and traversing machine-guns. Examples can be seen at Caxton Gibbet, Warboys, Wittering and Oakington.

[centre right] A shell-proof pillbox for heavy machine-guns, one of a pair on the hill above Duxford airfield [TL459473] and not found elsewhere.

[bottom] A bullet and splinter-proof pillbox at Wittering [TF052022]

0 0.5 1m

0 0.5 1m

Fig. 18 Designs for airfield defences. Top: Cross-section of the standard airfield Battle HQ (11008/41) showing the cupola giving all-round vision and the underground rooms. Centre Left: The FC Construction 'Oakington' or 'Mushroom' pillbox showing the domed roof, butterfly anti-ricochet screen, and the tubular rail for mounting and traversing machine-guns. Examples can be seen at Caxton Gibbet, Warboys, Wittering and Oakington. Centre Right: A shell-proof pillbox for heavy machine-guns, one of a pair on the hill above Duxford airfield (TL459473) and not found elsewhere. Bottom: A bullet and splinter-proof pillbox at Wittering (TF052022).

troops and Home Guard. Oakington provides a good example of this transition, with a string of pillboxes around the perimeter, but the beginnings of DLs in several places (**Fig. 17**). Fear of airborne assault persisted, particularly after the experience in Crete, until the end of the war, and airfields became the only places that hardened defences were permitted, and then only in conjunction with field-works and mobile forces. By May 1942, however, the Air Ministry was optimistically listing airfields which would have their garrisons withdrawn, but those in the front line stayed, and Cambridgeshire airfields all retained their defence forces.

Pillboxes on airfields were of a number of different designs (**Fig. 18**). At first they were mainly the DFW3/22 bullet-proof type mounting a single Lewis Gun, many of which survive at most of Cambridgeshire's airfields. Over time, there emerged some distinctive types confined to airfields. One was the FC Construction or 'mushroom' pillbox (**93**). This was a circular concrete pit with a tubular rail running around its lip to which were clamped two Vickers machine-guns. Over the pit was a domed concrete cantilevered roof which left a continuous gap of about 12 inches (30cm) through which

93 RAF OAKINGTON: an FC Construction, 'Oakington' or 'Mushroom' pillbox, one of several on the airfield perimeter (TL416662).

94 RAF DUXFORD: a shell-proof pillbox with seven loopholes for machine-guns. This example has recently been demolished but another similar pillbox may be seen to the north.

95 RAF SNAILWELL: a DFW3/22 pillbox with pre-fabricated loopholes (TL661659). It has subsequently been strengthened by the addition of a skirt, necessitating a dog-legged tunnel entrance.

96 RAF WATERBEACH:
an early version of a Battle
HQ based on a Stanton
shelter with a small
hexagonal cupola on top.
Now reportedly demolished.

97 RAF LITTLE
STAUGHTON: a
standard 11008/41 design
Battle HQ but with a
higher-than-normal cupola
(TL107621).

the guns could be fired. It was entered via a trench, and once DLs were developed, three of these pillboxes might be linked by zig-zag trenches. Oakington was one of the first airfields to receive these pillboxes and they are often described on Air Ministry plans as 'Oakington pillboxes'. They were also installed at Caxton Gibbet, Wittering and Warboys. Duxford has two different kinds of pillbox for machine-guns, one is a variation on the shell-proof DFW3/24 (**94**) with its seven loopholes, but the other is an exceptionally solid T-shaped pillbox for three machine-guns in Turnbull mounts. Snailwell has a screen of five pillboxes beyond the railway line which curves around the airfield's southern perimeter. Two of them are akin to the conventional DFW3/22, but the other three have had solid skirts built around their lower parts, up to the level of their six pre-fabricated loopholes, and pierced only by a tunnel entrance (**95**). There were square and rectangular pillboxes at Wyton and Wittering, one of those at Wittering being mounted on stilts to gain visibility over the adjacent fighter pen. As well as a conventional DFW3/22 pillbox, Sibson had two fifty-man air-raid shelters which were loop-holed for close defence. Peterborough had a pair of Allan Williams turrets mounted along the roadside near the main gate and officers' mess. Airfields assigned as Class I were allocated three Pickett-Hamilton forts, the disappearing pillboxes so beloved of Churchill but hated by those who might be required to use them. Duxford was one of five Class IIa fighter airfields added to the programme but no installation date had been scheduled by the time over 300 forts were being installed elsewhere, and it is unlikely they ever materialised.

The defence of the airfield was directed from a sunken Battle HQ sited to have a panoramic view of the flying-field. By 1941 there was a standard Air Ministry model (11008/41) which became universal, but Waterbeach had an earlier type which consisted of a hexagonal cupola mounted over a Stanton shelter (**96**). The new model consisted of a sunken structure containing a PBX, a runners' room and an office, with a raised concrete cupola with an all-round observation slit as the only visible part. Little Staughton's otherwise standard BHQ, now exposed to view, has been raised to increase its height over the flying-field (**97**). For some reason, Bottisham's masqueraded as a fighter dispersal pen, which would appear to achieve little beyond substituting one prospective target for another. Examples at Peterborough, Fowlmere and Oakington have been destroyed but that at Warboys survives.

The Army in the Second World War

Deployments of Local Units

The 50th SL Regiment was soon deployed to targets of greater importance than Peterborough, first to Cardiff to defend the docks, then to the Nottingham and Grantham GDA, and thence to the Isle of Wight. The 5th Battalion Northamptonshire Regiment joined 11th Brigade, 4th (Infantry) Division, sailing for France to join the BEF in January 1940. After Dunkirk, the battalion was sent to Lyme Regis (Dorset), on coast defence duties, and then to Christchurch (Dorset), Runfold (Surrey) and on up to Scotland for training. It sailed for North Africa as part of the TORCH landings in 1942, and fought through Sicily and Italy. The 1st and 2nd Cambridgeshires, along with many other East Anglian territorial formations, were initially engaged in anti-invasion duties and training with the 18th Division, whose HQ was at Sprowston (Norfolk). The 135th Field Regiment, as part of the Division's artillery, spent time in Norfolk and Scotland before being sent to Liverpool in 1941 to give help in blitzed areas. After further training in Wales, they were sent by ship to Singapore in November 1941 with the rest of the division. Those of 18th Division who survived the fall of Singapore were imprisoned, many being worked to death by the Japanese, or dying of tropical diseases, starvation or maltreatment. Some 400 men of the 135th Field Regiment under their CO, the grossly misrepresented Colonel Philip Toosey, spent time at Tamarkan Camp on the River Kwai, working on the infamous railway bridge. On repatriation in 1945, the regiment was not re-assembled and no successor unit was formed.

Camps and Depots

From the earliest mobilisation, through the re-forming after Dunkirk, the deployment of anti-invasion forces, and the preparations for training and despatching newly raised or reorganised formations to theatres around the world, the needs of the armed services for accommodation were extensive. As in the First World War, once the barracks and permanent camps had been filled then alternatives had to be found. Often the solution was to requisition a country house for use as HQ, officers' mess and quarters, with outbuildings for workshops and armoury, and surrounding parklands for a tented or hutted camp. Some such camps had serial use as at Quy Park, initially an assembly point for units of 2nd Armoured Division, and then the depot of the RAF Airfield Construction Service. In 1944, in the build-up to the D-Day Operations, the 2nd Northamptonshire Yeomanry was based at Quy with its Valentine and Matilda tanks as divisional troops with the 11th Armoured Division. Foreign forces in temporary exile also needed bases. Milton Hall near Peterborough, for instance, hosted the HQ of an AA division, then a Czech army depot for a while, followed by the SAS. Prior to D-Day, temporary camps such as those at Bainton or Marholm accompanied the use of battle training areas like Southey Woods near Upton.

Air Defence

Despite the presence in both cities of factories producing important munitions, neither Cambridge nor Peterborough suffered the intensity of bombing that might have been anticipated. Cambridge suffered twenty-one raids and Peterborough just eight, with most of the bombing over by mid-1941, and only sporadic raids in 1942. In 1944, a total of ten V1 'doodlebugs' fell on the county, an air-launched example of which landed in Castor (TL111978). Fortunately, only one solitary misguided V2 reached Cambridgeshire, falling on Fulbourn. It was nevertheless essential that AA defences were put in place from the very start, to defend both military and civilian targets.

AA Defences

Despite the grand designs of the 1935 Plan, integrating fighters and ground defences, the reality fell far short and provision of AA guns on the ground was sparse. Only those locations considered particularly important and especially vulnerable were given the few available modern 3.7-inch HAA or 40mm Bofors LAA guns. The HQs of AA Brigades were co-located with RAF Sector stations, hence 32 AA Brigade at Wittering, and 40 AA Brigade at Duxford, the latter subsequently removed to Sawston Hall and thence to Pampisford Hall, but the resources they could actually deploy were meagre. At the end of 1940, besides the two HQ stations which had four Bofors guns each, there were troops of the 30th LAA Regiment defending other Cambridgeshire airfields, but equipped only with Lewis Guns: 16 at Upwood, 12 at Wyton and 16 at Bassingbourn, whilst a troop of 149 LAA Battery manned 20 more at Peterborough. By 1941, the 30th LAA Regiment had added Oakington to its sites, with local HQs at no. 97 Cambridge Road, Ely and at The Manse, and later the Swiss Cottage Hotel, Fenstanton. Duxford had acquired two old 3-inch 20 cwt guns of First War vintage, to which were added a further pair despatched by rail from Leith, in January 1940. It would be another two years before any of these airfields received Bofors guns, when some new airfields might also get them, like the single Bofors at Castle Camps in May 1942. By this date there were more HAA guns emplaced to defend civilian or industrial targets, particularly after the start of a bombing offensive now remembered as the 'Baedeker' raids. Cambridge had

98 STANGROUND: a decaying BCF hut, one of two marking the remains of a HAA site defending Peterborough. In May 1942 it was armed with four mobile 3.7-inch guns and Mark 1 Gun-laying radar, and manned by 182 Battery of 136 HAA Regiment RA (TL223957).

five designated sites, only two of which were armed, one on the west side of the aerodrome, and the other 400 yards due west on Coldhams Common, each having two mobile 3.7-inch guns and GL radar, manned by 218 HAA Battery. Peterborough, seen as a more important industrial centre was protected by two batteries, each of four mobile 3.7-inch HAA guns with GL radar, on sites at the Grange recreation ground, Longthorpe and behind Horsey Hill Fort on the Pondersbridge road, where the remains of two BCF huts (**98**) are just about hanging on. The demands of the big cities and of other theatres of operations meant that once the risk of air-attack had diminished, the guns were stripped from the airfields for redeployment. In 1942, Wittering and Duxford whilst still notionally the responsibility of 78th HAA Regiment, both lacked HAA cover. In fact, 78th HAA Regiment, a Norfolk TA unit, was deployed to Egypt that year. The War Diary of the 40th AA Brigade refers to the Cambridge GDA in 1942, but there can have been little substance to this and Cambridge and Peterborough lost their HAA guns in April 1944 when every available weapon was needed for the defence of the ports and dockyards in the build-up to D-Day.

To make up for the constant shortage of conventional AA weapons, the 3-inch Un-rotated Rocket Projectile or UP had been developed in late 1940 and put into production the next year. These rocket projectors were usually grouped in ZAA batteries of four troops of sixteen, and the simultaneous firing of sixty-four rockets, each delivering the same weight of explosive as a 3.7-inch shell, came as close to creating an AA barrage as was possible. This was designed to be launched in front of an incoming bomber force as much as a distraction as an attempt to shoot them down. Later, by the end of 1943, twin-barrelled U2Ps were the most common weapon, but multiples of nine and twenty barrels would eventually be issued. The 101st Northamptonshire Home Guard ZAA Battery, RA, with its HQ in Unity Hall, Northfields Road, Peterborough, was formed in July 1942. Its projectors were based on open ground on the west side of Fulbridge Road (TF186015). This was manned by one of the three troops of the Peterborough-based 10th AA Regiment, Home Guard, the other two troops being based on Walpole Road, Cambridge, with HQ at no. 4 Bridge Street, and in Leicester's Victoria Park. Whilst releasing guns and regular crews for service elsewhere, the Home Guard ZAA regiments were very expensive in personnel as each watch, having already put in ten and twelve-hour days in the factory or on the land, could only be expected to stand to for one night in eight, leading to each battery having to recruit over 1,000 people, extra to existing Home Guard, ARP, AFS, and WVS membership. A list of railway sidings dated September 1942, records an AA School on Oundle Road, Peterborough, and this may have been set up to train the ZAA gunners. Orton Longueville Rectory is also listed elsewhere as an officers' billet, and this could have been for instructors. Operation Diver, the defence against the V1 'doodlebugs', pushed every available AA gun out to the coast in a continuous line running as far north as Holderness, in order to intercept the rockets before they could over-fly land. In early 1944, the 129th LAA Regiment of the 50th AA Brigade had moved its RHQ and three batteries into Yaxley, but its redeployment to Diver duties in the Weald of Kent, meant that ZAA batteries were left as the only local AA defence against any repeat of the 'Baby Blitz'.

99 PETERBOROUGH, Fulbridge Road: the canteen of the ZAA Battery manned by 10 AA Regiment, Home Guard.

HAA gun-sites were quite significant structures with up to four octagonal gun-pits with ready-use magazines built into dwarf walls. These emplacements were linked to semi-sunken magazines and crew-shelters, and the command post where the ranging and locating instruments were housed. Some way from the guns was a camp with office, garage, workshops, canteen and living huts, a veritable village of some 200 inhabitants. LAA sites were often any vantage point from which low-flying aircraft, preferably but not always enemy ones, might be engaged. In Peterborough the tower of Westwood Works provided such a platform for twin Lewis Guns initially, but subsequently for a 20mm Oerlikon. Peter Brotherhoods, next to the railway, added a purpose-built platform to their roof. In Cambridge Marshalls sought Bofors guns to defend their busy airfield but had to settle for a machine-gun on the roof of the control building. By September 1942 there are references to four LAA sites in Cambridge being manned by 158 LAA Battery and by 89 Battery the next month. All sorts of LAA weaponry was mounted, including cannon from crashed German aircraft and, especially on USAAF bases, four-gun turrets from damaged bombers, mounted on jeeps. ZAA sites, with their much lighter hold-fasts, consisted of simple concrete pads with crew-shelters and magazines alongside. Away from the rockets were the usual huts, the canteen at Peterborough's Fulbridge Road (**99**) site surviving into 2011.

Searchlights (SL)

In September 1939 the 40th AA Brigade at Duxford controlled four searchlight battalions, still badged at this date as REs. Two of these covered Cambridgeshire, the 36th Bn with companies based on Ely, Newmarket, Royston (Hertfordshire) and St Neots, and the 58th Bn with companies based at Marholm Rectory, Milton Park, Ramsey and Spalding (Lincolnshire). The 50th SL Regiment, raised in Peterborough, served elsewhere throughout the war and there is a reference to a SL Bn RE closing its HQ in Peterborough and being posted to the Norfolk coast at Weybourne in 1939. At this stage of the war searchlights operated in belts, with single lights spaced at intervals of roughly 3 miles (5km). In the Summer of 1940, these fixed sites were designated as anti-invasion 'Strong Points' and defended with coils of Dannert wire and, sometimes, a concrete pillbox. Lines of such sites can be traced across the county where the pillbox is the only surviving evidence of occupation. One such line runs from Girton (A14/M11 junction at TL412616), to Trinity Farm, then Quy (TL523613) and Swaffham Bulbeck (TL573614). In 1940, after a re-organisation, the 60th SL Regiment had its HQ at Beaupre Hall near Wisbech with a battery at Ramsey. By 1941 the 36th SL Regiment had its HQ at the West Fen Militia Camp in Ely, with its 345th Searchlight Battery at Barton Fields, Ely's other former Militia Camp. The 64th SL Regiment was at Ramsey, the 72nd at St Neots, the 60th at Hinxton Grange, whilst the 44th operated in the Wittering sector. The lights, by now, had been gathered into clusters of three, but in September 1941 this arrangement, too, was altered. Beaupre Hall was HQ of 345 Battery of the 36th SL Regiment when its twenty-four lights were ordered to de-cluster, being allocated new positions stretching from Wisbech in the north to Waterbeach in the south, and including sites in Ely, Littleport, Girton, Earith and Soham. The next month 33rd SL Regiment similarly de-clustered to take up forty-eight new sites straddling the Essex-Cambridgeshire-Suffolk border to form a new configuration of belts designated 'Indicator', 'Killer' and 'GDA'. A record of the re-deployment of the twenty-four lights of 323 SL Battery in 1942 in a circle around Cambridge is described in the unit's war diary as the 'Cambridge Lights' suggesting a box illuminating the approaches to the city in which fighters would be free to operate away from the HAA guns. The lights extend from Shelford in the south to Impington in the north, and from Comberton in the west to Fulbourn in the east, with an outer ring of sixteen lights and an inner one of eight. The frequency with which units were shunted around, and the policy chopped and changed, raises questions about their effectiveness.

Bombing Decoys

Most of the airfields which were open by the beginning of the war were provided with bombing decoys. These were sites, some distance away, intended to entice bombers to attack the wrong place, and came in two forms. 'K' decoy sites were for daylight operation and were equipped with dummy aircraft, contrived by the technicians of Shepperton Film Studios, and tended by a small ground-party of RAF personnel who ensured that signs of life were visible. 'Q' sites operated at night by simulating the landing lights of an airfield, and by using a Chance light to suggest aircraft taxiing manoeuvres. The lights would be extinguished just after the sound of incoming aircraft had been heard, giving them a chance to spot them and jump to the wrong conclusion. The crew operated the lights remotely from a hardened bunker. Most of the earlier airfields were provided with two decoy sites but as the war progressed, these were often needed for genuine airfields. For instance Somersham, having been a 'Q' decoy for RAF Wyton, later became a special duties airfield. Some of the surviving decoys doubled up to serve two or more airfields, the 'Q' site at Benwick serving both Upwood and Warboys for instance. Many of these decoys attracted bombs as occurred at Maxey in February 1941. After 1942, bombing attacks on airfields diminished, and decoys tended to be regarded as an unnecessary waste of trained manpower. Two control blockhouses still stand, one at the 'Q' site at Maxey serving Wittering (**100**), and one at Little Gidding for Polebrook (Northamptonshire).

100 MAXEY: the control blockhouse of the bombing decoy for RAF Wittering (TF147083).
Next to it is the 1960s underground ROC post, and the adjacent field held an RAF
high-frequency Direction-Finding station, in use into the 1960s, whose caretaker lived in the
nearby Air Ministry-issue bungalow (TF140077).

As the need to protect airfields receded, attempts to lure bombers away from civilian
and industrial targets were intensified. 'SF' or 'Starfish' sites, located on the periphery
of cities, were lit to suggest that enemy pathfinders had marked the site for the main
force to bomb. They consisted of networks of braziers of combustible material, laced
with accelerants which would simulate flash-fires – the whoosh factor. Cambridge
was provided with sites at Comberton and Babraham, and Peterborough had sites
at Stanground, where a blockhouse remains, and at Eye. Particularly important targets such as oil refineries, ports, factory complexes and railway marshalling yards were
given bespoke decoys, closely replicating the visual effects of the target. The marshalling yards at March, at the time amongst the most extensive in Europe, had a decoy
which simulated the lights of the yard and the fires and sparks produced by working
locomotives. Some of the effects were very simple including, for instance, lights in
boxes with weighted lids appearing to be doors closing. Others were more complex.
Most decoys were bombed at some time, suggesting that the effort of diverting bombs
from their real targets had been worthwhile. Somewhat surprisingly, March town and
the decoy site were each bombed just once.

Radar
Although there were no actual radar sites in Cambridgeshire, Brooklands House in
Cambridge was the administrative section and officers' mess of RAF No. 74 Wing
in 1941. This highly technical specialist unit was responsible for maintaining the East
Coast radar stations and for calibrating their equipment, by flying auto-giros out of
Duxford. The unit had begun in Leighton House, now part of the Perse preparatory
school, and expanded into Brooklands (101). In 1943, in preparation for the D-Day
landings, a re-organisation of RAF No. 60 Group, with its HQ at Leighton Buzzard

101 CAMBRIDGE, Brooklands House: HQ of RAF 74 Wing, responsible for calibrating the East Coast radar stations.

(Bedfordshire), split the country into two, and 74 Wing was disbanded, its stations going to 75 Wing which now covered the southern half of the country.

Royal Observer Corps

Cambridgeshire's nineteen aircraft posts monitored hostile aircraft activity through-out the war, reporting, from 1943, to the new control centre at Meadowfields, 730 Newmarket Road, Cambridge. This building still stands and is currently used as an ATC centre. It was built with a two-storey back part which allowed incoming infor-mation to be written up on glass panels in the gallery, visible to the controllers standing around the plotting table in the pit below. The Cambridge building is unusual in that it is not the usual horse-shoe of SECO hutting but a brick-built structure (**102**). Across the rear was a NAAFI canteen. From 1943 many of the ROC Centres had been linked directly to Ground Control Interception radar stations, and Cambridge's partner was Langtoft, just across the River Welland in Lincolnshire, some of whose staff were accommodated at Maxey House, south of the river. Much reliance was still placed on visual aircraft recognition and Spotters Clubs were formed. Youngsters were able to follow their plane-spotting interests in the ATC, and many cadets spent their nights watching for aircraft, as they proved more adept than some of the older observers.

Civil Defence Arrangements

Peterborough Council embarked on a programme of air-raid shelter construction from the start of the war. By Christmas 1939, the Town Hall had put in place an organisation comprising ARP wardens, auxiliary nurses, WVS members, rescue and

102 CAMBRIDGE, 'Meadowfields', no. 730 Newmarket Road: from 1943 the Royal Observer Corps 15 Group control centre.

demolition workers and fire-fighters. A network of Cleansing and Decontamination Centres, Wardens' Posts, Ambulance Stations, First Aid Posts and Auxiliary Fire Stations had been established. There was a Decontamination Centre in the Infirmary on Priestgate, now the Museum, where painted instructions may still be seen (**103**), and there was another built in 1940 in the Milton Street Police Station. The national guide-lines laid down that public shelters sufficient for 10 per cent of the local population should be provided for the use of those caught out in bombing raids. People would normally take refuge in domestic or work-place shelters. Examples of these could be found at Farrows' works in Old Fletton, which had 3 concrete shelters for up to 500 people plus fire-fighting and decontamination facilities; at London Brick where old tunnels were refurbished and brought into use as shelters; and at Baker Perkins Westwood Works which provided 26 shelters for 2,500 persons, some dug into the railway embankment near Spital Bridge. A programme of communal domestic shelter provision began with 65 fifty-person shelters in six locations to accommodate 3,250 people, soon increased to 107 shelters for 5,350, and then to 310 shelters for 9,000. Some 116 shelters for schools were ordered. In May 1941, 1,000 Morrison Shelters were distributed, and much of the system was expanded, with work being centred on the Corporation Depot in St John's Street and other district depots. Eventually there were shelter places for 30–35,000 people along with Emergency Feeding Centres for 6,000 in seven designated schools. Anderson Shelters, too, had been issued and a need for more of them was identified in Summer 1942. A large static water-tank stood on the Stanley recreation ground near Brook Street School, filled through a 12 inch (30 cm) diameter surface pipe from the river Nene. Similar arrangements to these

103 PETERBOROUGH, Priestgate Infirmary (now Museum): a notice outside the Gas Decontamination Centre.

104 RAF OAKINGTON: a Stanton air-raid shelter.

THE SECOND WORLD WAR

were made in Cambridge and, on a much smaller scale, in Huntingdon. Village halls such as that in Trumpington became ARP centres, communal kitchens and canteens for those working locally. Airfields were provided with their own air-raid shelters, the most common of which was the Stanton (**104**).

ARP wardens were provided with purpose-built Wardens' Posts for shelter and the storage of their paraphernalia used for tackling incendiaries and effecting rescue and salvage work. These were brick-built rectangular structures with thick concrete roofs. One stands in a park at the junction of Coleridge Road and Davy Road in Cambridge, and another can be seen on the corner of Queens Walk, London Road, Peterborough. Training for ARP personnel took place throughout the war, and a cache of practice incendiary bombs was recently discovered in a safe in Brooklands House, perhaps used by staff from the government offices, who would have stood nightly fire-watching duties.

However, it was not only the enemy's bombs which were to prove dangerous to the county's populace. On 2 June 1944, a train of fifty-one wagons nearly 400 yards long and carrying 400 tons of 250 and 500lb bombs, was travelling to Essex bomber airfields from the Midlands. As it was pulling into Soham Station, a fire was spotted on board. Thanks to the extreme bravery of railwaymen both on the train and in the station, wagons were uncoupled and the inevitable explosion was miraculously confined to forty-four bombs weighing 5 tons. Had the whole lot gone up then the town of Soham would have been obliterated. Two railwaymen were killed, and others were seriously injured, but injuries to townsfolk and damage to property were minimised.

Military Aviation in the Second World War

In 1939, aircraft from Upwood were deployed in France in support of the BEF, but for the next four years the RAF and USAAF units on the county's airfields would be concerned with defending against enemy bombing, or else carrying out bombing missions themselves over enemy territory. For a brief period in 1940, training and army co-operation aircraft from Cambridge, Peterborough and Snailwell, armed with makeshift bomb-racks, stood by to be used against the expected German invasion. Later on Bottisham and Snailwell were used for training purposes by the Belgian Air Force in exile, whilst Free French navy fliers were trained at Peterborough. Both Duxford and Wittering sustained heavy damage caused by the Luftwaffe's attempt to destroy RAF Fighter Command during the Battle of Britain. Wittering set up a remote Operations Room in Walcot Hall near Barnack, and moved its sick quarters to Stibbington Hall near Wansford.

Airfields
On the outbreak of war the programme of re-armament and re-orientation was far from complete. Unable to continue the construction of new airfields to pre-War standards, the Air Ministry adopted a scaled-down version. The new 'Austerity' stations, either 'Permanent', such as Oakington and Waterbeach, or 'Parent', like

105 RAF OAKINGTON: a T2 transportable hangar; one was once erected by twelve men in ten days.

106 RAF WITCHFORD: a B1 hangar for Ministry of Aircraft Production use.

Molesworth, would be finished with steel-framed 'J' hangars, and some hutted accommodation, although many buildings at the 'Permanent' stations were, in fact, little different from those finished earlier. Satellites such as Warboys, Bourn and Alconbury would be expected, initially, to operate without hangars at all although, ultimately, all the standard wartime airfields had at least two T2 hangars (**105**) for holding aircraft, and a MAP B1 hangar (**106**) for the use of civilian repair teams. Airfields planned from late 1940 onwards were allocated up to four T2s, but Graveley and Little Staughton were each given three, and Gransden Lodge only two. Sometimes extra hangarage was provided for specific purposes such as the two extra T2s for glider storage at Wratting Common, or Wyton's truncated T2 for holding Mosquitoes.

The majority of airfield buildings put up in the war were utility structures, either huts or 'tb'. 'Temporary Brick' meant walls were the thickness of half a brick, strengthened at intervals by brick buttresses; this form of construction was used even for watch offices and operations blocks. Only the secure stores for Norden bomb-sights, or for pyrotechnics and inflammables, were built in permanent brick with 9 inch (23cm) walls.

107 PETERBOROUGH, Nursery Lane: a T2 hangar, re-located from RAF Glatton and re-clad.

108 RAF ALCONBURY: the first watch office to design 7345/41 for use on Bomber Satellite airfields. Subsequently Alconbury was given a new general purpose 343/43 watch office and then a post-war tower by the USAF.

109 RAF LITTLE STAUGHTON: the watch office to design 13726/41.

110 RAF DUXFORD: the general purpose 343/43 watch office.

The other alternative was the wide selection of huts, the most common being the Nissen and its larger Romney version. There were proprietary brands such as that manufactured for Laing, the contractor, and various gabled timber huts sponsored by the different government departments involved – the Ministries of Air, Supply, and War Production. All these huts came in modular units to serve as small living spaces and offices, but could easily be combined to produce larger dining spaces, messes or workshops, and specialist training or briefing facilities. In contrast to the concentrated grid plan of the Expansion Period stations, these wartime utility airfields relied for protection on the principle of dispersal. Hangars, fighter-pens and hard-standings were distributed around the perimeter of the airfield with the technical area occupying its own space at one end, and the administrative site at the other. Communal sites, containing all the domestic functions, were scattered over a wide area on the fringes. Natural cover and contrived camouflage served to conceal both aircraft and activity. Little Staughton, now in use as an industrial estate, is a well-preserved example of such an airfield with many of these standard buildings still *in situ*. Other buildings have been recycled but survive off-site (**107**).

Initially, watch offices had been built to a number of wartime designs specific to the airfield's purpose thus Alconbury had a 7345/41 type (**108**), designed for a bomber satellite station, and Little Staughton, a 13726/41 (**109**) for bomber and OTU satellites but given the need for flexibility, a new multi-purpose watch office, the 343/43 (**110**) was introduced. All these buildings were of tb with Nissen or SECO additions. Huts, either Nissen (**111**) or tb (**112**), catered for most of the airfield's functions. Only occasionally did structures, such as Wyton's AA dome-trainer (**113**), depart from these norms.

Cambridgeshire was basically one large bomber-base, initially controlled from 2 Group HQ in Huntingdon and then from 1940 as 3 Group, from Exning House just over the Suffolk border. It comprised nineteen bomber airfields, five of which were in Cambridgeshire. In 1943, these airfields were re-organised into 'Bases', each with a main and two subsidiary airfields, so that squadrons might be rotated, an example being Waterbeach with Mepal and Witchford. In support of this structure were OTUs such as Bassingbourn (No. 11) and Upwood (No. 17), from which crews in training would join in with operational bombing sorties. From 1942 the Pathfinder Force, based at

111 RAF ALCONBURY: the Crew Locker and Drying Room which was used post-war by the USAF as squadron offices.

112 RAF LITTLE STAUGHTON: the tb Floodlight Tractor and Trailer Store (12411/41) which, along with the Fire-Tender Shed, stood alongside the watch office.

113 RAF WYTON: the anti-aircraft Dome Trainer which was painted inside to simulate the night sky, one of only a handful left.

Wyton with its HQ at Castle Hill House, Huntingdon (**114**), constituted 8 Group with nine airfields, all but one of them in Cambridgeshire. When the 8th USAAF arrived in 1942 it was allocated a significant number of bomber stations in East Anglia, including seven in Cambridgeshire and its HQ in Brampton. As fighters with longer ranges were developed then it became practicable to think in terms of at least partial fighter cover for bomber raids. The RAF had operated fighter stations in Cambridgeshire and the USAAF flew out of Bottisham, Duxford, Fowlmere and Wittering/Collyweston with Fighter Wing HQs at Sawston and Walcot Hall. More sites for airfields had been identified than were, in the end, needed, some being rejected on safety grounds, others on agricultural ones. Buckden was one of the latter, having been initially proposed as a potential 8th USAAF base.

One of the major causes of aircraft losses on bombing sorties was the problem of getting returning aircraft safely back to base. Aircraft might have been damaged by enemy action, crippled by equipment malfunction, in danger of running out of fuel, or just plain lost in the Fenland mists. One solution was the availability of the long runway at Wittering, another was FIDO. Graveley, a Pathfinder Force station, was the first airfield to be equipped with this fog dispersal system. Channels containing petrol burners were dug alongside the runway, and on foggy nights the burners were ignited and the resultant heat generated could lift the fog enough for the runway to be visible. Tests by aircraft of the Petroleum Warfare Department in early 1943 proved the viability of the scheme even in a combination of thick fog and heavy wet mist. The fuel costs were prodigious but aircraft and, more importantly, the lives of their crews were saved.

114 HUNTINGDON: Castle Hill House, HQ No 2 Group RAF Bomber Command, 1939–42, then HQ No. 8 'Pathfinder' Group from June 1943.

Logistics, Design and Construction

Whilst the actual air war was the major achievement, it must be remembered that the logistical operation which lay behind it was massive, particularly the part played by the railways and the construction industry. The construction of an airfield involved the delivery to the site of 4.5 million bricks, 37,000 tons of cement, 7,000 tons of rubble and 1,500 tons of girders and hangar sections. The construction task itself, consuming a third of the total labour force available to the country, was immense, as a new airfield could be expected see aircraft taking off from it within seven months of the first turf being cut, and the whole operation completed inside eighteen months with concrete runways, perimeter track, drains, sewers and buildings.

Kimbolton is an example of a typical bomber airfield built by W & C French Ltd. in 1941. Its three original concrete runways measured 3,970 feet (1,250m), 3,620 feet (1,115m) and 3,730 feet (1,150m), but were lengthened the next year to 6,000 feet (1,850m), 4,200 feet (1,295m) and 4,200 feet (1,295m). There were concrete hard-standings for aircraft – thirty-one pans and twenty loops, and hutted accommodation for 2,894 personnel. At the beginning of the war only nine airfields in the whole of Britain had concrete runways, so not only were new airfields requiring this level of provision, but also established ones, which had to move their operations elsewhere while the work was being carried out. Each airfield was a new town of 2–3,000 people dwarfing the local villages and as big as the local market town. Before the construction of the pipelines, the fuel for one night's bombing alone needed three trains of fifty tanker-trucks to deliver it, and so many petrol trains were necessary to deliver the daily requirements of the airfields that they had to be stabled outside Whittlesey at night in order to meet their commitments the next day. Added to the fuel on the already-overburdened railways, were the bombs, SAA, food and drink, and the comings and goings of personnel.

Some fighter airfields went through the war with only grass strips, but these were usually consolidated with steel track and PSP marshalling areas at each end of the runways, and steel mesh mats for parking aircraft around the edge. Fowlmere was a typical example of a wartime fighter station. The Technical Site was based around Manor Farm, utilising existing buildings such as a Dutch barn for the MT garage. A T2 hangar was built, supplemented by eight Blister hangars and fighter dispersal pens. Most of the airfield's operational and accommodation needs were met by tb structures and Nissen or Romney huts, more of which were built on the nine communal sites near to the village. There were two PSP runways, only 1,400 and 1,600 yards (1,260 and 1,440m) long, and a standard 343/43 watch office. Wittering's main runway ran perilously close to the Great North Road (A1) which skirts the eastern edge of the airfield. Early in 1942, to minimise the danger of over-shoots, the station commander, Basil Embrey, suggested traffic lights but this request being turned down; he solved the problem by joining up the Collyweston landing-ground to the west with the existing one, to produce a new grass strip 4,800 yards (4,430m) long.

The Secret War in Cambridgeshire, 1939-45

Lying some way from a vulnerable invasion coast but still conveniently close to London and to airfields flying missions to northern Europe, Cambridgeshire provided suitable locations for the preparation of clandestine operations. In 1939, Orwell Grange had been requisitioned by MI6 for its Section D (Special Operations), moving out of its Caxton Street offices as part of a massive de-centralisation exercise. It was subsequently used by SOE and the army for Special Forces training, and SOE's Norwegian section used Gaynes Hall, near St Neots, as STS 61. Holme Fen was the centre for the assembly of material to be supplied, often by parachute drop, to the various resistance organisations on the Continent of Europe. A production line was set up to fill canisters with weapons and ammunition, to pack radios safely, and to prepare post-1944 occupation currency (US francs) for circulation. Many of these supplies, along with SOE agents, were flown out of Tempsford (Bedfordshire) but training with the pilots and aircrew was carried out at Somersham airfield, originally laid out as a decoy. It is likely that some active SOE operations, particularly using Lysanders, were also flown from there, and possibly also from Horsey Toll, another local airstrip used by Lysanders. Holmewood Hall, in Holme village, was the HQ for these activities. Prior to D-Day, Milton Hall, designated SOE's ME65, was used for training the Jedburgh teams. These were jeep-borne, heavily armed, uniformed SAS troops who were dropped into France to support the French Resistance in their attempts to prevent German reinforcements from reaching Normandy in the early days of the invasion.

115 GODMANCHESTER, Farm Hall: the MI6 building which housed the German atomic scientists for Operation Epsilon (TL242701).

After VE Day, in order to keep them incommunicado pending the resolution of the war in the east, ten of the German scientists who had been working on the development of atomic weapons were brought to England to be quarantined, as no hint of even the very notion of atomic weapons should be allowed to leak out. They were kept isolated at Farm Hall, Godmanchester (**115**), a property owned by MI6. Operation Epsilon was an attempt to find out whether their (fortunate) lack of success had been genuine or simulated, and their conversations were tape-recorded. Eavesdropping Allied scientists, whose own efforts would be seen later in the year in Japan, came to the conclusion that it was not for want of trying that their German counterparts had failed to deliver one more Vengeance weapon to Hitler. Had they achieved their mission, the V2 rocket, later the basis for the US Saturn V, would have provided the ideal delivery vehicle.

Munitions Production

Peterborough

As an important centre for the engineering industry, Peterborough rapidly turned to meeting the needs of the armed service. The Westwood Works of Baker Perkins, coyly described in wartime promotional literature as 'a Midland factory', built Twin-6-pounder guns for mounting at naval ports to guard against the raids of E-boats; 6-pounder and the later 17-pounder AT guns; the work-horse 25-pounder gun and 4.5 inch and 5.5 inch medium guns. For the D-Day operation they developed turrets with 17 or 25-pounder guns for mounting on landing-craft. They re-designed or re-invented problem parts such as recuperator mechanisms, providing Royal Ordnance Factories with the solutions for incorporation in their output. Receiving ready-made barrels from the ROFs, they made the precision components needed both for their own products, and to be supplied for assembly elsewhere. Alongside these weapons, Baker Perkins continued to manufacture their trademark range of bakery equipment, which happened to include a mixer, the Nitro Incorporator, perfectly adapted for mixing high explosive.

Peter Brotherhoods, Perkins Diesels, Burdetts and Newalls all went over to wartime production. Frank Perkins in Queen Street made marine engines for use in RAF Air-Sea rescue launches. BTH in Woodston made parts for Wellington bombers, and even Symingtons, the corset manufacturers in Woodston, switched to making parachutes. Peter Brotherhoods made torpedoes for the Royal Navy, which were stored at the RAOC Depot in the former Sages factory. They were sent, from a dedicated siding, by rail to the Royal Naval Armaments Depot in a disused brick-pit in Warboys. The RAOC building was modified to accommodate any accidental explosions caused by their volatile contents, by introducing specially weakened walls which would blow out if necessary. Another brick-pit alongside the railway south of Fletton (TL194957) was adapted in 1943 as an aviation fuel depot, with underground tanks, gantry and pumps for loading rail tanker-trucks (with another such depot at RAF Bassingbourn).

London Brick contributed millions of Flettons to the airfield building programme, and provided land at Saxon Sidings, for a REME vehicle depot, a satellite of the central one at Chilwell (Nottinghamshire). The Ministry of Food constructed enormous grain silos at Dogsthorpe, begun in December 1942 and accessed by rail from Eye Green, and ran a Government Cold Store at Botolph Bridge.

Cambridge

A number of high-tech industries, such as Unicam and the Cambridge Instrument Company, making optical equipment and compasses for the Admiralty made Cambridge more important as a manufacturing centre than might have been thought.

In 1939 WG Pye, at its factory at no. 80 Newmarket Road, was active in two different areas developing equipment for the military. In the field of Radio Location it was responsible for most of the production of receivers for use in the new RDF or radar network. It also manufactured a two-way wireless for use by the infantry, producing 14,000 sets, and its designs for radios in tanks were also accepted. Work proceeded with devices such as OBOE which enabled bombers to find their targets, and a director of Pye was seconded to Bomber Command. The development of miniaturised radio transmitters and receivers enabled Pye to come up with a proximity fuse for AA shells which greatly increased the chances of them hitting enemy aircraft, absolutely vital when the V1 onslaught arrived.

Short Brothers, with an office in Kings College, ran a repair operation as SEBRO, commencing operations in Madingley Road, Cambridge in late 1940, repairing the Stirling bombers based locally at No. 3 Group stations. Initially, repaired aircraft were taken in

116 CAMBRIDGE, Newmarket Road: one of the three sites to which RAF 54 Maintenance Unit brought crashed aircraft for repair or scrap. It is now the East Barnwell Centre.

sections to Waterbeach, Oakington or Wyton for final re-assembly, checks and test-flying. In 1941 MAP provided four 'R' hangars at Madingley Road, and a further three at Bourn airfield which, being just down the road, was the obvious place to tow complete Stirlings for final processes prior to their being flown off. The works handled fourteen aircraft per month averaging a thirteen-week turn-around, with a through-put of around a thousand aircraft during the war years. Marshalls at Teversham, alongside training pilots, employed 3,000 people in their CRO operation repairing Witleys, Albemarles, and Dakotas. With three sites nearby on Newmarket Road (**116**), RAF No. 54 MU brought salvaged aircraft wrecks from across East Anglia for repair or cannibalisation.

Huntingdon

As elsewhere, Huntingdon's factories turned to war production as their peacetime markets dried up. P & H Engineering manufactured incendiary bombs, 200,000 of them altogether during the war, along with flare casings. Silent Channel made tyres for military vehicles, and processed rubber for use in ships' degaussing cables.

Acoustical Manufacturing Co. Ltd made radio parts, and the Huntingdon Hosiery Mill made 6.5 million pairs of socks for the armed services.

Weapons Development

The Air Fighting Development Unit, set up at Duxford in 1940 to evaluate the tactical abilities of new aircraft, moved to Snailwell in 1943. Lords Bridge began life in 1940 as No. 5 RAF Air Ammunition Park, run by No. 95 MU, with a slightly changed role as a Forward Ammunition Depot in 1942, but under the control of the USAAF as a Forward Filling Depot a large section was given over to the handling and storage of chemical weapons.

The Railways

The experience of the First World War had underlined the vital importance of keeping the railways going to transport commodities such as coal and oil, to move the products of the factories to their appropriate destinations, and to move large numbers of service personnel around. In September 1939 the LNER closed Peterborough's Great Northern Hotel and moved in their Civil Engineering department for the duration. The Surveyors Department occupied a house in Thorpe Road, and there was a telegraph office in St Leonard's Street. Peter Waszak has identified at least eleven private rail sidings established for wartime uses, both government and private. These range from food and fuel stores, to mineral extraction and munitions manufacturing. Elsewhere in the county, sidings were put in to service the WD Technical Stores Depot at Histon, 54MU's salvage yards on the Newmarket Road in Cambridge, and all the new airfields and depots.

Armoured Trains

A more specialist use of the railway was by the armoured trains which, from May 1940, had been assembled by Eastern Command as a solution to the problems of patrolling the less accessible parts of East Anglia. Each train was made up of a 2-4-2 tank engine (LNER F4) covered in boiler plate, two LMS three-plank drop-side wagons for storage, and two 24 foot (7.5m) coal wagons, modified as fighting trucks. Each of these two trucks was strengthened with a layer of concrete and boiler plate, and equipped with a 6-pounder Hotchkiss QF gun, a Boys 0.55 inch AT rifle and three Bren guns, of which two were on AA mountings. The crews were initially drawn from Royal Tank Regiment units but by early 1941 had been replaced by Polish troops. A total of twelve armoured trains (A-M) were fitted out with four spares (1-4), and they operated all over England and the east coast of Scotland. At different times Train G patrolled north of a Cambridge-Thetford line visiting Newmarket and Ely, Train A worked in the Cambridge-Hitchin-Bedford triangle, and Train M was based in Spalding (Lincolnshire) patrolling down to Peterborough, March and Wisbech. Late in 1941, Group 1, comprising five trains (A, C, D, F and G) was based in Cambridge, fanning out over large swathes of East Anglia, but supplemented by tracked carriers and armoured Bedford trucks, in order to facilitate better reconnaissance operations. The trains were broken up in spring 1943.

Hospitals and Welfare

At the start of the war Princess Mary's RAF Hospital (**117**) in Lynn Road Ely, which had opened in 1939, was the only actual military hospital in the county, but the RAMC maintained Reception Centres in Cambridge and Peterborough. Within a short time a number of voluntary Red Cross Convalescent Homes and Auxiliary Hospitals had opened, mainly in big houses such as Elton Hall, Hinchingbroke House, and the Palace in Ely. When the Americans entered the war, two 600-bed Emergency

117 ELY, Lynn Road: the Princess Mary's RAF Hospital, opened in 1939, and built in a light and airy International Moderne style.

Medical Service hutted hospitals, originally handed over to the RAF by the Ministry of Health, were transferred to the USAAF as US Eastern Base Section General Hospitals. One was at Histon, and the other was at Diddington Hall, near Buckden, served by its own railway siding. Pressure on general civilian hospitals meant that capacity had to be increased, Peterborough's Memorial Hospital, for instance, opened an annexe at Thorpe Hall in summer 1941. As medical techniques were improved in the laboratory of the battlefield, the Army Blood Transfusion Service made use of a freeze-drying plant in Cambridge. Welfare facilities for troops on leave or in transit proliferated with clubs being set up, such as Peterborough's Long Causeway in November 1939, and for US servicemen in Huntingdon's Freemasons' HQ in Priory House, in 1942. The NAAFI bungalow behind the ROC centre at no. 730 Newmarket Road, Cambridge, and what is now the Girl Guides' hut next to the bus station in St Ives are simply two remnants of the dozens of such facilities which once existed. In July 1942 the Peterborough City Council received a planning application for a NAAFI bakery, warehouse and offices in Padholme Road.

Prisoner of War Camps

Only towards the last third of the war were large numbers of POWs needing to be housed in secure camps. After D-Day, for instance, the quarterly return for German POWs recorded over 90,000 as opposed to under 8,000 in the previous quarter. It is unsurprising that existing camps, possibly vacated by the very troops now doing

the capturing, were pressed into service. The US army depot at Milton, its site under the A14/A10 interchange, and the two former Militia Camps at Ely fall into this category becoming POW Camps Nos 1025 (Milton), 26 (Barton Field) and 130 (West Fen). Cambridge had three other camps at Trumpington, also known as Hauxton, (Nos 45 and 180), near the present Park-and-Ride, and on Walpole Road, built in 1942. Old Huntingdonshire had camps at Huntingdon

118 FRIDAY BRIDGE: the distinctive water-tower, typical of such purpose-built prisoner-of-war camps.

(St Peter's Road), and Woodwalton Lane, Sawtry. In the north of the county there were camps at Friday Bridge (No. 90) later an international farm hostel, at Thorney, where a Handcraft hut on the Whittlesey road may represent a survival, and at Yaxley, now a mushroom farm. Friday Bridge was a typical example of the purpose-built camp with its distinctive water-tower (**118**), rows of pre-fabricated huts, separate compounds for prisoners' and guards' living accommodation, and communal kitchen and canteen facilities. Orton Hall was a camp for German POWs, both officers and other ranks, who were brought in to the railway station at Orton Waterville. Whilst German prisoners were invariably kept in secure camps, many of the Italians were parcelled out in small, often barely supervised groups, to work on the land, and accommodated in whatever buildings were available. Hinxton Grange was used as an out-station of the notorious Camp 020 at Ham (Richmond-on-Thames), run by the Home Office, where spies were interrogated, some of them prior to becoming XX agents. After D-Day, high-ranking Germans were debriefed there. Farm Hall at Godmanchester, was the setting for Operation Epsilon, the investigation into the activities of the most important German nuclear scientists. Most of these camps held POWs as late as 1947, when a newspaper article described the camp at Wansford, where prisoners converted Nissen huts as a church, and a 280-seater theatre. They had passes for Peterborough, and worked on local farms, forming a quarter of the work-force. Some travelled as far as Wisbech as fruit-pickers. Many were entertained by local families and entered into community life. At the end of the war many airfields, such as RAF Peterborough (Westwood Farm) had become camps, first for POWs, then, after their eventual repatriation, by squatters or displaced persons from all over Europe who took up places in the vacated camps.

nine

The Cold War and Beyond 1946–2012

If the media are to be believed it is a moot point whether we are currently living in a more or less secure world today. The relative certainty of the Cold War's mutually assured destruction has been replaced in many people's minds by the unpredictability of random terrorist action. Whilst both have induced high levels of paranoia amongst politicians, only the latter has inserted this into everyday life with widespread CCTV surveillance and the elevation of the trivial to the top-secret.

Military Aviation in the Cold War

During the 1950s, training continued at Bassingbourn, with the very first jet bomber conversion unit in the world at Cambridge and at Oakington in 1952. But the airfields whose development most clearly reflected the enormous changes in aerial strategy and tactics were the front-line operational bomber and fighter stations, primarily Wyton, Wittering, Duxford and Waterbeach.

Fighters against the Russian Bear

The end of the war saw a speedy reduction in the number of RAF operational squadrons and hence in the airfields needed to accommodate them. In 1945 there were only three squadrons of Meteors in service, but the RAF was quickly entering the Jet Age, and Molesworth became a Conversion Unit for both individual pilots and entire squadrons to ensure that the Meteors and Vampires coming out of the factories would be deployed effectively. Once these fighters became operational they were stationed to form a screen extending down the eastern side of Britain, positioned to intercept Russian bombers as they approached across the North Sea. In 1946 Duxford had been identified as a front-line Fighter Command airfield, but contingent on work being carried out on certain aspects, and in 1949 this up-grading commenced. The existing PSP runway was supplemented by a concrete 6,000 foot runway, with Operational Readiness Platforms (ORPs), suitable for use by jet fighters, at each end, and a new T2 hangar was erected. An Aircraft Servicing Platform (ASP) was laid each side of the up-graded Control Tower (281/51), and dispersed hard-standings with blast-walls, sufficient to hold three squadrons, were built around the edges of the flying-field. Along with bulk fuel storage tanks, a new armoury (**119**), now in use as a restaurant, was built.

119 RAF DUXFORD: the armoury built in the 1950s to arm jet-fighters.

This was where the Hunters, succeeding the Meteors, had their pre-prepared demountable cannon-packs installed on the same basis as racing-cars making pit-stops. On 1 March 1950, Waterbeach transferred to Fighter Command, with new work on the airfield necessary here as well, including two new ASPs, two ORPs, improved bulk fuel and weapons storage, and sixteen new dispersals with concrete blast-walls. Waterbeach squadrons were variously equipped with Meteors, Mosquitoes, Venoms, Vampires and Hunters through the 1950s, with Javelins operating from 1959 until 1963. Exercise *Fabulous*, staged in 1950, involved the permanent stationing of fighter aircraft, operationally fuelled and armed, in their concrete-walled dispersals, ready as an instant response to the constant threat of a Soviet bombing attack. It was through Waterbeach that each of Britain's operational all-weather fighter squadrons was rotated to maintain this state of preparedness.

The V-Force
The development of the aircraft which would deliver Britain's atomic bomb brought an even more urgent need for improved airfields (**120,121**). In 1951–52, a 9,000 foot (2.7km) concrete runway was laid at Wittering to accommodate the Bomber Command Development Unit from 1954–60, flying Lincolns initially, and then Canberras, testing the delivery of atomic weapons, and then Valiants equipped with the Blue Danube atomic bomb. By 1960, the V-Force was well-established and more Valiants came to Wittering, soon to be replaced by the Victors and Vulcans which stayed, in either operational or training mode, until 1970. Wittering was the first station to be given ORPs for four Vulcans to be held on fifteen minutes warning for take-off with armed nuclear

120 RAF WITTERING: the control tower designed for V-Bomber airfields, and built after 1955.

121 RAF WITTERING: the Gaydon hangar designed to hold V-bombers.

122 RAF WITTERING: the hut used by Vulcan crews, waiting at their dispersals, ready for instant take-off, their aircraft, armed with atomic weapons, parked on operational readiness platforms.

weapons (**122**). By 1970 after submarine-launched Polaris ICBMs had replaced the Blue Steel stand-off bomb as Britain's major nuclear deterrent, the Valiant squadrons were finally disbanded. Wyton was already long-established as a bomber station, and operational units remained there until 1950, when the station's primary role changed to one of aerial reconnaissance. In 1952 the main runway was lengthened to 9,000 feet (2.7km) in order to accommodate the aircraft of the 'V' Force, as Wyton was one of ten Class 1 Airfields equipped in 1962 with four ORPs to hold dispersed V-bombers, but it would appear that a dedicated atomic weapons storage facility never reached even the planning stage. With the RAF maintaining a nuclear capability as a back-up to Polaris, Brampton became HQ RAF Strike Command during the 1980s.

Intermediate Range Ballistic Missiles: THOR and CRUISE

Ten years into the Cold War, THOR, an IRBM carrying a nuclear warhead, had been selected as NATO's primary deterrent, but only able to reach Russian targets from launch-sites in Europe it was deployed in East Anglia. Acknowledged as no more than a stop-gap, filling in until an effective ICBM could be brought into service, it was given a projected life of just four years, which accounts for the ephemeral character of its site components. In 1958, Mepal was one of five sites, each armed with three missiles, forming one of the four THOR groups. Each group had a lead site, Mepal's was Feltwell (Norfolk), responsible for maintenance and training. The THOR missile was stored in a horizontal position on rails under a canvas cover,

123 MEPAL: the L-shaped blast-walls and conduits for electric cables and fuel-lines at this THOR IRBM site, now demolished.

and hoisted upright prior to firing. Each of the three firing positions had a pair (**123**) of L-shaped concrete blast-walls, (very) separate tanks of kerosene and of liquid oxygen for fuelling the rocket, and a theodolite pillar for setting the rocket's gyro-compass. Each emplacement was surrounded by anchor points embedded in concrete, open channels carrying cabling, gas pipelines, and lighting cables in steel conduits. The warheads were stored in a discrete fenced compound guarded by US technicians. The rockets could only be fired by being unlocked by designated RAF and USAF officers together on the receipt of coded orders. The sites were surrounded by security fencing lit up by lights visible from the sky for miles at night-time, clearly re-affirming the principle that deterrents must be visible in order to work. At the height of the Cold War, Molesworth was second only to Greenham Common as a USAF Cruise Missile base, targeted by the peace movement, and served by the A14, a new road specially built and opened in 1983 as the A1–M1 Link. Molesworth was de-activated in 1989 following arms limitation treaties signed with Russia in 1987, but remains a USAF base for processing electronic intelligence from all over the world, but particularly Africa. The missile storage bunkers may still be seen within their fenced and flood-lit guarded compound. Ramblers on the public footpath skirting the base, unless accompanied by dogs, may still be challenged by armed US servicemen.

Photo-reconnaissance (PR) and Intelligence Gathering

By 1955, Wyton's Mosquitoes had all been replaced by Canberras in the PR role, and the photograph factory (**124**), south of the main gate and now abandoned and derelict, was built to handle the deluge of aerial images, as a single sortie might return with 10,000 feet of film to be processed. After the 1960s the station's role lay wholly in PR and the collection of SIGINT and ELINT using mainly Canberras and Nimrods. Bassingbourn hosted the Joint School of Photographic Interpretation 1963–69, flying Canberras. After the end of the Second World War Alconbury remained operational under the USAF until 1993, with another replacement Control Tower added in the 1950s, and a single runway, 1.7 miles (2.7 km) long. A wide range of hangar-types may be seen including two re-clad wartime T2s, a USAF(E) Butler hangar (**125**) plus twenty-six Hardened Aircraft Shelters (HAS). In 1989, thirteen wider U2/TR1 HAS (**126**) for the U2 spy-plane with its longer wing-span, were completed at a cost of £25 million. They have a span of 135 feet (42m), a length of 105 feet (32m), and height of 32 feet 6 inches (10m). Some were never used and two have recently been declared Scheduled Ancient Monuments. Also from this period are two Nose-Docking Hangars for servicing the larger aircraft that could not fit into regulation hangars. A number of other significant Cold War structures include the un-protected photo-factory (**127**), and its replacement, the late 1980s Avionics building, with two underground levels and a massive rough-cast concrete roof, giving it its 'Magic Mountain' name. This temperature-controlled bunker was built to process the information gathered by the TR1 reconnaissance aircraft. Overtaken by the thaw in the Cold War, it was redundant almost before it was completed. It found a new, fortunately equally redundant, role in 2012 as the emergency standby morgue for the London Olympics (they thought

124 RAF WYTON: the photo-factory built in the 1960s to process the product of the photo-reconnaissance sorties.

125 RAF ALCONBURY: a USAF Butler hangar.

126 RAF ALCONBURY: one of the wider-than-normal Hardened Aircraft Shelters built for the TR1 reconnaissance aircraft.

127 RAF ALCONBURY:
the original photo-processing
facility, later superseded by the
'Magic Mountain'.

128 RAF ALCONBURY: a
watch-tower, one of several,
guarding the atomic weapons
storage area.

of everything). Watch-towers (**128**) are reminders of the need to secure the site with its atomic weapons storage. Soon after it was formed in 1953, JARIC (the Joint Air Reconnaissance Intelligence Centre) was established at Brampton Park (**129**), staying there until 2012, as The National Imagery Exploitation Centre or MI4. Following stand-down, parts of this organisation will re-locate to Wyton, moving into the Pathfinder Building, as the Defence Geospatial Intelligence Fusion Unit, part of the Joint Services Intelligence Group. Wyton became a Joint Services Command in April 2012, and amongst the other units co-located will be 42 Engineer Regiment (Geographic) consisting of fully trained combat engineers specialising, according to the MOD website, in geospatial intelligence.

129 RAF BRAMPTON: the thatched guard-room, more recently used as the chaplains' office. (Photo: Pam Osborne)

Air Defence

Owing to the intelligence on Soviet bomber capabilities gained during the Korean War, AA Command was stood down in 1955, and an alternative surface-to-air (SAM) defence weapons system was sought. Since 1945 there had been experimentation with guided missiles for AA application, and two such weapons emerged from this research.

Anti-Aircraft Missiles

Thunderbird (Red Shoes) was a mobile SAM used by the army until 1976 when it was replaced by Rapier. The responsibility for domestic air defence having been devolved to the Air Ministry, by 1958 the RAF had adopted the static Bloodhound (Red Duster) system. Fixed sites were established through Suffolk, Cambridgeshire, Norfolk and Lincolnshire, stretching up to South Yorkshire as a screen defending the bases of the THOR IRBMs and the V-bombers. The layout of these eleven Bloodhound sites was uniform. The two Fire Units, each containing sixteen missiles (**130**), consisted of launchers connected to hold-fasts serviced by underground ducts. The missiles were mounted on the launchers and fired from a control post containing the operations room. The old bomber airfield at Warboys was chosen to be re-fashioned as one of these Bloodhound bases and many of its buildings survived until recently. A fenced enclave, entered past a distinctive guard-room (**131**) and administrative building led to the double-gabled missile-assembly shed (**132**). The missiles stood, in two groups of eight, on their firing hold-fasts next to a skeleton steel tower mounting the radar. When THOR was withdrawn in 1963 to be replaced by the V-bomber force, the sites were closed down, but the more advanced SAM II units were brought back from

130 BLOODHOUND surface-to-air (SAM) AA missile. (Photographed at the RAF Museum, Hendon)

131 RAF WARBOYS: the distinctive guard-room of this Bloodhound site.

132 RAF WARBOYS: the Missile Assembly Building on this Bloodhound site.

Germany in 1975 with their HQ at Wyton. Right through the early 1980s, until their stand-down in 1991, Bloodhound missiles could be seen, lined up along the eastern edge of the airfield, pointing skyward with their Type 83 radars nearby.

The ROC and the UKWMO

In 1946 the ROC was re-formed in its original role as aircraft-spotters, and for five years observers operated from their old posts or makeshift alternatives. The lucky ones were based in semi-covered brick structures, some of which were raised on stilts, an example of which stood on the county boundary at Chrishall/Ickleton (TL448404). However it was felt that a purpose-built post should be provided for all, so Messrs. Orlit were commissioned to design a pre-fabricated concrete structure which could sit at ground-level (Orlit A), as at Wansford (TF078999) or raised up on stilts (Orlit B) (**133**), as at Buckden (TL199686). By 1955 over 400 had been built in a process of updating and re-distributing the ROC posts. The Cambridge centre at no. 730 Newmarket Road functioned as control of 15 Group, but a 1953 reorganisation of the ROC to conform to new Fighter Command areas saw the Group's surviving posts transfer to Bedford or Lincoln. Training evenings were held for ROC personnel on a weekly basis, as well as at weekends, and the annual national camps were held at RAF Waterbeach from 1950–54. Soon after this, however, the increasing speed of jet aircraft made recognition difficult and reporting far too slow, but the ROC was to adopt a new role. The threat of atomic war put the emphasis onto monitoring the presence, intensity and spread of nuclear fall-out and the ROC, stationed across Britain in over 1,500 posts linked by telephone or radio to regional controls, were ideally suited to the task. Orlit were again contracted to design a protected post, this time to be sunk underground. This new post was another concrete box, measuring roughly 20 feet (6m) by 8 feet (2.5m) by 8 feet (2.5m), and entered through a trap-door, leading via steel rungs down a 14 foot (4.5m) deep shaft. The three-man crew was equipped with instruments which would record the Ground-Zero of a nuclear blast as well as the required information about fall-out. On the surface (**134**) all that is visible is the entry-hatch, a ventilator, and the tops of the Bomb Power Indicator and the Fixed Survey Meter Probe. After 1956 there were twenty-five of these underground posts in the county, reduced to fifteen after October 1968. Of these, around half of them survive, including March (TL402953), Harston (TL430502), Ramsey (TL275849), Parson Drove (TF379098) and Upwell (TF504022). Because of the high water-table in much of Fenland, many were re-located to more suitable spots, that at Maxey (TF147083) having travelled over the Lincolnshire border from Market Deeping. Those posts that had remained in use after the cull of 1968, stayed active until the men and women of the ROC were stood down in 1991. During the 1980s a number of posts, amongst them St Ives, attracted the attentions of CND activists, alarmed by the posturing of the Thatcher-Reagan liaison, and the fastening of hatches was made more secure. In 1988, RIMNET was set up to monitor accidental releases of radioactive material after the Chernobyl incident two years previously. Reporting centres were based on the existing system of weather stations, mainly on MOD sites, including Mepal and Wittering.

The Army in the Cold War

Barracks and Drill Halls

As the RAF reduced the number of active airfields, the army jumped at the opportunity to relinquish some ageing barracks and decaying camps and move into civilised accommodation. In 1970, Bassingbourn became home to the Queen's Division providing recruit training for the Queen's Regiment, the Royal Regiment of Fusiliers and the Royal Anglian Regiment, and taking over the administration of the CUOTC's Barton Road rifle range. Since 1993 it has housed one of the five Army Training Regiments, but is scheduled to close by the end of 2013. Oakington served as the depot of the Royal Anglian Regiment until 1999, when the Home Office took it over as an Immigrant Reception Centre, but is now earmarked for development of a new township, Northstowe with up to 10,000 homes. Waterbeach was the base for the RE airfield construction units until 2012 when they left for RAF Kinloss in north-east Scotland. The airfield site is set to become yet another Cambridge satellite township.

The cement works in Coldhams Lane, Cambridge, was converted into a hutted TAC in 1947 for a REME unit, and later two TA signals units, and a company of the Royal Anglian Regiment (TA). The CUOTC's lease on Grange Road had expired, and there were plans for the redevelopment of Quayside, so they moved into the Coldham's Lane TAC in 1970, giving their RAC squadron room to train on its growing collection of armoured vehicles, and providing electronically controlled target devices for shooting practice. These premises were re-constructed in 1988.

133 BUCKDEN: an ORLIT 'B' Royal Observer Corps aircraft-spotting post (TL199686), from the 1950s. (Photo: Buckden Parish Council)

134 PARSON DROVE: a Royal Observer Corps radioactive fallout underground monitoring post from the 1960s.

135 CAMBRIDGE, Cherry Hinton Road: TA Centre housing, among others, a medical unit.

The wholly new TAC (**135**) at no. 450 Cherry Hinton Road was built in 1987 for a RAMC (V) field ambulance unit, now RHQ and HQ Company of 254 Medical Regiment. These share the premises with 'C' Squadron 21 SAS (TA). The London Road TAC in Peterborough has been modernised and extended over the years and now houses 158 (Royal Anglian) Transport Regiment (Volunteers) a logistics unit whose title memorialises its origins.

Secret Classrooms

So great was the reliance on eavesdropping during the Cold War that the intelligence services has developed an insatiable appetite for linguists, translators and interpreters. Large numbers of National Servicemen who happened to be, or were about to be, languages students, were taught a range of languages including Russian and Chinese. Cambridge University ran a course for the Joint Services School of Linguists, from 1951 until 1959, using teaching rooms in Newnham Terrace, The Hermitage in Silver Street and no. 5 Salisbury Villas, Station Road. Accommodation was spread between RAF Oakington and RAF Waterbeach, the Stella Maris (later Douglas Lodge) in Trumpington Road, and The Grove and Cecil Lodge in Newmarket. There was a mess for officer-cadets at Foxton Manor.

Defending against Nuclear Attack

Successive governments during the Cold War persisted in the delusion that it was possible to survive a nuclear attack and, of course, the corollary that it was desirable to survive one. It did not take much to work out that with Molesworth, Wyton, Wittering and Waterbeach around, Cambridgeshire would have been vapourised even before the four minutes were up. Although it was eventually realised that Civil Defence was maybe a bit optimistic, the government, especially under Thatcher in the mid-1980s, continued to require local authorities to plan for nuclear war. CD Centres were integrated into a wider range of emergency response, but bunkers were still being built when the Berlin Wall came down.

Nuclear Bunkers

After the end of the Second World War, Cambridge had been chosen to retain its status as the emergency administrative centre for eastern England under a Regional Commissioner. During 1953 a War Room was built for the Commissioner and his key staff on Brooklands Avenue (**136**). Within a few years this provision was deemed inadequate and a bigger Regional Seat of Government (RSG4) was built, in about 1962.

136 CAMBRIDGE, Brooklands: the Regional Seat of Government.

This new build, another monolithic concrete structure with walls 5 feet (1.5m) and a roof 7 feet (2m) thick, was joined onto the re-organised War Room. Together they contained offices for the Commissioner; his scientific, technical, legal and military advisers; a BBC studio; rooms for representatives of the major government departments, for local authority administrators and for co-ordinators of the emergency and other CD services; electricity generators and filtration plant; communications equipment; kitchens and bathrooms; dormitories for around 450 people and a double-height map-room surrounded, at its upper level, by rooms with interior windows overlooking the plotting-table. In 1965 a re-organisation into smaller areas left Cambridge as a Sub-Regional Control (SRC41), and in a further re-shuffle in 1972 Cambridge had apparently dropped out of the system, but the buildings were maintained throughout the 1970s and refurbished in the late 1980s.

Other related, but vastly less impressive, local authority structures in the county included an emergency control centre in the basement of Cambridge's Shire Hall, in use from 1967–87; a bunker built in 1983 in the basement of Castle Hill House in Huntingdon; and another emergency control centre in the basement of the South Cambridgeshire District Council offices in Hills Road, Cambridge, which was completed in 1986 by virtue of a substantial government grant. The basement of this Edwardian house was given a new concrete roof and steel blast-proof doors. The three rooms that make up the centre contain radio equipment, maps and filtration plant. East Cambridgeshire District Council had moved their offices into a former maternity hospital at The Grange, Nutholt Lane in Ely behind the old Shire Hall, and had installed their emergency centre in its basement by 1982. A short while later a new protected control room was added in the basement of a new extension. The centre included a small BBC studio, a map-room and domestic offices with a dormitory. With the construction of a new office building at Shire Hall in the late 1980s, an additional emergency bunker, now used for archive-storage, was laid under Castle Court.

Civil Defence

Civil Defence facilities include the South Cambridgeshire HQ at Abberley House, Great Shelford where a rescue training centre and emergency services' garages and stores operated from 1957–68; Peterborough's centre, in 'Gayhurst', a large detached house on Lincoln Road; Warkworth Lodge in Cambridge; and Soham's former fire-station. Large numbers of schools were designed with wide corridors to accommodate emergency medical services, and kitchens to provide communal feeding stations, examples in the Peterborough area included Southfields Juniors in Stanground, and Arthur Mellows Village College in Glinton. Some very surprised headteachers were to discover just how far their responsibilities might be extended in the eventuality of Armageddon.

Communications

Planning to cope with a nuclear attack inevitably involved a strong focus on both communications and transportation. In order to expedite military communications,

137 OVER: the microwave communications tower.

particularly information relating to a nuclear attack, a chain of microwave towers was built across the country, the best-known being the Post Office Tower in London's Tottenham Court Road. The major branch of this network was known as 'Backbone', and Morborne Hill near Stilton was a junction, feeding into Norfolk through a relay at Wisbech, and receiving via another relay at Over (**137**). Independent of public telephone systems, the Home Office maintained their 'Hilltop' radio stations, with a depot at Cheveley and a radio station at Great Gidding, in order to monitor internal security in the event of an emergency. Just as important as the air-waves were communications on the ground. A network of Military Road Routes was designed to ensure that the approaches to key military logistics centres such as Colchester, Harwich and Felixstowe were kept clear. During the Cold War period, Felixstowe functioned as a US Army Transportation Terminal, permanently manned by US personnel, handling personnel movements and 35,000 tons of military stores annually. These included explosives and nuclear warheads being brought in to supply the air bases in East Anglia, and the Cruise missile base at Molesworth. The A45, code-named 'YAK' and later to be extended and improved as the A14, was a vital link in this network. There was also a complementary network of designated Essential Service Routes (ESR), roads which would be kept clear of civilian traffic in order to allow free passage for the military, the emergency services and internal security forces. Under the terms of Martial Law, imposed by the Regional Commissioner, the TA would be deployed to aid the police in enforcing restrictions and prohibitions, and to carry out summary justice, particularly against looters. The ESRs in Cambridgeshire were the M11 and A11; the A15 from Yaxley to the Lincolnshire border; the old A14 Roman Road from Royston to Godmanchester; and the A604, A45, and A428, as predecessors of the new A14. Government stores were sited to enable the emergency distribution of their stocks of food, fuel and medical supplies to be organised. Such stores were located in Godmanchester, Burwell and Huntingdon. The old AA and RASC depot in Caxton had become a Ministry of Supply stationery store, surviving the nuclear holocaust clearly being contingent on completing the right forms.

Munitions and Weapons Development

At the end of the war Lords Bridge, the former FFD, and Rectory Farm, Orwell were both used as RAF chemical weapons storage sites, and run by No. 95 MU. No. 91 MU administered another such site at Marsh Close, Comberton Heath. By 1948 the stocks were in process of disposal, mainly by incineration, a fairly haphazard procedure. At Orwell, for instance, petrol was poured over the mustard gas bombs, incendiaries added, and then the whole lot was ignited by rounds fired from a Sten Gun. The ashes were then covered in bleaching powder. These methods were time-consuming so large quantities of mustard gas bombs were dumped in the Irish Sea off Stranraer. At the Comberton site, drums of mustard gas were decanted into a pit and burnt, the drums themselves then being decontaminated in a furnace, but the land was so blighted that not until 1989 could it be declared safe. Lords Bridge (**138**) was re-activated from 1948 until its final closure in 1957, but it would be another forty years before the land could be regarded as safe.

Marshalls at Teversham, alongside their airport operation, have continued their involvement in aircraft repairs and maintenance, with a particular focus on TriStars (especially tankers), V-Bombers and Hercules transport aircraft which come to Cambridge from all over the world. Hangars now cover over a million square feet (100,000 square metres), the largest being capable of holding two Boeing 747s.

Wittering housed the RAF Bomber Command Development Unit, until 1960, and has its own nuclear weapons storage on-site. Wyton was home to the Electronic Warfare and Avionics Unit from 1970 until after 1987. Perkins Diesels in Peterborough has explored the development of multi-fuel engines for tanks (what a terrible waste of whisky!).

In 2013, as the nation's armed forces are reduced with their new roles appearing to stabilise as police action and intelligence-gathering, so their real estate requirements have shrunk dramatically, making for a generally lessened impact on the landscape.

138 LORDS BRIDGE: the decontamination centre at this chemical weapons storage depot.

Appendix 1

Iron Age Forts

Appendix 2

Mediaeval Castles
and Other Fortified Sites

Early Earthwork Castles

Aldreth, vanished earthwork castle of 1071	
Benwick, probable location for castle used in 1144 campaign	
Bourn Hall, possible ring-work	TL322561
Braham's Farm, Ely St Mary, earthwork used in 1070 campaign	TL534777
Burwell, unfinished moated castle of 1144	TL587661
Cambridge, motte and bailey of 1068	TL446593
Castle Camps, probable ring-work and small bailey	TL627424
Chatteris, possible site of castle in use c.1140	
Caxton, The Moats, may date from 1144 campaign	TL294587
Eaton Socon, motte & bailey of c.1140	TL173588
Ely, Cherry Hill, motte and bailey of 1071	TL541799
Fordham, possible site of castle in use c.1140	
Great Staughton, possible motte inside bailey	TL116630
Huntingdon, motte and two baileys, built 1068	TL242715
Huntingdon, siege castle of 1174	TL236714
Kimbolton, motte, probably of twelfth-century date	TL094674
Knapwell, Overhall Grove motte, probably dating from 1140s	TL337632
Orwell, possible motte	TL361504
Peterborough, Tout Hill, motte of c.1070	TL194987
Rampton, Giant's Hill: unfinished moated platform of 1144	TL431681
Ramsey, Booths Hill, motte and bailey of c.1140	TL293848
Sapley, low oval motte and bailey	TL248775
Southoe, ring-work of twelfth-century	TL178638
Southoe, ring-work occupied eleventh–fourteenth century	TL184644
Southoe, Boughton, mentioned 1140–53, possibly Diddington	TL198647
Swaffham Bulbeck, Four Mile Stable, possible motte and bailey	TL589597
Swavesey, rectangular earthwork, possibly from 1144 campaign	TL359689
Willingham, Belsar's Hill, Iron Age fort re-used 1070 and 1139	TL423703
Wisbech, built 1071 as oval earthwork castle	TF462096
Wood Walton, motte and bailey of c.1140, motte now removed	TL210826

Stone Castles

Bassingbourn, John of Gaunt's House, castle licensed 1266	TL325451
Cambridge, rebuilt in stone, 1285–99	TL446593

Castle Camps, large-scale construction works, 1265 and 1331   TL627424
Cheveley, square moated enclosure, licensed 1341   TL678613
Kimbolton, quadrangular moated castle, late thirteenth century, replaced motte   TL100677
Kirtling, square moat built by 1219   TL686575
Maxey, quadrangular moated castle, licensed 1374   TF129088
Wisbech, re-built in stone, 1087   TF462096
Woodcroft, quadrangular, moated castle of c.1280   TF140045

Early Mediaeval Stone Manor Houses

Barnack, stone manor (possible twelfth-century aisled hall), destroyed 1830   TF078050
Hemingford Grey, moated Norman manor, first-floor entrance   TL289705

Strong Houses

Buckden Palace, late fifteenth-century brick house of bishops of Lincoln   TL193677
Chesterton Tower, built c.1330 by proctor of St Andrews   TL463598
Elton Hall, courtyard house of late fifteenth century with gatehouse   TL088930
Ely, Bishop's Palace, brick house of 1490 and later   TL530803
Guyhirn Tower, vanished house of Bishop Morton
Leighton Bromswold, manor house of late fifteenth century, gatehouse 1616   TL116752
Little Downham, Bishop's Palace, late fifteenth century on earlier site   TL519843
Longthorpe Tower, hall and strong tower of 1300   TL165984
Northborough Manor, hall-block with gatehouse, 1330   TF151079
Torpel, possible hunting-lodge   TF107053

Ecclesiastical Buildings

Biggin Abbey, residence of bishops of Ely, stone range of fifteenth century   TL487616
Downham Palace, late fifteenth-century reconstruction of earlier palace   TL519843
Ely: Porta (1397), Sacrist's Gate, Steeple Row Gate & Goldsmith's Tower
    (c.1500 and earlier)
(Hinchingbrooke House, gatehouse of c.1500 from Ramsey Abbey   TL228714)
Peterborough, Outer Gate (twelfth century, licensed 1309), Abbot's Gate (early thirteenth
    century), and precinct walls (eleventh–fifteenth century)
Ramsey, fortified during Anarchy, rump of gatehouse of thirteenth century   TL290850
St Neots Priory, precinct wall and gatehouse (demolished)   TL182603

Moated Sites (some examples)

Burrough Green, Park Wood, moats and banks   TL642549
Carlton, Lopham's Hall   TL647521
Conington, Bruce's Castle, the de Brus manor recorded 1242   TL184486
Conington Round Hill, mystery site (motte, garden, gun-battery?)   TL153853
Ellington Thorpe, twelfth-century moat with timber aisled hall   TL155704
Elton Manor, owned by Ramsey Abbey   TL084940
Molesworth, manorial site   TL072761
Sawtry, Archers Wood, manorial earthworks   TL175813
Swaffham Bulbeck   TL555627
Torpel Manor, earthworks of manorial complex   TF111054

West Wickham, Hill Farm	TL624490
West Wickham, Yen Hall	TL616504
West Wratting, Scarlett's Farm	TL605516
Wintringham, moated timber-framed manor house of 1175–1250	TL219598
Winwick	TL106808

Moats at Barton TL4055, Fowlmere TL4245, Ellington Thorpe TL1570, Southoe TL1763, Sawtry TL1781, and Wintringham TL2259 have all been excavated.

Appendix 3

Civil War Sites

Burghley House	TF050060
Cambridge Castle	TL446582
Chesterton, Mount Ararat, flanked redoubt	TL470600
Conington Round Hill	TL153853
Earith Bulwark	TL393750
Elford Closes, Stretham	TL502722
Huntingdon Castle	TL241715
Huntingdon, battery off the Hartford road	TL248723
Huntingdon, Bowling Green sconce, and bastion (inferred)	
Leverington	TL445107
March, Cavalry Barns sconce	TL421957
Northborough Manor	TF151078
Sawtry, Tort Hill, gun-platform	TL173841
Stanground, Horsey Hill fort	TL224960
Stonea Camp	TL447930
Upware fort	TL536701
Wisbech Castle	TF462096
Woodcroft Castle	TF140045

Drill Halls and Other Premises used by Volunteer Forces

Cambridge

* 14 Corn Exchange Street, HQ and Orderly-room, 3rd Volunteer Battalion Suffolk Regiment, 1888; HQ and 'A'–'D' Companies 1st Battalion Cambridgeshire Regiment 1908–14; HQ Cambridgeshire Regiment until 1970s Lion Yard re-development
* Grange Road, base for CUOTC from 1860–1971, included armoury, NCO's house, forge, magazine and later garaging
* 19 Rose Crescent, HQ and Orderly-room, CUOTC to 1888
* 2 Wheeler Street, HQ and Orderly-room, CUOTC to 1891
* 82 Norwich Street, HQ 'A' Squadron Loyal Suffolk Hussars, 1904
* 22 Market Street, HQ and Orderly-room, CUOTC to 1929
* 39 Green Street, Offices and HQ of 1st Eastern General Hospital until 1913
* 50 Norwich Street, HQ 'A' Squadron Loyal Suffolk Hussars, 1912
* 196 East Road, drill hall, Cambridgeshire Regt, 'A' Squadron Loyal Suffolk Hussars and 1st Eastern General Hospital, 1914; 1st Battalion Cambridgeshire Regiment, 250th Field Company, RE, and Cambridgeshire and Isle of Ely Territorial Association offices, 1929; demolished in 1983; crest preserved at Cherry Hinton TAC
* Pembroke College, Old Library, temporary Orderly-room, CU OTC to 1918
* Trinity College: HQ 1st Eastern General Hospital, 1915–18
* Quayside, HQ and Orderly-room of CU OTC, from 1929
* Coldhams Lane, converted cement works as TAC from 1947, in use by CUOTC and signals unit; rebuilt 1988
* 450 Cherry Hinton Road: TAC built 1987, in use by RAMC unit and 'C' Squadron 21 SAS (TA)

Ely

* Lynn Road, Shire Hall: Armoury and Orderly-room 'H' Company, 3rd Volunteer Bn Suffolk Regt 1888
* Silver Street, Militia Barracks built c.1855: 68th or Cambridgeshire Regiment of Militia until 1881, when it became 4th Bn Suffolk Regt; 'H' Company, 1st Bn Cambridgeshire Regt 1908–14; 'B' Company, 1st Bn Cambridgeshire Regt 1920–39
* Barton Road, drill hall: 'B' Company, 1st Bn Cambridgeshire Regt from 1939

Godmanchester

'D' Squadron, Bedfordshire Yeomanry, 1908–14; 'A' and 'B' Companies, Huntingdonshire Cyclist Battalion, 1914–18 (no obvious dedicated premises)

Huntingdon

* Cowper Road, Militia Barracks: 2nd or Huntingdonshire Regiment of Militia, 1855–81; 'H' Company 4th (Huntingdonshire) Volunteer Bn, Bedfordshire Regt, 1900–14
* St Mary's Street, drill hall: 'H' Company 5th (Huntingdonshire) Bn, Bedfordshire Regt, 1908; HQ Huntingdonshire Cyclist Bn, 1914–18; in use to 1945; now sale-room
* Bridge House (Old Bridge Hotel): officers' mess Huntingdonshire Cyclist Bn; drill ground 'D' Squadron, Bedfordshire Yeomanry 1908–14
* 3 Cromwell Walk, ACF building + indoor range next to 'Volunteer' PH

Kimbolton

Castle is presumed to have been the venue for Earl of Manchester's Huntingdonshire Mounted Rifles formed 1861, and joined by Cambridgeshire Mounted Rifles in 1863; drill station for 'D' Squadron, Bedfordshire Yeomanry, 1900–14

March

* Magazine Lane, Napoleonic drill hall and powder store: 5 Corps Cambridgeshire Volunteer Rifles, 1860; demolished after the Second World War
* High Street: Orderly-room 'G' Company, 3rd Volunteer Bn Suffolk Regt, 1888
* Gas Lane, drill hall in converted C19 chapel; 'G' Coy 1st Bn Cambridgeshire Regt
* Gas Lane, drill hall post-WWII: ACF; also explosives/inflammables store

Newmarket

* Fordham Road, armoury and drill hall: 'H' Company, 1st Battalion, Cambridgeshire Regiment, 1912; 'D' Company, 1st Battalion, Cambridgeshire Regiment, 1929

Peterborough

* Royal Hotel (probably in Westgate): 6th Corps Northants. Rifle Volunteers, 1862
* Thorpe Road, Sessions House: armoury, 6th Corps Northants. Rifle Volunteers, 1862
* Wentworth Hotel, Wentworth St: drill space, 6th Corps Northants. RVs, 1860s
* Church St, Corn Exchange: drill space, 6th Corps Northants. Rifle Volunteers, 1860s
* Cumbergate: Orderly-room, 6th Corps Northants. Rifle Volunteers
* Queen Street, drill hall, 6th Corps Northants. Rifle Volunteers, 1868; 336 (Northants) Bty RFA, until 1927; demolished c.1975 for redevelopment
* St Leonard's Street, drill hall, Northants RE Volunteers, 1867; unit disbanded 1908; 'B' Squadron Northamptonshire Yeomanry; demolished 1911 for Crescent Bridge
* London Road, Fletton, 'Coffee Palace' (1898), 'G' Coy 5th Bn Bedfordshire Regt 1900–1914; 'F' & 'G' Companies Huntingdonshire Cyclist Bn 1914–18
* Broad Bridge Street, The Saracen's Head Public House: HQ of the re-formed, 'B' Squadron, Northamptonshire Yeomanry, 1902
* London Road, Fletton, TA hut, for 'D' Coy 5th (Huntingdonshire) Bn (TA) Northamptonshire Regt; 1921–1930; demolished
* Lincoln Road, Millfield, drill hall, HQ, 'A', 'B' & 'C' Companies 5th Battalion Northamptonshire Regiment & 336 (Northamptonshire) Battery, RFA, 1927; now City Youth Centre
* 'Shortacres', London Road, Fletton: HQ 402 Bty 585 SL Regt RA (TA), 1939; in use as TAC, 2013
* Northfields Road, Unity Hall: classroom for 135 Field Regiment, 1939
* Lincoln Road, Millfield: PSA Hall canteen 135 Field Regiment, 1939

Ramsey

★ High Street, drill hall, built 1911 for 'Hunts Territorials': 'H' Company 5th
  (Huntingdonshire) Bn, Bedfordshire Regt; drill station 'D' Squadron, Bedfordshire
  Yeomanry, 1908–14; 'E' Company, Huntingdonshire Cyclist Bn 1914–18; 'A' Company, 5th
  Battalion, Northamptonshire Regiment, 1920–39; demolished 2001

St Ives

★ Free Church Passage/Bull Lane, drill hall: drill station for 'H' Company 5th
  (Huntingdonshire) Battalion Bedfordshire Regt, 1900–14; 'C' Company, Huntingdonshire
  Cyclist Battalion, 1914–18

St Neots

★ High Street, Corn Exchange: 'J' Company, 1st Cambridgeshire Corps, Rifle Volunteers,
  1876; drill station for 'D' Squadron, Bedfordshire Yeomanry, 1902; drill station for 'D'
  Company 5th Battalion Bedfordshire Regt. 1900–14; base 'D' Company, Huntingdonshire
  Cyclist Battalion, 1914–18
★ Ware Road, drill hall: 'C' (machine-gun) Company, 5th Battalion Northamptonshire Regt,
  1922–39; demolished c. 1990s

Whittlesey

★ Inhams End, Orderly-room 'F' Company, 3rd Volunteer Bn Suffolk Regt, 1888
★ Station Road, Public Hall built 1880: 'F' Company, 1st Battalion Cambridgeshire Regt,
  1908–14, now club
★ Station Road, drill hall, in use c.1914–1945+, demolished 1960s; ACF hut on site

Wisbech

★ North Brink, Corn Exchange, Orderly-room 2nd Corps Cambridgeshire Rifle Volunteers,
  1860; 'E' Company, 1st Battalion Cambridgeshire Regiment, 1912; drill station 'D'
  Squadron Norfolk Yeomanry, 1908–14
★ Great Church Street, Orderly-room 'E' Company, 3rd Volunteer Battalion Suffolk
  Regiment, 1888
★ 4 North Terrace, drill hall, 1893+ until c1933, 'C' Company, 1st Battalion Cambridgeshire
  Regiment
★ Sandylands, drill hall, 'C' Company, 1st Battalion Cambridgeshire Regiment, 1937; TAC
  until c.2000

Yaxley

★ drill station for 'G' Company 5th Battalion Bedfordshire Regiment, 1914
★ Girls' School, mobilisation venue 'H' Company, Huntingdonshire Cyclist Bn 1914
★ Chapel Street, drill hall, 'D' Company 5th (Huntingdonshire) Bn Northamptonshire
  Regiment, 1920–39; burned down around 1963
★ NB other locations in Cambridgeshire, Isle of Ely, Huntingdonshire, or Soke of
  Peterborough, providing drill stations for Rifle Volunteer or Territorial units: Benwick,
  Burwell, Chatteris, Coates, Doddington, Glinton, Great Shelford, Madingley, Sawston,
  Soham, Somersham, Sutton, Thorney and Upwell

Appendix 5

Airfields and other RAF and USAAF Aviation-related Sites

Notes

* Drawing or Type Numbers used in several places show sequence/year of production: the Watch Office for All Commands was built to the 343rd design to emerge from the Air Ministry drawing office in 1943 – hence 343/43. The term 'tb' refers to buildings with walls a single brick in width and officially 'temporary brick'.
* Where structures are recorded as surviving, that refers to the latest sighting pre-2013.
* Figure 19 shows major airfield locations using each entry's number:

1 Alconbury opened in 1938 as a satellite for Upwood, part of RAF 2 Group, equipped with Fairey Battle light bombers. Mainly temporary buildings were put up with the administrative area around Alconbury House. After Upwood's aircraft were deployed to France, Wyton, with its Blenheims, took over as parent airfield. Wellington's four-engined bombers soon moved in and in 1941, three runways were laid. In 1942 the runways were extended (1 x 2,000 yards and 2 x 1,400 yards). That year the VIIIth USAAF (Station 102) arrived flying B-24 Liberators. Stukeley Hall became the officers' mess and the existing Nissen huts and tb buildings stayed in use, the original Crew Locker and Drying Room (16657/41) in parallel linked Nissen Huts survives as Building 25, having been subsequently used as a USAF Wing HQ with an annexe housing an Automatic Digital Network terminal, used for monitoring the supply of spare parts. The first watch office (7345/41) still stands with a Nissen crew – briefing room attached. This was superseded by a standard watch office (343/43) which also survives in 2013. In 1944 the 482nd Bomb Group came off operations in order to operate a Pathfinder School, one of whose experimental radar workshops can still be seen. The separate 2nd Strategic Air Depot was known by the USAAF as Abbots Ripton. The USAF stayed at Alconbury until 1993 flying U2 reconnaissance aircraft and processing their product in a succession of dedicated buildings culminating in the semi-underground Avionics building, only completed in time for the end of the Cold War. Much of the airfield is now in commercial use, there is still a USAF enclave, and a new town is planned.

2 Bassingbourn opened in March 1938 to house the training unit for 2 Group's light bombers. It is a typical Expansion Period airfield with four 'C' hangars (two each of 5043/36 and 5044/36), the usual workshops (4923/35), stores (4287/35), guardhouse (662/36), station HQ (1723/36), officers' mess (8699/37), sergeants' mess (7858/38), institute (8055/38), sick-bay (7503/37) and armoury (4839/35). The watch office was a 'Fort' type (207/36) with a tower, later given a first-floor wrap-around extension, with fire-tender shed and night-flying equipment store alongside (7292/36). The site also contained married quarters, sports facilities, dumps for bombs and fuel, specialist stores and synthetic training provision.

Much of this remains. In 1939 the station became No. 11 OTU equipped with Wellingtons, which operated until late 1942 when the B-17s of the VIIIth USAAF 91st Bomb Group arrived to carry out missions against industrial targets in Germany. After the war the station saw a number of units including No. 204 Advanced Flying School in 1952, and 231 OCU with its PR Canberras in 1953. Flying ceased in 1969, but most of the original buildings remain, now used by an army training regiment but scheduled to close.

3 Bottisham began in 1940 as a satellite for Waterbeach and served mainly as a landing-ground for No. 22 EFTS at Cambridge. From summer 1941 it was used by Army Co-operation Command and two Sommerfield track runways were laid, and a watch office was built. The drawing number listed on the Air Ministry plan (15371/41) seems to refer only to a reduction in area, so the watch office may have been the standard single-storey fighter satellite one (17658/40). Later, some dispersal revetments, a T2 hangar (3653/42) and five Blister hangars (9392/42) were added. In 1943 the airfield was up-graded for the P-47s of VIIIth USAAF 361st Fighter Group (Station 374), soon to receive Mustangs. The station closed in 1946 and was sold in 1958. A few tb huts, once used by the defence detachment, remain north of the A14.

4 Bourn commenced operations as a satellite of Oakington whose Stirling bombers used the airfield from 1941, carrying out raids over Germany. Early in 1944 *Oboe*-equipped Mosquitoes were employed on precision-bombing raids over France, and then, equipped with H2S they marked for raids, particularly on Berlin. It ceased to be an operational base from 1947, and had largely been returned to agriculture by 1961. Short Engineering Bros. Repair Organisation (SEBRO) had a factory on Madingley Road, repairing Stirling bombers from 1941. The aircraft were towed by road to Bourn for final assembly prior to being flown off. Later, in 1945, Liberators of RAF Transport Command were also overhauled here. The airfield had the usual two T2s, with a site earmarked for a third, and a B1 hangar, but the MAP 'R' Hangars which can still be seen on the site, were used by SEBRO, together with the surviving works canteen building. The majority of the buildings were Nissen, Romney and Laing huts or tb, with a Blister hangar for the Free Gunnery Trainer (7316/42), and some adapted farm-buildings for the MT compound.

5 Brampton was never a flying field but housed a number of important establishments until recently. Brampton Park was home to evacuee children in 1939, and a year later was acting as a clearing-house. Brampton Grange was HQ RAF 7 (Training) Group until October 1942 when it became HQ 1st Bombardment Wing, VIIIth USAAF and then, from September 1943, 1st Bombardment Division with Combat Wings at Polebrook (Northants), Bassingbourn, Molesworth and Thurleigh (Beds). The Grange was inadequate so Brampton Park was taken over as the Officers' Club with Nissen huts as dining-room and a Red Cross Aero Club. Many personnel were still accommodated under canvas. After the war, the RAF moved into Brampton Park which has served as HQ Strike Command, Logistics Command and JARIC. The grounds contain offices, a MT compound, and a thatched cottage, surely the RAF's strangest guard-room. The site is being vacated by the RAF in 2012.

Bury see Upwood

Cambridge (Whitehill Farm) was begun by Marshalls as a private airfield in 1930.

6 Cambridge (Teversham) was opened in 1938 by Marshalls as the civil aerodrome serving Cambridge. It housed a number of flying training organisations including No. 22 E & RFTS, 1938–39, No. 22 EFTS 1939–52, No. 4 Flying Instructor School 1940–44, and

No. 22 Reserve Flying School, 1951–54, flying Chipmunks. During the war Marshalls was one in an extensive network of Civilian Repair Organisations, and handled Airspeed Oxfords and Whitley bombers. At the centre of the airport complex, now confined to the south side of Newmarket Road, stand the original 1938 hotel, flying control and hangar. An assortment of wartime and post-War hangars and workshops surround this core, with Handcraft huts and two of the original five Blister hangars, MAP A1 sheds, Boulton & Paul VR1 sheds, imported T2s and the more recent hangars which have housed Concorde, Tristars and Hercules. Next to Hangar No. 1 is the original fire tender shed and stores, but two Bellman hangars put up for the flying school in 1938 have been replaced by later structures. Marshalls continues to function as a busy airport and aircraft maintenance centre.

Cambridge (Newmarket Road)

RAF 54 MU occupied three sites centred on the area to the west of the airport and was concerned with salvaging wrecked aircraft, from across the whole of East Anglia. One of these sites, may still be seen, a YWCA hostel in 1945, but now occupied by the East Barnwell Community Centre.

Cambridge

Short Bros operated a Civilian Repair Depot (CRO) known as SEBRO in Cambridge, on a site, east of the M11, now occupied by the Schlumberger Centre, on Madingley Road. A number of hangars were constructed for this facility in 1942, including four MAP 'R' hangars, demolished around 1960. Aircraft, almost exclusively Short Stirling bombers, were repaired and towed along the A45 to Bourn airfield for final assembly, flight testing, and onward delivery to bomber stations.

7 Castle Camps was started in September 1939 as a satellite for Debden, the Fighter Command Sector Station in Essex, housing Hurricane squadrons engaged in the Battle of Britain, with tented accommodation. In 1941 runways were laid, and eight Over Blister hangars (13087A/41), some aircraft dispersal pens and a Bellman hangar (6411/39) were built. Dozens of Nissen, Thorn, Laing and Romney huts along with tb buildings met the airfield's technical, training and domestic needs. A very few buildings were in permanent brick, one being the surviving PBX (13727/41) next to Coopers Farm. Also in brick was the watch office of uncommon design (MS2650). In 1942 the first Mosquitoes arrived, serving as night-fighters intercepting enemy bombing raids. Through 1943 the Mosquitoes acted in a bomber support capacity. After that, the airfield, by now a satellite of North Weald (Essex) hosted a variety of units including a Radar Calibration Squadron, and more Mosquito night-fighters, Mark XIV Spitfires and Tempest Vs. The airfield closed in early 1946. A few Nissen and curved asbestos huts and tb buildings survive on communal and technical sites.

8 Caxton Gibbet started life as home to the Cambridge University gliding club in 1935, but in May 1940 was transferred to the Air Ministry, intended as a dispersal field for Duxford. It actually became a Relief Landing Ground for the trainee pilots of No. 22 EFTS at Cambridge. With Cambridge under pressure, some Laing huts were provided for ground instruction, and No. 4 Flying Instructor School used the airfield for night-flying exercises. As Cambridge increased both its intakes of trainees and trainee-instructors, at the same time increasing their flying time, it became necessary to further develop the facilities at Caxton Gibbet. Two Over Blister and five standard Blister hangars were constructed, together with more Laing hutting (1032/41) for staff accommodation. The Swansley Wood domestic site also provided hutted overspill accommodation, some of which may remain, for personnel from the adjacent Bourn airfield. From early in 1946 the airfield reverted to agriculture.

Collyweston see Wittering

Cottenham was a Landing Ground during the First World War.

9 Duxford started the post-First World War period as No. 35 TDS, subordinate to neighbouring Fowlmere. Three pairs of GS hangars and a number of workshops, barrack-rooms and specialist buildings such as the chapel remain. The complementary Aircraft Repair Shed was wantonly destroyed during the filming of the 'Battle of Britain' movie. In 1920 Duxford became No. 2 Flying Training School and then, in the 1923 review it was selected as a Fighter Command Sector Station, whilst hosting the University Air Squadron and the Meteorological Flight. At the height of the Battle of Britain the RAF and RNAS Air Fighting Development Units arrived from Northolt, staying until 1943, experimenting on Typhoons and modified fighter/bombers. In early 1943 the VIIIth USAAF 78th Fighter Group (Station 357) arrived flying Mustangs in support of pre-D-Day operations. In late 1944 a PSP runway had been laid, but only in 1951 was one installed in concrete, for the Meteors, Hunters and Javelins which used the airfield until it closed in 1961. Concrete ORPs were added at each end of the runway. To the buildings of the 1919 development, others had been added during the reconstruction of the later-1920s. These include the operations block (1161/24 and 757/27), the sergeants' mess (288/25) and works services building (1132/27). A further expansion in the mid-1930s brought Types 'B' and 'C' Barrack-Blocks (852/32 and 451/32), the station offices (352-3/30), guardhouse (1266/32), officers' mess (2969/34), six-bay petrol-tanker shed (2773/34), institute (852/32) and sick quarters (213/30). A number of other structures, including the fire-fighting MT shed (2802/38), dining room (6848/39) and eight blister hangars were added during the course of the war, and older buildings were camouflaged with paint schemes. From 1949 Duxford, was upgraded to become a front-line Fighter Command airfield, flying Meteors succeeded by Hunters. Finally Javelins flew from Duxford as part of the Quick Reaction Alert system but Duxford was reckoned inadequate for use by Lightnings, so closed in July 1961, although trial bore-holes were sunk in preparation for silos to hold the un-developed Blue Streak IRBM. Duxford now serves as an outpost of the Imperial War Museum.

10 Fowlmere was built in 1918 as No. 31 TDS with the same set-up of buildings as Duxford, but everything was demolished in 1923. Early in 1940 a fighter airfield was started on a different site as a satellite of Duxford flying Spitfires throughout the Battle of Britain. Late in 1941 a US Eagle squadron moved in with Hurricanes. In March 1943 two Sommerfield runways were laid along with eighty concrete pads by W & C French, and a T2 hangar (3653/42) supplemented the seven blisters. The technical area was centred on Manor Farm with the main stores and MT section in converted farm-buildings. The 339th Fighter Group VIIIth USAAF (Station 378) brought their P-51s to carry out bomber escort duties, cover for airborne operations and ground strafing missions. By the end of 1945 the action was over and the land was quickly returned to agriculture. A re-clad T2 hangar is thought to be on a different site from the one it originally occupied.

11 Glatton (now Conington) was built by US Army 809th Engineer Battalion to open as Station 130 in January 1944. The 457th Bomb Group of VIIIth USAAF flew pre-D-Day raids on targets in northern France, and then into Germany. The airfield closed in early 1946. The site was unusual in that Rose Court Farm was allowed to continue in occupation in the middle of the triangle of runways. The airfield had two T2 hangars, a watch office (12779/41) and hutted accommodation for almost 3,000 personnel, round about the average for a bomber station. The Braithwaite water tank on its tower can be seen from the A1, and a standby-set house (8760/42) stands near the church. An engineering works

on the Pondersbridge-Ramsey St Mary's road, possibly Peck's, is reputed to have re-homed Glatton's MT shed, and one of its T2 hangars (3653/42), re-erected off Peterborough's Fengate for use by British Road Services in the 1960s, still stands on Nursery Lane as a self-store centre.

12 Gransden Lodge opened as a satellite of Tempsford (Bedfordshire) in 1942. A Wireless Investigation Flight conducted tests on GEE the navigation aid. Other experiments included work on H2S by the Bombing Development Unit, and then by the Pathfinder Navigational Training Unit in 1943. Although vacated by early 1946, one 2,000 yard runway was kept in use for emergency landings in the 1950s. There were two T2 hangars and a site prepared for a B1, un-built by October 1944. The surviving watch office was the standard model for bomber satellites (13726/41). The operations block is one of the only other surviving buildings.

13 Graveley too was a satellite of Tempsford (Bedfordshire), opening in March 1942, but soon coming under the control of Wyton as part of the Pathfinder force, flying Halifaxes, and replacing Alconbury. A year later, as an independent command, it flew off Halifaxes and Lancasters on strategic bombing missions. Graveley was the only airfield in this part of the country to be equipped with FIDO which enabled aircraft to land in the fog. It closed in late 1946, but returned to use as a Relief Landing Ground for Oakington ten years later until the late 1950s. Three T2 hangars and a B1 were provided, and a watch office for bomber satellites (7345/41) with an extension (4170/43).

Hardwick Farm was identified in 1911 as a landing ground for aircraft supporting the military manoeuvres. During the First World War it operated as a private FTS. Its location is variously given as TL370571 which is the location for the present-day farm, and 346595 which lies in the middle of what was, thirty years later, to become Bourn airfield. (Not to be confused with Hardwick bomber airfield in Norfolk.)

Horseheath was a Landing Ground in the First World War, and a bombing decoy site in the Second.

14 Horsey Toll started as a private flying field in 1929 and was part of the Civil Air Guard scheme in 1938. In 1941 Morrisons Engineering Ltd of Croydon (Surrey) took over the airfield as a Civilian Repair Organisation specialising in the repair and adaptation of Hurricanes, handling over 600 of the different marques in the course of the war. A road was laid from the A605 with a concrete bridge crossing Oxney Dyke, and W & C French with local builders Messrs. Cracknell and Messrs. Hawkins, built three new MAP hangars, an A1, a Super Robins and a Robins 'B', which still stand. There is a three-bay MT garage, workshops for repairing instruments and engines, and a canteen. The site now stores heavy plant.

15 Kimbolton was built by W & C French as a satellite of Molesworth. In late 1942 the 379th Bombardment Group of VIIIth USAAF (Station 117) took over both Molesworth and Kimbolton carrying out nearly 10,500 sorties in 330 operations, the most of any VIIIth Air Force unit, over France and Germany until June 1945 when operations ceased. The airfield had two T2 hangars, a standard watch office (12779/41) and hutted accommodation. The RAF ran a recruit training centre for a short while after the war. A few Nissen huts and a tb double Link Trainer (4188/42) remain.

16 Little Staughton opened late in 1942 as an Advanced Air Depot of the VIIIth USAAF (Station 127), functioning as such through 1943. It had three concrete runways, three T2

hangars and a number of Robins hangars, now re-located from their original positions. The watch office (13726/41) and its accompanying Nissen hut Fire Tender Shelter (12410/41) and tb Night Flying Equipment Store (12411/41) still form a recognisable group. A Butler Combat Hangar and Butler Warehouses were added by the USAAF. Virtually all the airfield buildings were either tb or hutted and many of these remain, representing an almost complete survival of a utility airfield of the period. Tb buildings include the Squadron CO's office (7895/41), guardhouse (18366/40), dinghy shed (2901/43), armoury (18365/40), gas defence centre (48/40) and the gas respirator store and workshop (13730/41). Nissen huts were used as maintenance staff workshops (12777/41) and general purpose huts. The main workshops (5540/42) and main stores (2883/43) each comprised a pair of Romney huts linked by a tb annexe. The airfield was returned to RAF 8 Group in January 1944, when Pathfinder missions over France and Germany commenced, continuing until September 1945 when flying ceased. The airfield is now an industrial estate which, over the years, has hosted aviation-related enterprises.

Lords Bridge was an odd combination of bomb dump, chemical weapons repository and, from 1942, a Forced Landing Field for 22 EFTS and No. 4 FIS at Cambridge. The site opened as a RAF Forward Ammunition Depot in November 1939 run by 95MU storing up to 8 kilotons of high-explosive bombs for 2 and 3 Groups, Bomber Command, in two groups of six-cell HE magazines. Pyrotechnics for the Pathfinder Force were also stored in Nissen huts. From August 1942 until January 1944 it was VIIIth USAAF Station 599 storing a range of bombs, SAA and chemical weapons. USAAF use meant that stocks of 2,000lb and 4,000lb bombs were returned to Reserve Depots. Prior to the D-Day softening up operations, an extra 17,000 bombs were stored at Lords Bridge, and stocks of chemical weapons for retaliation against first-use by the enemy. In 1944, Lords Bridge was equipped to carry out the delicate and highly-dangerous operation of filling gas-bombs weighing up to 65lbs. The depot had bulk underground tanks holding 250 tons of each of the *Runcol* and *Pyro* produced by ICI at Rhydymwyn (Clwyd) and Runcorn (Cheshire), as well as buildings in which the filling took place, along with bath-houses and de-contamination facilities. After the war Lords Bridge dispersed some of its stock of HE bombs to dormant airfields including Bourn, Wratting Common, Witchford and Gransden Lodge. By 1948 Lords Bridge was the only serviceable depot but all were put under Care and Maintenance until at least June 1954, finally closing in 1957. The site then became Cambridge University's Astronomical Observatory, but remnants of the depot's administration compound including the decontamination centre, an MT garage, as well as some of the twenty or so Pyrotechnic Stores, can still be seen. The filling depot itself was only handed over in 1997 after the land had been thoroughly cleansed.

17 Mepal opened in early 1943 as a sub-station of Waterbeach operating Lancasters against targets in Germany. It had a standard bomber field layout with one B1 and two T2 hangars, a watch office (12779/41) and mainly tb buildings and huts, scattered over twelve or more sites to the east of the flying field with its three runways. Flying ceased in 1946, but in 1958 it was selected as a site for three THOR missiles, an IRBM carrying a nuclear warhead with a range of under 2,000 miles (3,200 km). Mepal was in a group with HQ at Feltwell (Norfolk) and with other sites at North Pickenham (Norfolk), Shepherd's Grove and Tuddenham (both Suffolk).

18 Molesworth operated in the First World War as a Home Defence airfield used by No. 75 Squadron, until late 1917, when the airfield was abandoned. A new airfield was planned in 1939 and built through 1940 opening in May 1941. Briefly occupied by a number of units during 1942, no missions were flown. In February 1942 it was selected for use by the USAAF (Station 107) and the runways were extended and two T2 hangars added to the

'J' hangar (5836/39) already there along with a watch office (518/40). The majority of the buildings which housed the 3,000 personnel of the 303rd Bombardment Group were of temporary brick. Apart from the watch office, the only permanent brick buildings were the pyrotechnic and bombsight stores (2847/37 and 1906/42). The Group's B-17s carried out missions over France and Germany until April 1945. In 1945 it reverted to RAF 12 Group, Fighter Command as a pilot and squadron Conversion Unit for Meteors into 1946, followed by intermittent use as a Relief Landing Ground. After a period under Care and Maintenance it went to USAFE in 1952, its runways being extended for use as a transport base. In July 1987 it was handed over to 303 Tactical Missile Wing, IIIrd US Air Force, as a cruise missile base. The storage bunkers are protected by earth traverses, wire fences and watch-towers. It now processes ELINT.

19 Oakington was an Expansion Period airfield, with work starting in 1939, and which opened in July 1940 while still unfinished. Blenheims were replaced in October 1940 by Stirlings which were flown from here throughout the war, having adopted the Pathfinder role in August 1942. The station had been built to Expansion Period standards but for its two 'J' hangars and a 'villa' type watch office (5845/39). In early 1941 the three concrete runways were completed, making it easier for the bombers to operate effectively, and one B1 and two T2 hangars were added, the first as an aircraft repair shed, and the latter to accommodate the eight Mosquitoes of No. 1409 Meteorological Flight. Transport Command took over in July 1945 operating until 1950. It was then the turn of Training Command with No. 1 Flying Training School, 1950–51, using Graveley as a Relief Landing Ground. After they left it became No. 206 Advanced Flying School, 1951–54 and No. 5 Flying Training School, 1954–62 using Vampires and Meteors. From then No. 5 FTS continued but with Varsities until the school closed in 1974. After that, the Army Air Corps took over, training on Scout, Gazelle and Lynx helicopters. Most of the station survived until well into the 2,000s being occupied by The Royal Anglian Regiment, and then by a Home Office immigration centre, but the whole site is earmarked for development as a new township, linked to Cambridge by the bizarre guided bus, and most of it has already (2013) been demolished.

20 Peterborough (Westwood Farm) began life as No. 1 Aircraft Storage Unit in 1932, with one 'A' hangar and five more projected. The extra hangars never materialised but the aircraft park operated until 1935 with nine canvas Bessoneau hangars. Soon after No. 7 SFTS had been formed using Hawker Hart Trainers, six Bellman hangars (959/37) had been built. An officers' mess (7035/30), sergeants' mess (325/30) and station office (714/30), all three of which survive, ground instruction blocks, synthetic training facilities and hutted accommodation made up this atypical station. In 1940 No. 7 SFTS left for, Kingston, Ontario to become to 31SFTS, and a series of schools training Fleet Air Arm, Polish and Free French pilots occupied the station. In 1946 flying ceased and most of the site has been absorbed into Peterborough New Town. One of the Bellman hangars has been re-erected at Sibson.

Portholme Meadow, Godmanchester, was home to No. 211 TDS for a few months in 1917, prior to a move to Scopwick (Digby), Lincolnshire, as No. 50 TDS in 1918.

Quy Park had been requisitioned by the army early in the war, but by 1943 part had become the depot of the RAF Airfield Construction Service. Training activities revolved around the handling and transporting of heavy plant, and work with the Transport Research Laboratory to investigate site testing and the development of stable surfaces for airfields. Detachments maintained home airfields, built some of the Advanced Landing Grounds used by the 2nd

Tactical Air Force before D-Day, constructed further advanced landing grounds in France and Holland, and built airfields all over the world in Iceland, Malta, North Africa, Singapore and Kowloon.

Sawston Hall (Station 371) served as HQ VIIIth USAAF 66th Fighter Wing with eleven airfields under command including Duxford and Fowlmere.

21 Sibson opened in July 1940 as a Relief Landing Ground for Peterborough. Over the next year it was used by a variety of training units but reverted to Peterborough which based two Flights of trainee pilots there in 1943. Within a year most activity had moved to quieter skies. It closed fully in late 1946 and is now used as a privately run parachute school. There is a T1 hangar which may not be on its original site, and a Bellman which is a post-War import from Peterborough. Buildings, mostly tb, remain from the communal sites to the west of the B621. High Leys Cottage, among other existing buildings on the site, was adapted for RAF use in the war.

22 Snailwell was initially opened in 1941 as an Army Co-operation Command station flying Lysanders. Throughout 1942–43 Typhoons operated from here flying anti-shipping missions, and trials of aircraft to support ground operations were carried out. Snailwell also served into 1943 as a satellite for the VIIIth USAAF fighters from Duxford, and as a IXth USAAF base for tactical fighter units, as Station 361. In late 1944 the RAF (Belgian) Initial Training School moved in, staying into 1946 when the station closed. Nothing now remains of this once busy airfield which had a Bellman hangar, a watch office (12779/41) and Blister hangars.

23 Somersham began as a bombing decoy for Wyton (TL342765) but also functioned as an airfield for covert flights, probably by SOE personnel, using Lysander aircraft. This was centred on TL358763, with a Nissen hut and cottage close by at TL 356765. It was also used for parachute drops of canisters, presumably for practice, by Stirlings.

24 Steeple Morden opened in September 1940 as a satellite of Bassingbourn, whose bombers were engaged in missions over Europe. It was then allocated to VIIIth USAAF (Station 122) as a bomber base, runways being laid in autumn 1942, and at least one hangar, probably a T2, erected, but was soon deemed unsuitable. It was used by PR aircraft and then by Fighter Groups until after the war when it closed down, and was returned to agriculture. The operations block and some Romney huts survive.

25 Upwood (actually Simmonds Farm, Bury) was initially a Home Defence aerodrome, and then a training station for Nos 190 and 191 Night Training Squadrons until 1919 when it closed. It re-opened on a new site in January 1937 as a light bomber airfield flying Battles, and then Blenheims as an OTU, by 1941 using Warboys as a satellite. It is the archetype Expansion Period airfield with four 'C' type hangars and, originally a 'Fort' type watch office. In 1943 the Pathfinder Navigational Training Unit moved in and the airfield was given three concrete and tarmac runways, and a replacement watch office (12779/41). Mosquitoes equipped with Oboe were stationed here until the end of the war flying over 4,000 sorties. For the ten years after the war heavy bombers, Lancasters, and then Lincolns, were based here, followed by Canberras, whose brief stay until late 1959, included participation in the Suez operation of 1956. The USAF(E) carried out NCO training in the original officers' mess, and the RAF School of Education was in residence from 1964–73. Part of the site is still (2013) occupied by an emergency USAF hospital, geared to receiving large numbers of wounded, flown in from overseas. Many of the buildings of the

Expansion Period remain including the hangars (4292/35), guard-room (469/38), officers' mess (570–572/37), sergeants' mess (3484/36), armoury (4829/35), institute (1482/36) and a number of barrack-blocks (1132/38 and 2357/36). Much of the technical site such as the station workshops (6957/37), and the synthetic training structures, including the link trainer (12386/36), also survive. There are three concrete runways, 6,000, 4,800 and 4,200 feet long (1,850, 1,475 and 1,300m), and bomber dispersals. Sadly the buildings have been subject to official vandalism in the guise of urban warfare training, and opportunities for their constructive re-use have been missed.

Walcot Hall (Station 372) near Barnack first served as Wittering's remote Operations Room and, from 1942, as HQ VIIIth USAAF 67th Fighter Wing with seven airfields under command stretching through Norfolk and Suffolk to Northamptonshire and the north of Lincolnshire.

26 Warboys was originally planned as a satellite of Upwood but opened in 1940 as a bomber airfield flying Stirlings, and then, in 1942, Wellingtons, as part of the Pathfinder Force. By early 1943 resident squadrons had been converted to Lancasters, and in June, the Pathfinder Force Navigational Training Unit was formed at Upwood, but opted to use the concrete runways at Warboys, operating until 1945, but from 1944, flying H2S- and Oboe-equipped Mosquitoes. As an airfield built in wartime, its buildings were utilitarian. There were the usual two T2s and a B1 hangar, and a Bomber Satellite watch office with attached briefing-room (15898/40). One of the few permanent brick buildings was the WT Station serving Wyton (7905/38). Virtually all the other buildings were of tb or hutting. Several of these huts remain at Old Hurst including the Sergeants' Mess on communal site 2, and the former officers' quarters on communal site 10, now the village hall. Having virtually closed in 1945 Warboys came back to life in 1959 as a Bloodhound SAM site, protecting the THOR IRBM sites. This occupied a new enclave in the middle of the flying field with its own guard-room and HQ building. A double-gabled shed was built to service the Ram-jet motors which powered the missiles. The site closed in 1963.

27 Waterbeach was planned as an Expansion Period airfield in 1939, and opened in January 1941 flying Wellingtons. Although many of the buildings were to pre-War standard such as the 'Villa' type watch office (5845/39) and much of the domestic and technical sites, compromises were made with the hangars which ended up as two 'J' types, two T2s, a T1 and a B1. Early in 1942 the Wellingtons were replaced by Stirlings, which stayed until late 1943 when they, in turn, were substituted for Lancasters which saw out the war, carrying out hundreds of sorties as part of 3 Group's Main Force. The station then went to Transport Command flying Liberators repatriating thousands of troops from all over the world. On 1 March 1950 came another transfer, this time to Fighter Command, and the airfield was up-graded accordingly. In 1963 the RAF handed the airfield over to the army which installed 39 Regiment RE, specialising in airfield construction. In 1994 Stirling House, the administrative centre for maintenance of US, NATO and MOD property was built. The REs are now destined for RAF Kinloss in the Highlands, and Waterbeach will most probably become a new township.

28 Witchford was a standard wartime bomber airfield which opened in June 1943 flying Stirlings in raids over Germany. From November 1943 Lancasters were flown against targets such as Berlin, Magdeburg and Schweinfurt, suffering the highest loss rate of any Lancaster unit. The airfield was built with the usual allocation of two T2 and one B1 hangars, and a general-purpose watch office (343/43). All the accommodation and technical functions were in tb buildings or huts. One re-clad B1 hangar and some Nissen huts remain on an industrial estate. Off the Witchford by-pass are some BCF huts and a tb building, part of a communal site.

29 Wittering initially known as Stamford, started life as a Home Defence fighter station in 1916, but had been planned as No. 1 Training Depot Station, functioning as such throughout the war. It was provided with the standard three double GS Sheds and an Aircraft Repair Shed, along with mainly hutted accommodation. Although placed under Care and Maintenance in 1920 it was recalled to service in 1924 as the new home of the Central Flying School, and was completely modernised prior to opening in 1926 as RAF Wittering. In 1935 No. 11 SFTS was set up but, within three years, Wittering's role had changed as it became a Fighter Command Sector Station. In the early years of the Second World War the station was active both flying sorties to protect industrial targets in the Midlands against enemy bombers and also developing air-fighting techniques with a variety of aircraft, particularly night-fighters. As the balance of the war changed, so did Wittering's role, and in 1943 the Air Fighting Development Unit moved in, one of a number of such units which trialled aircraft and tested tactics. The station boasted the longest grass runway of any, an early prototype for emergency runways elsewhere such as Woodbridge (Suffolk). Wittering (Station 368) also enjoyed shared use for a while, with the VIIIth USAAF's 20th Fighter Wing who overflowed out of Kingscliffe (Northamptonshire). In 1944, Collyweston became home to the Gunnery Research Unit which moved up from Exeter, to join the resident collection of captured enemy aircraft which toured the country. At the end of the war Collyweston was integrated into the Wittering airfield, where it remains. Wittering continued its development role with the Fighter Leaders School (1944); the Central Fighter Establishment (1944–45); and the Fighter Interception Unit (1944). After the war fighter squadrons alternated with training units such as the Flying Training Command Instructors' School in 1946, and No. 1 Initial Training School, 1948–50. The airfield was up-graded in the mid-1950s, initially as a Fighter Command base, with a new runway and other improvements which included an off-site radio station across the A1 in Burghley Park (TF060043). A change of plan saw four ORPs being built for the V-Bombers which were around until 1970. Fighters then returned, the Hunters staying until 1978, followed by the Harriers, which remained until 2012. The airfield displays a rich cross-section of RAF architecture from all this activity: barrack-blocks, station offices, parachute store and guard-room from the Home Defence period of the 1920s; two 'C' type hangars and fuel-tanker sheds from the Expansion Period; the operations block from the Second World War; the control tower, designed for 'V' Bomber stations in 1955, a Gaydon hangar, and Blue Danube storage from the 1950s; Blue Steel building, atomic bomb preparation and storage compound, and V-Force operations control building from the 1960s.

30 Wratting Common opened in mid-1943 flying Stirlings as part of RAF 3 Group's Main Force, attacking targets in Germany. As well as its normal complement of two T2 and one B1 hangars, it received an additional pair of T2s specifically for the storage and maintenance of Horsa gliders prior to the D-Day airborne operations. The station finished the war operating Lancasters. Following use by storage and maintenance units the airfield closed in late 1947, and was returned to agriculture. The B1 hangar and one of the T2s survive along with some huts.

31 Wyton opened in 1916 as a training station, with No. 31 Training Squadron of 7 Wing, in occupation until 1918. The airfield lay on the south side of the A141 road opposite the existing estate cottages near Hungary Hall. The site was abandoned and the buildings demolished. Chosen as the location for an Expansion Period airfield in 1935, it opened in July 1936, becoming HQ 2 Group RAF Bomber Command in 1938, its squadrons being equipped with Blenheims. It had four 'C' type hangars and a 'Villa' type watch office (2328/39), along with all the other standard buildings of its genre. During the Second World War Wyton flew sorties in Blenheims, Wellingtons and Stirlings until August 1942 when it became 8 (Pathfinder) Group HQ, its administrative centre moving to Castle Hill House

in Huntingdon in 1943. The Pathfinder squadrons flew Lancasters and Mosquitoes from Wyton until the end of the war. The station's role soon changed to photo reconnaissance using, mainly, Canberras. During the 1980s the airfield was defended by Bloodhound II SAMs. In 1992 the airfield closed to flying and the four pavilions of the Defence Logistics Organisation, Equipment Support (Air) were built. Currently (2013) the Defence Geospatial Intelligence Fusion Unit is moving into the Pathfinder Building. In April 2012, the station became a Joint Services establishment and will be receiving 42 Engineer Regiment (Geographic), RE. Although nothing remains from the earliest period of Wyton's history, despite continuous updatings and changes of role, much from the Expansion Period survives. From the Second World War, a shortened T2 hangar for Mosquitoes, a rare AA Dome Trainer, and numerous huts remain. Much evidence of the 'V' Force era has been covered over by the DLO blocks but these more recent additions have contributed another layer to the fabric of this long-time RAF station.

Yelling near St Neots was a Home Defence landing-ground during the First World War and would have been equipped with little more than a hut and a petrol tank, beside a grass landing-strip.

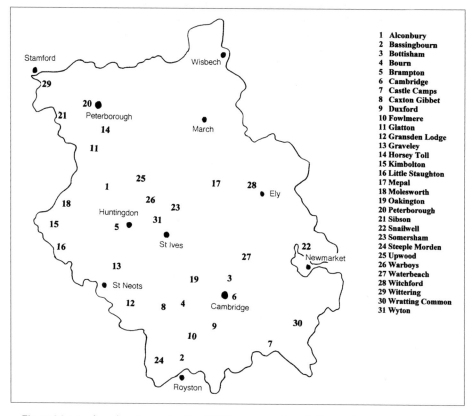

Fig. 19 Map to show locations of major airfield using numbers in Appendix 5.

Appendix 6

Designation of Airfields under Taylor Report, 1940

(levels of airfield defences and garrison allocations determined by Taylor's criteria)

IIa: Duxford, Castle Camps, Fowlmere and Wittering (existing fighter stations)

IIa: Alconbury, Bassingbourn, Oakington, Upwood, Graveley, Wyton (existing bomber stations)

IIa: Bourn, Snailwell, Molesworth, Kimbolton, Little Gransden, Little Staughton, Steeple Morden, Waterbeach and Warboys: (bomber stations under construction)

IIb: Peterborough (within 5 miles of VPs)

III: Caxton Gibbet, Cambridge and Sibson

Appendix 7

Air Defence: Bombing Decoys

Alwalton	Q/K site for RAF Wittering	TL152949
Babraham	SF site for Cambridge	TL518522
Benwick	Q site for RAF Upwood and Warboys	TL345918
Boxworth	Q site for RAF Oakington and Tempsford	TL330663
Coldham	QL/QF site for March railway yards	TL452211
Colne	Q site for RAF Wyton	TL389776
Comberton	SF site for Cambridge (relocated)	TL398569
Comberton	SF site for Cambridge (relocation)	TL399573
Eye	QL then SF site for Peterborough	TF264009
Fulbourn	SF site for Cambridge	TL527545
Grafham	Q site for RAF Molesworth	TL177688
Great Eversden	Q site for RAF Duxford	TL337536
Haddenham	Q/K site for RAF Wyton and Waterbeach	TL467775
Horseheath	Q/K site for RAF Duxford	TL587482
Little Gidding	Q site for RAF Polebrook	TL116817
Littleport	Q site for RAF Mildenhall	TL584852
Maxey	Q site for RAF Wittering	TF143077
Rampton	Q site for RAF Oakington	TL466697
Soham	Q site for RAF Waterbeach	TL566730
Somersham	Q site for RAF Wyton	TL345760
Stanground	QL then SF site for Peterborough	TL233958

Appendix 8

Locations used by
Home Guard (HG) Units

Ailsworth, Manor house cellars: HQ 'A' Coy 2 Northants (Soke of Peterborough) Bn
Cambridge, Barton Road: rifle range
Cambridge, 4 Bridge Street: HQ 101 Cambridgeshire ZAA Battery HG
Cambridge Guildhall: Cambridge HQ HG Group/Zone Commander (5,6 and 7 Bns.)
Cambridge, Downing Place, Music School: HQ 5 Cambs Bn; and Zone QM's Stores,
Cambridge, Mill Road, 8–9 Broadway: HQ 'A' Coy 5 Cambs Bn
Cambridge, Hills Road, Boys' Grammar School: HQ 'B' Coy 5 Cambs Bn
Cambridge, Grange Road, University Library: HQ 'C' Coy 5 Cambs Bn
Cambridge, Castle Hill/Shire Hall Keep and Battle HQ 5 Cambs Bn HG
Cambridge, Chesterton Road, Little Theatre: HQ 'D' Coy 5 Cambs Bn
Cambridge, Milton Road: HQ 'E' Coy 5 Cambs Bn
Cambridge, Chesterton Road, Cambridge Instrument Co: HQ 'F' Coy 5 Cambs Bn
Cambridge, Chesterton: 32 AA Brigade School, 1943
Cambridge, Station, District Manager's Office: HQ 'G' (LNER) Coy 5 Cambs Bn
Cambridge, East Road Drill Hall: garrison armoury
Cambridge, 1 Regent Street, Post Office: HQ + 'C' Coy 6 Cambs (34 GPO) Bn
Cambridge, Bridge Street, Quayside: HQ 8 University STC (Mobile Reserve) Bn
Cambridge, Midsummer Common, Ferry House: HQ 7 Cambs (Mobile Reserve) Bn
Castor, Riding School: Battle HQ 2 Northants (Soke of Peterborough) Bn HG
Chatteris, The Wheatsheaf PH then Church Rooms: HQ + 'D' Coy 3 Isle of Ely Bn (then to March)
Ely, Barton Road, Drill Hall: miniature range.
Ely, Egremont Street, Badminton Hall: HQ + 'A' & 'B' Coys 2 (Isle of Ely) Bn
Eye: HQ No. 3 Platoon, 2 Northants (Soke of Peterborough) Bn
Fulbourn, Queens Farm: HQ 'A' Coy 3 Cambs Bn
Grantchester, (Toft Hall, Toft): HQ 'A' Coy 4 Cambs Bn
Great Shelford: HQ 'F' Coy 3 Cambridgeshire Bn
Haddenham: HQ 'D' Coy 2 (Isle of Ely) Bn
Helpston Quarry: grenade range used by 1 & 2 Northamptonshire Bns
Hildersham: HQ 'C' Coy 1 Cambridgeshire Bn
Impington, Wood House: HQ 'C' Coy 1 Cambridgeshire Bn
Littleport: 'C' Coy 2 (Isle of Ely) Bn
Longstowe Park: battle training centre
Madingley, (Childerley Hall): HQ 'B' Coy 1 Cambridgeshire Bn
March: 'C' & 'D' Coys 2 Isle of Ely Bn then HQ 3 (Isle of Ely) Bn
March, Whitemoor: firing range

Newborough, Bull Inn: HQ No. 2 Platoon, 'D' Coy, 2 (Soke of Peterborough) Bn

Newmarket, Doric Cinema: training centre, 2 (Cambridgeshire & Suffolk) Bn

Newmarket, Egerton House: Battle HQ 2 (Cambridgeshire & Suffolk) Bn

Newmarket, High Street, Jockey Club: HQ 2 (Cambridgeshire & Suffolk) Bn

Offord Manor: Battle HQ, South Huntingdonshire Bn

Peterborough, Dogsthorpe Manor: Billiards Room, HQ 'C' Coy 2 Northants (Soke of Peterborough) Bn

Peterborough, Dogsthorpe Manor Farm: HQ 'D' Coy and No. 1 Platoon, 2 Northants (Soke of Peterborough) Bn; also training area

Peterborough, Dogsthorpe Brickyards: range used by 1 & 2 Northamptonshire Bns

Peterborough, Lincoln Road, Gayhurst: Civil Defence Centre

Peterborough, Lincoln Road, Fox & Vergette Horse Repository: HQ Peterborough Home Guard, May 1940

Peterborough, Northfield Road, Millfield, Unity Hall: HQ 101 HG ZAA Battery, later HQ 10 HG AA Regt. (Cambridge, Leicester & Peterborough)

Peterborough, Lincoln Road Drill Hall: HQ 1 Northants (City of Peterborough) Bn

Peterborough, London Road Drill Hall: HQ 1 Huntingdonshire Bn

Peterborough, London Road, Drill Hall, (31 Priestgate from 1942): HQ 'A' Company, 1 Huntingdonshire Bn

Peterborough, Park Road, The Kings School: HQ 'C' Coy 1 Northamptonshire (City of Peterborough) Bn

Peterborough, 25 Priestgate, Milton Estates Office: HQ 2 Northamptonshire (Soke of Peterborough) Bn

Peterborough, Mountsteven Avenue, Walton Senior School: Battle HQ 2 Northamptonshire (Soke of Peterborough) Bn

Peterborough, Westwood Works: HQ 'B' Coy 1 Northants (City of Peterborough) Bn

Quy, Bush Farm: 0.22" rifle range & ammunition store, 3 Cambridgeshire Bn

Quy Vicarage: platoon HQ, 3 Cambridgeshire Bn

St Ives, Bridge Street: original HQ 2 South Huntingdonshire Bn

St Ives, Broadway, Wych House: HQ 2 South Huntingdonshire Bn HG

St Ives: Enderby's Printing Works: first night-time HQ 2 South Huntingdonshire Bn

St Ives, London Road, Dolphin Inn: Battle HQ, 2 South Huntingdonshire Bn

Sawston, Brooklands: HQ 'B' Coy 3 Cambridgeshire Bn

(Uffington House, Gun-room & Loose-box: HQ 'B' Coy 2 Northamptonshire (Soke of Peterborough) Bn) site in Lincolnshire

Werrington, Lincoln Road, Cock Inn: HQ 'C' Coy 2 Northamptonshire (Soke of Peterborough) Bn (formerly Bn HQ)

West Wickham: HQ 'D' Coy 3 Cambridgeshire Bn

Appendix 9

Command and Control in the Second World War

Babraham Hall: HQ 22 Armoured Brigade, 1940
Cambridge, Brooklands: Administrative section of RAF No. 74 Wing, 1941–43
Cambridge, Montague Road, St Regis House: HQ Cambridge District, Eastern Command
Cambridge, 'Binsted', no. 5 Herschel Road: HQ Cambridge Area, Eastern Command
Cambridge, King's College: HQ Cambridge sub-Area (then to no. 62 Grange Road)
Cambridge, no. 62 Grange Road: HQ Cambridge sub-Area, Eastern Command
Cambridge Guildhall: Cambridge HQ Home Guard Group/Zone Commander
Cambridge, Trinity College: US planning for D-Day, 28–31 March 1944
Duxford: Sector HQ and Operations Room 11 Group RAF Fighter Command, 1940
Huntingdon Castle Hill House: HQ No. 2 Group RAF Bomber Command, 1939–42
Huntingdon, Castle Hill House: HQ No. 8 (Pathfinder) Group RAF Bomber Command from June 1943
Huntingdon, Brampton Grange: HQ No. 7 (Training) Group RAF Bomber Command until October 1942
Huntingdon, Brampton Grange: HQ 1st Air Division, VIIIth USAAF, with Combat Wings at Bassingbourn, Molesworth, Thurleigh and Polebrook
Huntingdon, Brampton Park: HQ 1st Air Division, VIIIth USAAF
Huntingdon, St Mary's drill hall: HQ Huntingdon sub-Area, Eastern Command
Madingley Hall: HQ II Corps and 2 Armoured Division, 1940
Newton Hall: HQ 2 Support Group, 2 Armoured Division, 1940
Sawston Hall: HQ 66th Fighter Wing VIIIth USAAF
Walcot Hall, Barnack: remote Operations Room for RAF Wittering, 1940–42
Walcot Hall, Barnack: HQ 67th Fighter Wing, VIIIth USAAF, from 1942
Wittering: Sector HQ and Operations Room 12 Group RAF Fighter Command, 1940
Wyton: HQ No. 8 Pathfinder Group RAF Bomber Command until June 1943

Appendix 10

Military Hospitals and Welfare

First World War

Abbots Ripton Hall, auxiliary hospital
Balsham, Park House VAD hospital
Buckden, Buckden Towers VAD hospital
Burghley House, VAD hospital (affiliated 5th Northern General Hospital, Leicester)
Cambridge, Addenbrookes Hospital (overspill for 1st Eastern General)
Cambridge, 1st Eastern General Hospital (RAMC, TF) 1500-bed hospital, open-air hutted hospital built on King's and Clare Colleges' cricket-grounds
Cambridge, 39 Green Street, HQ 1st Eastern General Hospital, then to Trinity College
Cambridge, Barnwell, military VD hospital, 1916
Cambridge, Cherry Hinton, military VD hospital
Cambridge, Huntley VAD hospital
Cambridge, St Chad's Hospital
Cambridge, Wordsworth Grove Red Cross hospital
Ely, Silver Street VAD hospital
Fordham, The Manse VAD hospital
Fulbourn VAD hospital
Great Shelford VAD hospital
Huntingdon County Hospital
Huntingdon, Lawrence Court relief hospital
Huntingdon, Brunswick Villas Red Cross hospital moved to…
Huntingdon, Walden House Red Cross hospital
Kimbolton Hall VAD hospital
Linton, Manor House hospital
Newmarket, Severalls House hospital
Newmarket, Sussex Lodge hospital
Peterborough, Milton Hall auxiliary hospital
St Ives VAD hospital
St Neots VAD hospital
Sawtry, Whitehall VAD hospital
Shepreth VAD hospital
Whittlesford VAD hospital
Willingham VAD hospital
Wimpole Park, VAD auxiliary hospital
Wisbech, North Cambridgeshire Hospital
Wisbech, Selwyn Hall VAD hospital

Second World War

Babraham, Gog Magog Hills Red Cross Convalescent Home/Auxiliary Hospital
Burghley House, convalescent ward in the Orangery
Cambridge, freeze-drying plant used by Army Blood Transfusion Service
Cambridge, 4 Gresham Road, Red Cross Convalescent Home/Auxiliary Hospital
Cambridge, Silbury, Grange Road Red Cross Convalescent Home/Auxiliary Hospital
Cambridge, 730 Newmarket Road, NAAFI bungalow behind ROC centre
Cambridge, Trumpington Hall Red Cross Convalescent Home/Auxiliary Hospital
Conington Castle, Red Cross Convalescent Home/Auxiliary Hospital
Diddington Hall, US Eastern Base Section General Hospital, 600-bed EMS (rail)
Elton Hall, Red Cross Convalescent Home/Auxiliary Hospital
Ely, The Palace Red Cross Convalescent Home/Auxiliary Hospital
Ely, Princess Mary's RAF Hospital, 1939
Great Shelford, The Grange Red Cross Convalescent Home/Auxiliary Hospital
Hinchingbroke House, Red Cross Convalescent Home/Auxiliary Hospital
Histon, US Eastern Base Section General Hospital, 600-bed EMS
Huntingdon, Priory House, Freemasons' HQ, club for US servicemen, 1942
Peterborough, Long Causeway, soldiers' club, November 1939
Peterborough, The Lindens, Red Cross Convalescent Home/Auxiliary Hospital
Peterborough, Midland Road, Memorial Hospital
Peterborough, Padholme Road, NAAFI offices and warehouse
Peterborough, Paston Hall, Red Cross Convalescent Home/Auxiliary Hospital
Peterborough, Thorpe Hall, annexe of Memorial Hospital, 1941
St Ives Market-place, NAAFI hut (now Girl Guides)
Soham, The Moat Red Cross Convalescent Home/Auxiliary Hospital
Stibbington Hall, sick quarters for RAF Wittering

Cold War

Ely, Princess Mary's RAF General Hospital
Upwood, USAFE 500-1,000-bed Medical Centre
Upwood, RAF Aviation Medicine Training Centre, 1960, to North Luffenham 1964
Waterbeach, proposed USAFE Contingency 500-1,000-bed hospital

Appendix 11

Second World War
Prisoner-of-War Camps

Cambridge, Walpole Road, 1942
Ely, Barton Field, Camp 26
Ely, West Fen Militia Camp, Camp 130
Friday Bridge, Wisbech, Camp 90
Godmanchester, Farm Hall, Operation Epsilon debrief of German nuclear scientists
Histon, Milton Road, Camp 1025
Hinxton Grange, used by Camp 020 (Ham, Richmond-on-Thames)
Huntingdon, St Peter's Road
Kingscliffe, Bedford Purlieus, POW and Displaced Persons camp
Orton Longueville, Orton Hall
RAF Peterborough, POW and Displaced Persons camp
Sawtry, Woodwalton Lane
Thorney Camp
Trumpington, Camps 45 and 180
Wansford Camp
Yaxley Camp, now mushroom farm at TL 193930

Bibliography

ABERG, F.A.: *Medieval Moated Sites*; 1978, York, CBA Research Report 17

ABRAHAM, B: *Short Bros (Rochester & Bedford) Ltd*; 2006, in airfield Review 113, Thetford

AKEROYD, A. & CLIFFORD, C: *Huntingdon, Eight Centuries of History*; 2004, Derby

ANNISS, G.: *A History of Wisbech Castle*; 1977, Ely

BENNETT, E.: *Willow Hall, planned as a German HQ*; 30/7/1944, Sunday Express

BOWYER, M.: *Action Stations 1: East Anglia*; 1979 & 1990, Wellingborough

BOWYER. M.: *Action Stations 6: Cotswolds & Central Midlands*; 1983, Wellingborough

BOWYER, M.: *Action Stations Revisited, No. 1 Eastern England*; 2000, Manchester

BRADFORD, L.; personal communication re Devil's Ditch Civil War battery, 1980s

BROWN, A.E. & TAYLOR, C.C.; *Seventeenth Century Sconce at March*; Proceedings of the Cambridge Antiquarian Society, LXX, 1980

BROWNE, D.: *Roman Cambridgeshire*; 1977, Cambridge

CAMBRIDGESHIRE & ISLE OF ELY TERRITORIAL ASSOCIATION: *We Also Served*; 1944, Cambridge

CATTERMOLE, M. & WOLFE, A.: *Horace Darwin's shop: a history of the Cambridge Instrument Company 1878–1968*; 1987, Bristol

CESSFORD, C.: *Excavation of the Civil War bastion ditch of Cambridge Castle*; Proceedings of the Cambridge Antiquarian Society, XCVII, 2008

CHORLTON, M.: *Airfield Focus: Mepal & Witchford*; 2001, Peterborough

CHORLTON, M.: *Plane to Plane: The Story of Frederick Sage & Company, Limited Walton, Peterborough 1911–1936*; 2004, Cowbit

CLIFFORD, C. & AKEROYD, A.: *Huntingdonshire in the Second World War*; 2007, Stroud

COCROFT, W.: *Cold War Project Survey Report, Regional Seat of Government 4, Cambridge*; 1997, RCHME, Cambridge

COCROFT, W. & THOMAS, R.: *Cold War, Building for Nuclear Confrontation 1946–89*; 2003, Swindon

COOKSON, J.E.: *The English Volunteer Movement of the French Wars 1793–1815: Some Contexts*; in The Historical Journal 32.4 (1989), Cambridge

CRISP, G.: *The Supply of Explosives and Ammunition to the RAF in WW2*; in Airfield Review Vol. 10 Nos. 1, 1988 & 2, 1989 and No. 124, 2009

DELVE, K.: *The Military Airfields of Britain: East Midlands*; 2008, Ramsbury

FINCHAM, G.: *Durobrivae*; 2004, Stroud

FRANCIS, P.: *British Military Airfield Architecture;* 1996, Yeovil

FRANCIS, P. and CRISP, G.: *Military Command and Control Organisation*; 2008, Swindon (in CD form for English Heritage)

FRANCIS, P.: *Airfield Defences*; 2010, Ware

FRANK, Sir C.: *OPERATION EPSILON: The Farm Hall Transcripts*; 1993, The Institute of Physics Publishing, London

FRERE, S.S. & St JOSEPH, J.K.: *The Roman Fortress at Longthorpe*; in Britannia 5, 1974, London

GRAY, D.: *The Uncommon Soldiers, Peterborough & District 1914*; 2006, Peterborough

GRAY, D.: *Peterborough at War 1939-45*; 2011, Peterborough
HOWARTH, P.: *Caxton Gibbet EFTS Relief Landing Ground*; 2010, in Airfield Review, 126, Hoxne
JONES, D.: *Summer of Blood, The Peasants' Revolt of 1381*; 2009, London
KENYON, J.: *Castles, Town Defences & Artillery Fortifications in the United Kingdom & Ireland: a Bibliography 1945-2006;* 2008, Donington
KEYNES, G.L. & WHITE, H.G.; *Excavations at Earith Bulwark*, Proceedings of the Cambridge Antiquarian Society, 50, 1908
KING, D.J.C. & ALCOCK, L.: *Ringworks of England and Wales;* in Taylor, AJ (ed): *Chateau Gaillard* lll, (1966), 1969, Chichester
KING, D.J.C.: *Castellarium Anglicanum (index & bibliography)*; 1983, New York
KIRBY, T. & OOSTHUIZEN, S. (eds): *An Atlas of Cambridgeshire and Huntingdonshire History*; 2000, Cambridge
LIDDIARD, R.: *Castles in Context;* 2005, Macclesfield
LLOYD, C.L.: *A History of Napoleonic & American Prisoners-of-War, 1756-1816*; 2007, Woodbridge
MALIM, T.: *Stonea and the Roman Fens*; 2005, Stroud
OSBORNE, M.B.; *Cromwellian Fortifications in Cambridgeshire*, Huntingdon, 1990
OSBORNE, M.B.: *20th Century Defences in Britain: Cambridgeshire*; 2001, Market Deeping
OSBORNE, M.B.: *Defending Britain;* 2004, Stroud
OSBORNE, M.B.: *Always Ready, the drill halls of Britain's volunteer forces*; 2006, Leigh-on-Sea
OSBORNE, M.B.: *Pillboxes in Britain and Ireland;* 2008, Stroud
PALMER, W.M.; *Cambridge Castle*, 1928, Oleander Books, reprinted 1976
PICKSTONE, A. & MORTIMER, R.: *War Ditches, Cherry Hinton: Revisiting an Iron Age Hill-fort*; 2012, Proceedings of the Cambridgeshire Antiquarian Society, Volume CI
RCHM (E): *North-East Cambridgeshire*; 1972, HMSO
RCHM (E): *West Cambridgeshire*; 1968, HMSO
RCHM (E): *City of Cambridge*; two volumes, 1959, HMSO
RCHM (E): *Huntingdonshire*; 1926, HMSO
RCHM (E): *Peterborough New Town*; 1969, HMSO
REX, P.: *Hereward the Last Englishman*; 2005, Stroud
REX. P.: *The English Resistance, the Underground War against the Normans*; 2006, Stroud
RIDDELL, E. & CLAYTON, M.: *The Cambridgeshires 1914-1919*; 1934, Cambridge
SAINSBURY, J.D.: *The Hertfordshire Batteries RFA 1908-1920*; 1996, Welwyn
SAINSBURY, J.D.: *The Hertfordshire Yeomanry Regiments RA Part 1 The Field Regiments 1920-1946*; 1999, Welwyn
SIMONS, G.: *Airfield Focus: Peterborough*; 1996, Peterborough
STRACHAN, H.: *History of the Cambridge University Officers Training Corps*; 1976, Tunbridge Wells
SUBTERRANEA BRITANNICA: *www.subbrit.org.uk/rsg/sites*
TAYLOR, A.: *Castles of Cambridgeshire*; nd Cambridge
TAYLOR, C.C.; *Fieldwork in Medieval Archaeology*, 1974, London
TAYLOR, C.C.: *Moated sites: their definition, form and classification*; in Aberg, 1978
TAYLOR, C.C.; *The Bulwark, Earith, Cambridgeshire*, in Proceedings of the Cambridge Antiquarian Association, Vol. LXXXVII. 1998, Cambridge
TEBBUTT, C.F. & RUDD, G.; *Earthworks on Tort Hill, Sawtry,* Proceedings of the Cambridgeshire Antiquarian Society, LXX, 1980
WASZAK, P.: *A German Prisoner of War in Peterborough*; in Peterborough Local History Society Magazine, 22, October 2002, Peterborough
WASZAK, P.: *Peterborough Wartime Sidings*; in Nene Steam, Winter 2002-3, Peterborough
WILSON, W.: *Soldiering on and off* (2nd Hunts Bn Home Guard); 1963, St Ives
WOODGER, A.: *Northborough Manor*; 1976, Bourne
WORSWICK, J.: *The Wyton Octagon*; 2000, in Airfield Review, 87, Stockport
YOUNG, R.: *St Neots Past*; 1996, Chichester

Index

Page numbers in *italics* denote illustrations

If you enjoyed this book, you may also be interested in …

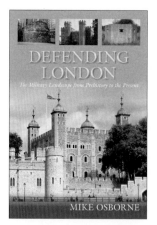

Defending London: The Military Landscape from Prehistory to the Present
MIKE OSBORNE

Defending London describes the various elements of London's military heritage, and places them in their historical, archaeological and social context. From the castles and strong houses of the mediaeval and Tudor monarchs and statesmen, to the pseudo-fortresses of the Victorian militia and rifle volunteers; the airfields of the anti-Zeppelin fighters of the Royal Flying Corps, to the anti-nuclear defences of the Cold War, and beyond.

9780752464657

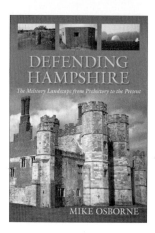

Defending Hampshire: The Military Landscape from Prehistory to the Present
MIKE OSBORNE

For 2,000 years, Hampshire has been at the heart of the nation's defences against foreign invasion, as well as being heavily involved in civil conflict. In the front line during two World Wars it has accommodated the infrastructure for training and deploying vast numbers of troops and material, providing a springboard for the D-Day invasion. Much of the county's military heritage is still represented in the landscape today: Roman forts, mediaeval castles, Victorian barracks and drill halls, military airfields, anti-invasion defences, radar sites, bunkers and nuclear attack monitoring posts.

9780752459868

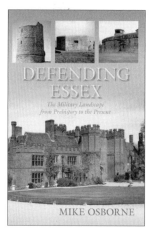

Defending Essex: The Military Landscape from Prehistory to the Present
MIKE OSBORNE

Essex, the county with the longest coast-line in England and dominating the eastern approaches to London, has been in the front line against numerous foreign invasions and civil disorders from the Spanish Armada to the two World Wars and from the Peasants' Revolt to the English Civil War. Many reminders of these scenes of conflict may be seen in the landscape – Iron Age forts, a Roman walled town, mediaeval castles, coastal fortifications from Napoleonic times and earlier, and Victorian barracks and the drill halls of the Volunteers.

9780752488349

Visit our website and discover thousands of other History Press books.

www.thehistorypress.co.uk